changing toronto

changing toronto

Julie-Anne Boudreau,
Roger Keil, and
Douglas Young

Governing Urban
Neoliberalism

A Garamond Book

University of Toronto Press

LIBRARY AND ARCHIVES CANADA CATALOGUING IN PUBLICATION

Boudreau, Julie-Anne
  Changing Toronto : governing in-between the global and the local / Julie-Anne Boudreau, Roger Keil and Douglas Young.

Includes bibliographical references and index.

ISBN 978-1-4426-0133-8 (bound). — ISBN 978-1-4426-0093-5 (pbk.)

  1. Toronto (Ont.) — Politics and government.   2. Toronto (Ont.) — Social conditions.   3. Toronto (Ont.) — Economic conditions.   4. Toronto (Ont.) — Environmental conditions.   I. Keil, Roger, 1957–   II. Young, Douglas, 1952–   III. Title.

JS1789.3.A2B68 2009   320.9713'541090511   C2009-901855-1

We welcome comments and suggestions regarding any aspect of our publications — please feel free to contact us at news@utphighereducation.com or visit our internet site at www.utphighereducation.com.

North America
5201 Dufferin Street
Toronto, Ontario, Canada, M3H 5T8

2250 Military Road
Tonawanda, New York, USA, 14150

ORDERS PHONE: 1-800-565-9523
ORDERS FAX: 1-800-221-9985
ORDERS EMAIL: utpbooks@utpress.utoronto.ca

UK, Ireland, and continental Europe
NBN International
Estover Road, Plymouth, PL6 7PY, UK
TEL: 44 (0) 1752 202301
FAX ORDER LINE: 44 (0) 1752 202333
enquiries@nbninternational.com

This book is printed on paper containing 100% post-consumer fibre.

The University of Toronto Press acknowledges the financial support for its publishing activities of the Government of Canada through the Book Publishing Industry Development Program (BPIDP).

Edited by Betsy Struthers
Designed by Metapolis

Printed in Canada

Contents

three Tory Toronto: Neoliberalism in the City 53

four Making the Megacity 69

five Diverse-City 85

Preface

And up above us all, leaning into sky, our Golden Business Boy will watch the North End die, and sing "I love this town," then let his arcing wrecking ball proclaim, "I hate Winnipeg."

The Weakerthans, *One Great City*

This sentiment, expressed lyrically by the Winnipeg band The Weakerthans about their great city, applies well to our own view of Toronto. Having lived here for many years (although Julie-Anne Boudreau now resides in Montreal), the three authors have watched those who say they love this city destroy and rebuild many parts of it in their image. We, too, both love and hate Toronto, depending on the angle from which we choose to look at it. In this book, we have assembled our views on recent changes in the southern Ontario global city region, paying particular attention to the decade of 1995–2005. These views are necessarily complex, not uni-linear, conflicted, and often incomplete. But we hope they shed new light on the developments that continue to determine the rhythm of our everyday lives in Canada's largest metropolis. Our approach is political, in the sense of urban politics. We borrow here from David Harvey (1999: 127):

I have long argued that urbanization should be understood as a process rather than as a thing. That process necessarily has no fixed spatial boundaries, though it is always being manifested within and across a particular space. When I speak of urban politics, then, it is in the broad sense of political processes at work within a fluidly defined but nevertheless explicit space.

The title of this book, *Changing Toronto*, is meant to capture the dynamic nature of urbanization. Toronto is changing, and it is our hope that this book contributes to understanding who or what is changing it, how and at what scale, and what the impact of those changes is on the lives of the people who live and work there. We project our views through three compatible and mutually reinforcing lenses of environmental, economic, and social change in Toronto during these fast-moving times of neoliberalism and globalization. As critical urbanists, we believe that the first step towards creating a socially and environmentally just urban world is to understand the urban world we currently live in. We would like to enlist this book in that kind of social and environmental change.

Many people have helped us put this book together. We thank Cenk Aygul for his help researching Chapter 4, Sara Macdonald for her research help with Chapter 9, and John Grundy for his research assistance with Chapter 10. The manuscript would not have come together without the excellent editorial work of York University graduate students Nicole Lulham, Nate Prier and Melissa Slupik.

We also thank our fellow travelers who have worked with us, and/ or provided comments on sections of research that went into this book: Ahmed Allahwala, Jon Caulfield, Gene Desfor, Pierre Hamel, Nik Heynen, Bernard Jouve, Stefan Kipfer, Punam Khosla, Sara Macdonald, and Joseph Roman.

Finally, we would like to acknowledge financial support for some of the research that this book is based on. The research for chapters 8 and 10 was supported by a small grant from the Faculty of Environmental Studies at York University. The research for Chapters 9 and 10 was supported by SSHRC Standard Grant #410-2003-1207, "Metropolitan Governance and International Competitiveness: Montreal and Toronto Case Studies." And Chapter 7 is based partly on Douglas Young's unpublished dissertation, "Rebuilding the Modern City After Modernism in Toronto and Berlin" (2006) as well as on research done as part of the In-Between Infrastructure research project funded by Infrastructure Canada.

Julie-Anne Boudreau, Roger Keil, Douglas Young
Toronto, February 2009

List of Figures, Tables, and Maps

Figures

Tables

Acknowledgements

Many people have helped us put this book together. We thank Cenk Aygul for his help researching Chapter 4, Punam Khosla for assistance with Chapter 8, Sara Macdonald for her research help with Chapter 9, and John Grundy for his research assistance with Chapter 10. The manuscript would not have come together without the excellent editorial work of York University graduate students Nicole Lulham, Nate Prier and Melissa Slupik.

We also thank our fellow travelers who have worked with us, and/or provided comments on sections of research that went into this book: Ahmed Allahwala, Jon Caulfield, Gene Desfor, Pierre Hamel, Nik Heynen, Bernard Jouve, Stefan Kipfer, Sara Macdonald, and Joseph Roman. The reviewers of the manuscript have been generous in their comments on an earlier draft and we thank them for their constructive input.

We would also like to express our gratitude to the team of editors for this book who gave us excellent support throughout the project: Tracey Arndt, Anne Brackenbury, Anna Maria Del Col, Beate Schwirtlich, Betsy Struthers and Greg Yantz.

Finally, we would like to acknowledge financial support for some of the research that this book is based on. Chapter 8's research was supported by a small grant from the Faculty of Environmental Studies at York University. The research for Chapters 9 and 10 was supported by SSHRC Standard Grant #410-2003-1207, "Metropolitan Governance and International Competitiveness: Montreal and Toronto Case Studies."

Chapter 7 is based partly on Douglas Young's unpublished dissertation, "Rebuilding the Modern City After Modernism in Toronto and Berlin" (2006) as well as on research done as part of the In-Between Infrastructure research project funded by Infrastructure Canada.

Julie-Anne Boudreau, Roger Keil, Douglas Young Toronto, March 2009

Credits

Parts of some chapters in this book have been previously published. Chapters 2 and 3 borrow from Roger Keil, "'Common-Sense' Neoliberalism: Progressive Conservative Urbanism in Toronto, Canada," *Antipode* 34:3 (2002): 578–601; and Roger Keil, "Toronto in the 1990s: Dissociated Governance?," *Studies in Political Economy* 56 (Summer 1998): 151–68.

Parts of Chapter 4 are revised versions of Julie-Anne Boudreau, *The MegaCity Saga* (Montreal: Black Rose Books, 2000), and of Roger Keil and Douglas Young, "A Charter for the People? A Research Note on the Debate About Municipal Autonomy in Toronto," *Urban Affairs Review* 39:1 (2003): 87–102.

Parts of Chapter 5 were published in Julie-Anne Boudreau, "Toronto's Reformist Regime, Municipal Amalgamation and Participatory Democracy," in *Metropolitan Democracies: Transformations of the State and Urban Policy in Canada, France and Great Britain*, ed. Philip Booth and Bernard Jouve (Aldershot: Ashgate, 2005) 99–115; and in Roger Keil, "Scale, Raum, Stadt: Differenz und Alltagsleben in Toronto," *DISP* 161 (2005): 60–70.

Parts of Chapter 6 are reworked versions of Douglas Young, "TorontoPlan: A New Official Plan for a New City," which appeared in the journal *Urban Planning Overseas*. The Chinese version of this special journal issue was published in May 2005 and the English version in July 2005.

Chapter 8 includes material that was previously published as Douglas Young and Roger Keil, "Urinetown or Morainetown?: Debates on the Reregulation of the Urban Water Regime in Toronto," *Capitalism, Nature, Socialism* 16:2 (June 2005): 61–83; this was reprinted in Nik Heynen, James McCarthy, Scott Prudham, and Paul Robbins (eds.), *Neoliberal Environments: False Promises and Unnatural Consequences* (London and New York: Routledge, 2007). It also contains work from Roger Keil and Julie-Anne Boudreau, "Metropolitics and Metabolics: Rolling out Environmentalism in Toronto," in *In the Nature of City: Urban Political Ecology and the Politics of Urban Metabolism*, ed. Nik Heynen, Maria Kaika, and Erik Swyngedouw (London and New York: Routledge, 2006): 41–62.

Some of Chapter 9 has been previously published as Roger Keil and Douglas Young, "Transportation: The Bottleneck of Regional Competitiveness in Toronto," *Environment and Planning C: Government and Policy* 26(4): 728–51.

Parts of Chapter 10 are a reworked version of John Grundy and Julie-Anne Boudreau, "'Living with Culture': Creative Citizenship Practices in Toronto," *Citizenship Studies* 12:4 (2008): 347–63.

Chapter 11 is partly based on Julie-Anne Boudreau and Roger Keil, "La réconciliation de la démocratie locale et de la compétitivité internationale dans le discours réformiste à Toronto: Essai d'interprétation sur le néolibéralisme normalisé," *Politiques et Sociétés* 25(1): 83–98.

Chapter 1: Lyrics from "One Great City," by John K. Samson. Copyright © 2003, used by permission.

Chapter 12: "Flypaper" Lyrics: Words and Music by Kevin Brereton. Copyright © 2006 UNIVERSAL MUSIC PUBLISHING, A Division of UNIVERSAL MUSIC CANADA INC. All Rights in the U.S. and Canada Controlled and Administered by UNIVERSAL-SONGS OF POLYGRAM INTERNATIONAL, INC. All Rights Reserved. Used by Permission.

"Urinetown" Lyrics: from URINETOWN, Music and Lyrics by Mark Hollmann, Book and Lyrics by Greg Kotis. Copyright © 2001 by Mark Hollmann and Greg Kotis. All Rights Reserved. Used by Permission.

"I See A River" Lyrics: from URINETOWN, Music and Lyrics by Mark Hollmann, Book and Lyrics by Greg Kotis. Copyright © 2001 by Mark Hollmann and Greg Kotis. All Rights Reserved. Used by Permission.

The following figures are credited to:

Roger Keil: 1.2, 2.1, 2.2, 2.3, 5.1, 5.2, 6.4, 7.1, 8.2, 9.1, 9.2, 9.3, 9.4, 9.5, 10.4, 12.1.

Douglas Young: 3.1, 6.1, 6.2, 6.3, 7.2, 8.1, 8.3.

Julie-Anne Boudreau: 4.1, 10.1.

John Grundy: 10.2, 10.3.

Ute Lehrer: 1.1

Metapolis: 0.1, 7.3, 7.4

Figure 0.1: Municipality boundaries, urban area, and shorelines from Geography Division, Statistics Canada, 2006 Boundary Files, Catalogue no. 92-160-XWE/F. Generalized Greenbelt Boundary (2005) adapted from Greenbelt Plan Outer Boundary, copyright © Ontario Ministry of Natural Resources and Ontario Ministry of Municipal Affairs & Housing.

Figure 4.1: Adapted from the GTA Task Force (1996) and Filion (2001)

Figure 4.2: Printed with permission of Jian Ghomeshi.

Figure 4.3: Printed with permission of Mike Colle.

Figure 7.3: Municipality boundaries, urban area, and shorelines from Geography Division, Statistics Canada, 2006 Boundary Files, Catalogue no. 92-160-XWE/F.

Figure 7.4: Road network from Geography Division, Statistics Canada, 2007 Road Network File, Catalogue no. 92-500-XWE/F.

Figure 7.5: Census 2001: City of Toronto. Copyright 2003 City of Toronto. All rights reserved.

Figure 7.6: Census 2001: City of Toronto. Copyright 2003 City of Toronto. All rights reserved.

Figure 11.1: Reprinted with permission from *The Globe and Mail*.

Figure 11.2: Reprinted with permission from *Eye Weekly*.

Figure 11.3: Reprinted with permission from David Miller.

All tables in Chapter 7 include data taken from the 2001 Census. Source: Census 2001: City of Toronto. Copyright 2003 City of Toronto. All rights reserved. Date of publication: May 2003.

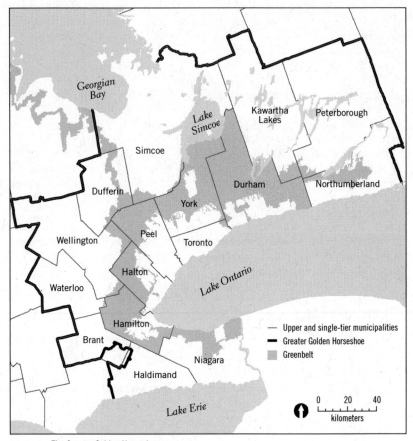

FIGURE 0.1 The Greater Golden Horseshoe.

1

Canada Urbana:
Perspectives of Urban Research

Ulrich Beck (2007) identifies three major risks world society faces today: terror, climate change, and globalization.[1] It is tempting to apply this grand vision to the state of Canadian cities, which are facing similar challenges. Having become the major containers of the country's still growing population (mostly through immigration), cities have become the sites of the nation's concerns and contestations over what we could call, rephrasing Beck's risks slightly, human security, environmental sustainability, and economic stability. This is even more true for the three Canadian "global cities" (Brenner and Keil 2006)—Montreal, Toronto, and Vancouver—that articulate the country's economy, culture, and populations into the global flows and scales that constitute the conditions of urban life today. Whereas 25 million, or more than 80 per cent, of Canadians live in metropolitan centres, these three urban regions account for much of the country's economic activity, cultural shifts, and demographic change. The larger regions of the Greater Golden Horseshoe, Vancouver/Victoria, Calgary-Edmonton, and Montreal grew by 8 per cent between 2001 and 2006. In their boundaries live 53 per cent of Canada's population. It is here where urban Canada is redefined most visibly as the face of an urban nation.

The majority of the world's population is now urban. That this means different things to different populations is obvious. In one powerful thrust

---

1 In an interview with a Swiss newspaper, Beck adds human genetic engineering and nanotechnology to the list.

of development, the world has turned into a "planet of slums:" The rising
number of squatters in the bidonvilles, favelas, and barrios of the global
South live apart from a presumed trajectory which equates urbanization
with (Western) modernization (Davis 2006). While not modernized in
the Western sense, they are modern nonetheless, as they are entangled in
one integrated post-colonial urban world, where place and modernity are
coincident (Robinson 2006). Constructions of class difference, racialization, and imperial degradation are rampant throughout that urban world,
and the geography of North and South often belies that integration
through its insistence on distance and boundaries. In another powerful
thrust of urbanization, people have moved away from cities into the suburban and exurban fringes of major urban regions, which are spreading
across fertile farmlands, arid deserts, and drained wetlands at a scale
unimaginable even to the keenest prognoses of megaurbanization only
one generation ago (Gottmann 1961; Vicino et al. 2008). The "100 mile
cities" of the Western world that stretch forever into contiguous corridors
of (sub)urbanity are now home to the majority of national populations
in all major industrial countries. In Canada, several such conurbations
house millions of Canadians along the American border: the Quebec
City to Windsor corridor in particular (including Ottawa), but also the
Calgary-Edmonton urban corridor, and the lower mainland of British
Columbia. Winnipeg, although rather stagnant in terms of population
growth, provides the bellybutton of Canada's urban body, as Halifax in
the East as well as Saskatoon in the West are dimples in the line-up.

To urban centres in Canada, the three-pronged risks of human security,
environmental sustainability, and economic stability appear as problems
of complex urban governance (Keil 1998b) in which social cohesion,
sustainability, and economic competitiveness are played against each
other in multitudinous ways. Place-specific strategies for growth are often
developed compatibly with strategies for ecological modernization and
social welfare (Desfor and Keil 2004).

The various think tanks and task forces that clamour for attention
in the nation's mind have put the urban on the agenda for debate. The
Conference Board of Canada calls "Canada's hub cities a driving force
of the national economy" (Brender and Lefebvre 2006). Mike Harcourt's
"External Advisory Committee on Cities and Communities" concludes
that "urban quality of life is the key to sustaining economic prosperity

because appealing cities attract investments, technology, and highly qualified labour" (Canada External Advisory Committee on Cities And Communities 2006, xv). In his book on "the new city" in Canada, John Lorinc claims that the task at hand is not only urgent but will have to be a long-term strategy of social change as "the urban agenda that has taken root in Canada's largest cities is all about understanding the critical importance of trying to anticipate how our cities will change as the result of our collective political action—not just between now and the next election, but over decades and beyond" (Lorinc 2006, 327).

How difficult it is to sustain such attention on urban matters has been personified in the fate of three political pioneers of its urgency: Jack Layton, the leader of the New Democratic Party (NDP), a one-time Toronto city councillor and subsequent chair of the Federation of Canadian Municipalities; Paul Martin, one-time prime minister of Canada who—with Layton pushing him firmly in that direction—termed the urban agenda as the political program for his short-lived government; and Glen Murray, one-time mayor of Winnipeg and arguably the most visible urban commentator in the country. Still, Murray is not mayor anymore, Martin is not prime minister, and Layton has all but been silent on urban issues in recent years. The urban agenda, as present as it is on the minds of many Canadians, has been sidelined in the official political arena and has receded once again to the domain of civil society and elite interventions (Broadbent, 2008). Even at the onset of a global economic crisis when major infrastructure investments and other supportive actions for the living environments of Canadians are being recommended by most commentators, the federal government, with close to no representatives in major urban areas, has been hesitant to support significant shifts in public policy towards an urban agenda.

As the political champions of the urban agenda fall silent or by the wayside, a few forums of urban debate and demand still exist. Prime among them is the Big City Mayors conference, which continues to remind higher levels of government of the growing unevenness in the governance of the Canadian federal system. Their regular meetings usually result in a mix of stern protest and hopeful reassertion. The current period of political struggles over Canada's urban future is characterized by path dependencies that originate in prior mobilities (ways to get around) and moorings (modes of creating place) (Hannam *et al.* 2006) of social

Scale

Scale has become an important concept in the social sciences. The concept, as used by researchers today, denotes more than the common metric measure with which it is commonly related. Instead, it implies a process of social production of space, of which the production of scales—i.e., dimensions of socio-spatial activity—is an important part. It is assumed that there is a more or less hierarchical order of scales in place that stratifies society and the state, economic activities, and politics. Some social theorists have challenged a rigid hierarchical understanding of scale and have instead promoted a "topological" theory, which posits that places are made in the absence of scalar hierarchies through a manifestation of flows that cut through all dimensions of human existence from the body to the global (for more on the scale debate, see Keil and Mahon 2009).

forces in the country. Most cities have undergone what some have called profound processes of neoliberalization (Brenner and Theodore 2002). For Toronto, which will be the chief focus of this book, these processes have been analyzed in three related processes as the city was forged, in the decade after 1995, into a competitive city: the entrepreneurial city, which resembles more a business firm than a public institution; the city of difference, which makes ethnic diversity into a marketable commodity in the interurban competition; and the revanchist city, where more often than not the socially disadvantaged are also criminalized and where the middle classes have largely obliterated the spaces of the poor through gentrification and social exclusion (Kipfer and Keil 2002).

What happens in cities regarding their economic growth, social and environmental sustainability, and human security is governed by processes that combine dynamics at different scales of socio-spatial activity. This seems to be particularly true for the case of Canada with its complex system of federalism, which necessitates multi-level cooperation between governments and social institutions. The governance of Canadian cities has exploded the boundaries of municipal politics. More than ever, for example, it has been framed in explicitly metropolitan or regional terms. The amalgamation of Toronto and the merger of Montreal, in particular, have signaled strongly that Canada's urban agenda is largely seen by provincial decision-makers and local economic forces as regionally scaled. To some degree, as we will demonstrate for the Toronto case, these trends have also been mirrored by civil society action and social protest. In his work on metropolitanization in Europe, American urban theorist Neil Brenner insists "that urban governance has served as a major catalyst, medium, and arena of state rescaling processes" (Brenner 2004, 174). In more practical terms, Patrick Le Galès explains:

> This kind of reorganization occurs in all cities where there is simultaneous experimentation with different scales of proximity in service management: the municipal scale, the inter-municipal scale of the conurbation, and beyond these to the scale of the city region, which extends urbanization. This last scale, in general, uses a fairly light touch in coordinating things, but it may be the place where the coordination of public policy—transport, the environment, or to attract business—is learned. (Le Galès 2002, 247)

Boudreau et al. have written for the Canadian case:

> Big cities bring pressures for a new configuration of intergovernmental relations.
>   In this institutional and political flux, the main challenge of public policy-making is to stabilize a place for exchanges between institutions. There seems to be an emerging political space at the metropolitan scale, where collective action and claims for local democracy unfold. The recent reforms have created more and more organized local and metropolitan societies. Metropolitanization also means an internal reconstitution of the political sphere and its articulation with civil society. There is a diversification of local and metropolitan responsibilities and activities, from the production of local services to, among other things, a proactive role in economic development. (Boudreau *et al.* 2006, 7–8)

In Europe this increased diversification through metropolitanization leads, among other things, to a concentration of important and lucrative economic activities "within major metropolitan regions" and to an intensification of "territorial disparities between core urban regions and peripheral towns and regions" (Brenner 2004, 180). Yet we can also find these tendencies in Canada, where urbanization has bifurcated into a pattern of globalized, successful, growing, dynamic city regions (such as Calgary-Edmonton, Montreal, Ottawa, Toronto, Vancouver, and, with reservations, Winnipeg) while there is also a large number of declining towns, mostly in the old industrial and resource economy belts of the East and the North (Bourne 2004; Simmons and Bourne 2003).

Lastly, our book recognizes the tremendous urban morphological change we have experienced in Canadian cities today. The new global-ized urban regions are growing differently from how they grew in the past. We will argue that large numbers of Canadians now live in "in-between cities" between the glamour zones of the gentrified downtowns and the traditional suburbs.

Urban Neoliberalization and the Canadian City

The main theoretical argument put forth in this book is that urban neoliberalization can be read as a specific intersection of global—in the sense of both general and worldwide—shifts in the structure of capital-ist economies and states with the everyday life of people in cities. As a state strategy, urban neoliberalization creates not only new conditions for economic growth (or, in other terms, the accumulation of capital) but also inevitably more fissures in which urban resistance and social change can take root. The twin domains of environmental sustainability and social cohesion are centrally—and usually negatively—affected by neoliberalization, as economic competitiveness gains prime status in government agendas. There are two partially contradictory yet inter-twined modes of explanation that are useful to consult when it comes to the workings and effects of neoliberalism. One is the neomarxist political economy approach, especially its regulationist tradition; the other is a certain Foucauldian strand in social theory, which concerns itself with the emergence and spread of new technologies of power, particularly in the urban. It will be argued here that, while each is insightful and with merit for different reasons, they may best be complemented with a look at changes to the construction of urban everyday lives.

This theoretical argument is explicated using a case study that we be-lieve lies at the basis of the current state of metropolitanization in Canada more generally and in Toronto more specifically: the neoliberalization of the urban through deliberate policy decisions of a programmatically interventionist, yet substantively anti-statist, neoliberal government. Gov-ernments at all levels—from the national Liberal governments of Chré-tien and Martin and Stephen Harper's Conservatives, to Mike Harris's Ontario Tories and Gordon Campbell's Liberals in British Columbia, to various municipal governments across the country—have been creating a policy context through which the everyday lives of urban Canadians, and specifically Torontonians, were changed in many ways leading to long-term shifts in power and spatiality.

Why Focus on Urban Neoliberalization?

Urban politics regulates many of the contentious issues of globalizing societies: economic growth in an age of globalized markets, migration, and settlement; police and social control; social services; environmental regulation; schools and education; and so on. To a certain degree, cities have become the political place where the dirty work of globalization is being done. The local state becomes an ever more important key to social control. Not surprisingly, while advertised internationally by conservative American research institutes, the recipes for social control espoused by the state focus on the urban dimension of the control and the capacities of the local state to intervene in social matters. New York City under Mayor Rudolph Giuliani gained some notoriety in sweeping the streets clean of homeless people, drug addicts, and other undesired elements. The so-called "broken windows" theory creates an atmosphere of draconic state intervention in community affairs in cities where fear and violence are rampant. Policies of "zero tolerance" and "three-strikes-you're out" have targeted predominantly minority and marginalized youth (often locking them up indefinitely for small infractions) while making little more than a dent in urban violence and delinquency. These policies have a decidedly urban dimension.

The reconstruction of aspects of urban politics in public discourse into an arsenal of authoritarian measures to regulate social problems is paralleled by a broad media attack on the poor, the homeless, the marginal, the alternative, and their political advocates. While there are periodic rituals of public solidarity in cities with homeless people and children in poverty, the overall tone of public discourse on the urban "Other" has become noticeably rougher since the 1990s. Again cities, often correctly hailed as the multicultural, multi-class, multi-sexual orientation strongholds of globalized postmodern society, are also at times the focal point of reactionary politics. A case in point was the unprecedented campaign of the Toronto press against the radical poverty advocacy organization Ontario Coalition Against Poverty (OCAP) and its charismatic leader

[handwritten annotation: PURPOSE: TO ENRICH INNOVATION THRU INTRODUCTIONS OF COMPETITIVENESS / OPPORTUNITY, AT COST OF 'COMFORT' STRUCTURES THAT DEFINE WORK, CLASS]

Neoliberalism and Neoliberalization

Neoliberalism is a theory and practice of running the economy in a way that frees markets from state and bureaucratic controls. Historically, neoliberalism was a reaction to both the widely experienced authoritarian practices of the mid-twentieth century and the Keynesian-Fordist regime of accumulation that characterized the post-World War II societies in the West. In that latter regime, state intervention in the economy (e.g., the creation of welfare state provisions, monetary regulation, market controls, etc.) dovetailed with a social mode of regulation that often entailed complex compromises between capital and labour in a largely growing political economy. Critics such as Milton Friedman and Friedrich Hayek chided the "virtuous cycle" economies thus created and developed an economic theory which gained ground in the 1970s when the postwar economic order suffered a major recession. Neoliberal theories were first put to practice in Chile under the dictatorship of Augusto Pinochet. Later, the governments of Margaret Thatcher in Britain (after 1978) and Ronald Reagan in the United States (after 1981) put neoliberal doctrines to work, freed the markets from many so-called "constraints," and reformed the monetary system. Such processes of neoliberalization were seen by detractors as thinly veiled strategies of upsetting the power of the working class, who had kept the balance of power during Fordism as social struggles led to welfare state provisions and social safety nets and incomes were tied to the rise of company earnings. Indeed, market liberalization under Thatcher, Reagan, and fellow neoliberals like Ontario's Mike Harris in the 1990s came in tandem with strong state measures against the poor, the working class, and marginal groups. In cities, neoliberalization was often synonymous with workfare, strict police control, and tight fiscal austerity. The person who most visibly symbolized these policies was New York City Mayor Rudy Giuliani. Internationally, neoliberalization coincided with the growing imperial power of the United States in a post-Cold War environment. The so-called Washington Consensus, a package of mechanisms based on neoliberal principles, was meant to create "structural adjustment" in crisis-prone economies of the global south. These policies had the tendency of wrecking entire countries while spreading devastation among the poor in cities and the countryside. The World Bank, the International Monetary Fund (IMF), and various American financial institutions became the global pace setters of neoliberalization after 1990. As David Harvey wrote:

> Neoliberalism is in the first instance a theory of political economic practices that proposes that human well-being can best be advanced by liberating individual entrepreneurial freedoms and skills within an institutional framework characterized by strong private property rights, free markets, and free trade. The role of the state is to create and preserve an institutional framework appropriate to such practices. The state has to guarantee, for example, the quality and integrity of money. It must also set up those military, defence, police, and legal structures and functions required to secure private property rights and to guarantee, by force if need be, the proper functioning of markets. (Harvey 2005, 2)

While pure neoliberalism exists nowhere, there have been various pathways towards neoliberalization in places as diverse as Chile, Britain, New Zealand, the United States, and China at national, supra-national (World Trade Organization, International Monetary Fund, World Bank, United Nations), and sub-national (cities and provinces) scales. "The process of neoliberalization has ... entailed much 'creative destruction' not only of prior institutional frameworks and powers (even challenging traditional forms of state sovereignty) but also of divisions of labour, social relations, welfare provisions, technological mixes, ways of life and thought, reproductive activities, attachments to the land, and habits of the heart." (Harvey 2005, 3)

John Clarke. While all Toronto papers have chastised OCAP and Clarke for their confrontational, direct action approach to anti-poverty politics for some time, the demonstrative squatting of a downtown park in the summer of 1999 brought out particularly violent reactions by pundits across the city. One neighbourhood paper made Clarke the subject of a front page article with the headline "Poverty Pimp." In an inside article short on information about the surge in homelessness and poverty in Tory (Progressive Conservative) Toronto (see Figure 1.1) but long on red-baiting, misrepresentations, and badmouthing, OCAP and Clarke were accused of exploiting the homeless for the purpose of a radical Marxist agenda (McLeod 1999).[2]

The Political Economy of Urban Neoliberalism

The advance of neoliberalism has been an often coordinated, politically directed, rarely self-propelled, and violent process of change in the global architecture of capitalist production, trade, and consumption. Yet neoliberalization has not been an even process by which the theories of market liberalization were spread smoothly across societies and states. Instead, it has been contested, with resistance as well as local circumstances and conditions playing a major role in defining what aspects of the new regime would be implemented at various locales (Leitner et al. 2007). As many would agree, after a quarter century of neoliberal advance,

---

2 The weekly *Toronto Eye* magazine broke the ranks of the united press front in Toronto and documented many instances of the "war on John Clarke," whom they considered "the most unpopular man in Toronto" in the summer of 1999.

FIGURE 1.1 Homeless person sleeping on sidewalk, financial district, Toronto. During both the 1990s recession and the subsequent recovery, homelessness remained a constant reminder of the highly uneven distribution of wealth in neoliberal Toronto.

this phenomenon is now historical in at least two ways. It denotes a not entirely defined *era* of recent developments in world capitalism, and, in debates among critical social theorists and activists, it is a *keyword* with a history of its own.

In the first sense, neoliberalism denotes that period of time that started roughly with the governments of Ronald Reagan in the United States and Margaret Thatcher in Britain. This period "swept aside" previously held doubts about the value and power of markets and introduced "its mantras of private and personal responsibility, and initiative, deregulation, privatization, liberalization of markets, free trade, downsizing of government, draconian cut-backs in the welfare state, and its protections" (Harvey 2000, 176; see also Harvey 2005). The progression and success of neoliberalism as a set of policies, ideologies, and what Larner (2000) calls "governmentalities" (see below) has summarily been associated with the emergence of a new regime of capitalist accumulation variably called post-Fordist, neo-Fordist, neo-Taylorist, flexible, liberal productivist, etc. (Lipietz 2001; Jessop 2001a, 2001b). Among political economists, the short history of neoliberalism has already produced internal periodizations. Peck and Tickell (2002), for example, have introduced the useful distinction between "roll-back neoliberalism"—the dismantling and deregulation of postwar Fordist-Keynesian modes of regulation—and "roll-out neoliberalism"— the active creation of new institutions and regulations of the state and society.

Simultaneously, neoliberalism—together with its "cousin" globalization—has become a major reference point for social theory overall. In attempting to pinpoint the special characteristics of our current period, theorists have, for instance, looked at the relationship of neoliberalism as a political project with "a new technological revolution (the 'information revolution'), new managerial achievements, and the new hegemony of finance" (Duménil and Lévy 2001, 141). As scholars have assessed the impact of neoliberalism on human societies worldwide, they have pointed to two interlocked yet counterposed dynamics: on the one hand, the continued and accelerated destruction of human and natural communities (more pressure on sustainability and human security) and the sheer unlimited—and seemingly unopposed—potential for capitalism to unleash its disciplinary regime onto societies (boundless and often unregulated economic growth and globalization) (Hardt and Negri 2000; van der Pijl 2001), and the renewed capacity of communities around the world to resist the negative consequences of the related processes of neoliberalization and globalization on the other hand (Bourdieu 1998; Hardt and Negri 2000; Harvey 2005; Klein 2000, 2007; Purcell, 2008).

In all of this, debates on *space* have figured prominently in geography and urban studies in particular and the social sciences in general (among the most prominent and influential voices have been Neil Brenner, David Harvey, Doreen Massey, Neil Smith, and Edward Soja). After much neglect in the traditional non-geographic disciplines, space has now become a general point of interest in the social sciences. More recently, following influential work by Lefebvre (1991), authors in the English-speaking world have moved from a widespread debate on the social production of space to a new interest in *scale* (see Keil and Mahon 2009 for an overview). One aspect of this larger theoretical and empirical debate has been the specific interrelationships of urbanization and neoliberalization or, more specifically, globalization.

Taking Brenner's and Theodore's postulations on the "urbanization of actually existing neoliberalism" as a point of departure, this book will look at a specific case of neoliberal urbanization in Toronto, Canada. Two specific points relevant to our own discussion below deserve mentioning: first, we agree with Brenner and Theodore (and others) that neoliberalism comes in many guises, spatial scales, historical trajectories, etc.; this means that neoliberalism—just like globalization—is not a monolithic affair that impresses itself onto local, regional, or national states, civil societies, and economies. Neoliberalism exists through the practices and ideologies of variously scaled fragments of ruling classes who impose their specific projects onto respective territories and spheres of influence. And we agree, secondly, that there is no such thing as a pure form of neoliberalism which is being "applied" to various places, but that there is rather "contextual *embeddedness* ... defined by the legacies of inherited institutional frameworks, policy regimes, regulatory practices, and political struggles" (Brenner and Theodore 2002, 351).

The Foucauldian Critique:
Explaining Urban Neoliberalism with Changing Technologies of Power

Theorists critical of traditional political economy approaches have introduced an alternative view of its emergence as a globally visible set of new technologies of power. With explicit reference to the work of Michel Foucault, it has been suggested that neoliberalism can be understood as either policy, ideology, or governmentality (Larner 2000). Particularly important in our context is the notion of neoliberalism as *governmentality*, which refers to the many ways in which neoliberalism emerges on the basis of a restructured political subject: "Neo-liberal strategies of rule ... encourage people to see themselves as individualized and active subjects responsible for enhancing their own well being" (Larner 2000, 13). In this view, citizens as active agents or clients operate on a governance terrain, wherein previous distinctions between state, civil society, and market are largely blurred since "marketization" rules each of those domains and the relationships among them. More than pure ideology or a set of practices thought of as imposed from outside or above, neoliberalism as governmentality becomes an overarching frame of reference for contradictory discursive events which link the everyday life of individuals to the new world of "advanced liberalism."

 Engin Isin (1998) has looked at neoliberalism not merely as a prescription for state retreat, but rather as a complex set of *changing*

technologies of power. He argues that current capitalist societies have undergone three related shifts towards such new technologies. First, there are new relationships between expertise and politics, placing more emphasis on performance, efficiency, and marketability of knowledge. Second, there is a shift in the technologies of power towards privatization and away from accountable public processes. And thirdly, Isin suggests a shift towards a new specification of the subject of government, whereby citizens are redefined as clients and autonomous market participants who are responsible for their own success, health, and well-being. Nikolas Rose (1999) has argued in similar fashion that when looking at governance in this manner, we need to distinguish analytical, normative, and descriptive aspects of governmentality in neoliberalism.

Developments in Toronto since the 1990s have been a case in point. Governments at the time set in motion a set of practices, driven by right-of-centre ideologies, which "liberated" economic growth through marketization and privatization of previously public services and through an application of "neoliberal" modes of governance (performance indicators, streamlining, etc.) to bureaucratic processes. These new practices are based on and accepted by new subjects, and collectives have emerged in a new frame of societal reference where individuals and communities expect to "do their share" in protecting themselves against the ups and downs of markets. The introduction of neoliberal technologies of power is often intended by governments and corporations, and it is accomplished to a large extent by re-regulating the everyday lives of people in urban settings.

The Urban, the Everyday, and Neoliberalism

We can argue, then, that *urban* neoliberalism refers to the *contradictory re-regulation* of everyday life in the city (Figure 1.2). Built on models of technologies of power developed in the previous era, the everyday now has become a tight space where individuals (divided and collectivized by class, "race," gender, etc.) are suspended in a web of control and opportunity, rights and responsibilities, further massification, and controlled isolation. Insofar as they are aggressive extensions of their Fordist-Keynesian predecessors, neoliberal societies are characterized by their propensity to engulf the individual and social collectives with rules that are accepted by them as naturalized forms of behaviour. Neoliberalism as a mode of

FIGURE 1.2 Landscape of everyday life, West Toronto. This residential neighbourhood was built on a former industrial site. It displays the architecture typical of many infill sites in the city, where an uneasy mix of private homeownership and the quest for density lead to townhouse megacomplexes and large homes piled on top of one another.

regulation must be understood as regularizing urban everyday life in ways that represent and reproduce the specific form of globalized unrestrained capitalism that has been taking shape in and after the Fordist crisis (Harvey 2005). Yet in contrast to the Fordist period, in the current era the mall replaces the assembly line as the major conveyor belt of the regulatory regime. This process is part of the overall global and total production of social space, which characterizes our period and gives global capitalism a new lease on life (Lefebvre 2003). "The urban," as an important part of this spatialization of industrial society, plays a key role in the regulation of current society:

> There is nothing more contradictory than "urbanness." On the one hand, it makes it possible in some degree to deflect class struggles. The city and urban reality can serve to disperse dangerous "elements," and they also facilitate the setting of relatively inoffensive "objectives," such as the improvement of transportation or of other "amenities." On the other hand, the city and its periphery tend to become the arena of kinds of action that can no longer be confined to the traditional locations of the factory or office floor. The city and the urban sphere are thus the setting of struggle; they are also, however, the stakes of that struggle. (Lefebvre 1991, 386)

The coincidence of economic and cultural hegemony and socio-political control has certainly reached new heights in this current era and has grown into a global strategy. Yet, while the state becomes increasingly a punitive (rather than a caring) institution in the restructuring process, with police brutality at high levels and fear of crime on everyone's mind, it gradually loses the control it might have had over the means to protect its citizens from attack, as witnessed through recent events in the United States from Oklahoma City in 1995 to New York City in 2001 (Keil 2007). Once more, we see the collusion of economic growth through neoliberalizing processes of capital accumulation with violations to human security and sustainability, especially in urban communities. Those communities, however, have begun to articulate new modes of contestation (Leitner *et al.* 2007; Purcell 2008).

Everydayness and Urban Resistance

At the basis of neoliberal urbanism remains the restructuring of the political economy linked to a changing set of technologies of power. Related to both processes are two overlapping critical discourses. On the one hand, there is the traditional discourse of the social, leading to political strategies against exploitation and inequality; on the other, there is a cultural critique, which deals with aspects of autonomy and self-realization. A combination of both critiques lies at the basis of a new understanding of politics in the neoliberal city (Boltanksi and Chiapello 2006). Urban politics, as Stefan Kipfer (1998, 177–78) following Lefebvre has observed, is a dynamic and thoroughly contradictory social space: "[c]aught up in the contradictions between the macro-structures of capital and state and the micro-worlds of everyday life, urban politics is no mere local affair" but rather is multi-scalar, potentially universalist, and, most importantly perhaps, transformational. Urban society, hailed by Lefebvre (2003) in the heydays of the 1960s as the possible site and process of positive social change, at first glance seems to have become the controlled, marketized, consumerist stage of the complete capitalization of everydayness under neoliberalism. The urban plays a specific role in the grounding of neoliberal modes of regulation. Yet, the reproduction of capital through the production of urban space is not a linear, capital-driven process. Urban cultures and subcultures have been produced by

and have produced, have-been subjected to and have resisted, have suc-
cumbed to and have fought back neoliberalism in its many urban guises.
Cities under neoliberal rule continue to be huge mass production and
consumption nexuses—much in the tradition of the Fordist city. In this
context, the social critique remains a powerful strategic pre-condition
for urban resistance through class struggle and collective consumption
mobilizations. Yet cities also have become machines of differentiation,
fuelled by contradictory processes of social struggle and conflict. In some
of these events, both social and cultural critiques are fully developed as
discourses of radical change. In others, they are exercises in co-optation
and integration.

Urbanized Neoliberalism in Canada

Today's Canadian neoliberalism has to be seen against the backdrop of
the country's traditional "uneven spatial development" (Peck 2001, 224)
and its specific history of Fordism and post-welfarism (Peck 2001, 213–60;
Teeple 1995; Shields and Evans 1998; Jenson 1989). One also needs to take
into account the tradition of austerity politics, which has characterized
federal governments, provincial governments, and urban governments
since the mid-1980s (Shields and Evans 1998). Provincial governments
have also been on the forefront of the neoliberal restructuring. The neoliberal medicine was prescribed across the country by NDP, Progressive
Conservative (PC), and Liberal governments alike (Peck 2001; Shields
and Evans 1998). At the urban scale for more than a decade, Metropolitan Toronto and its successor local state, the new City of Toronto, have
been spearheading both new public management budget discipline for
social activist and environmental organizations in the city's governance
perimeter and leaner service delivery as mainstays of neoliberal policies
(Conway 2000; Kipfer 1998).

The Structure of the Book

This chapter has introduced the volume's substance and main conceptual
and theoretical arguments. Chapter 2, "The City That Works (No More):
The Crisis of the Mid-1990s," lays out the chief issues that have kept the
city and its people occupied in the past 20 years. Creating an arc between

the pre-amalgamation Toronto of the late 1980s and early 1990s to the regionalized mega-city of the past decade, this chapter creates the context in which the following substantially themed chapters and chronological narratives are to be understood. In the early 1990s, it became increasingly clear to politicians and other decision-makers that the peculiar spatial compromise that characterized the region in its two-level metropolitan government had run its course. Development in the regions outside of Toronto exploded, and the economic base of the inner city was eroded as large-scale socio-economic restructuring occurred, including the dramatic loss of industrial employment. As social problems accumulated in the city, the region was booming, even as the recession early on in the decade even took the edge off some of the suburban growth spurts. This chapter explores this story of the growing dysfunctionality of the Metro model and discusses, with a focus on a 1994 referendum on the issue, some of the political debates that carried the day. The work of the Golden Commission and its discursively influential, if politically ignored, report will conclude this analysis.

In Chapter 3, "Tory Toronto: Neoliberalism in the City," we examine how, in Ontario, an explicitly neoliberal provincial government (which holds all the constitutional power over municipal matters) under PC Premier Mike Harris created a particularly aggressive form of neoliberalization. The neoliberal reforms of the Tory Common Sense Revolution affected Toronto in a variety of ways from boundary redrawing to downloading of government responsibility. It is a case study of "real existing neoliberalism" (Brenner and Theodore 2002) in an urban context.

The next chapter, "Making the Mega-City," begins by narrating how the Harris government decided to amalgamate Metro Toronto with six local municipalities in 1998, how residents reacted, and how this became a turning point in Toronto's recent history. The chapter then turns to how amalgamation was implemented and its consequences at City Hall. Our main objective is to reflect on the legacy of amalgamation. How did amalgamation and the fierce struggle against it affect the political dynamics in Toronto? Did the suburbs win over downtown, as many opponents to amalgamation feared? What happened to social mobilization during the struggle against amalgamation and after? How did the Mega-City saga shape Toronto's (self)identity?

Chapter 5, "Diverse-City," deals with the notion of ethnic diversity. We often hear that Toronto is the most multicultural city in the world. In this chapter, we reflect on what it means for everyday life in the city. We look at how diversity served as a rallying identity in the post-amalgamated hallways at City Hall as well as in the streets of the new mega-city. While the new City adopted "Diversity, our strength" as its motto, neighbourhoods across the Greater Toronto Area (GTA) were undergoing important demographical shifts that sometimes uncovered problems of racism and discrimination. The diverse-city has in many ways been instrumentalized not only to consolidate a post-amalgamation identity, but also to empower Toronto in the Canadian and international economic and political arenas. The objective to manage, regulate, and encourage diversity is at the core of the New Deal for Cities and Communities and the new *City of Toronto Act*. Capitalizing on diversity is the other aspect of this instrumentalization, whereby the diverse streets of Toronto and the highly skilled labour pool of immigrants are sold as a major competitive advantage.

Planning in the Toronto region is the subject of Chapter 6. Planning has undergone a two-fold change in the period 1995–2005. It has been restructured with new goals and new ways of achieving them, and it has been rescaled in an attempt to better address planning issues. This chapter describes how planners and politicians in the post-amalgamation City of Toronto seized the opportunity in drafting of a new Official Plan to dramatically reorient planning in Toronto. The new Plan's loosened regulatory framework is intended to make Toronto stand out among competitor global cities as an attractive place to invest, and a newly constructed planning discourse is intended to sell Torontonians on the virtues of the large-scale intensification that the Plan encourages. This discourse rests on the twin pillars of curbing suburban sprawl by building tall within the City and of creating, at the same time, beautiful new buildings appropriate to a global city. Evidence suggests that not all Torontonians are sold on the merits of the new approach. Ironically, while the City has loosened planning regulation, the Province of Ontario has stepped in to restrict development in other parts of the region. Two pieces of provincial legislation introduced in 2005 are examined—one of them created a large Greater Golden Horseshoe Greenbelt in southern Ontario; the other, called *Places to Grow*, will guide patterns of development on either side of the Greenbelt. These provincial interventions acknowledge the need for coordinated action on planning issues of regional concern and, at the same time, up-scale the definition of "the Toronto region" to encompass a large chunk of Southern Ontario.

Chapter 7 explores Toronto's "in-between city," the once-modern suburbs of the 1950s and 1960s that lie in-between the fashionable downtown and waterfront, and the booming edge cities of the 905. These places are in-between cities in another sense—they defy traditional perceptions of, on one hand, inner city and, on the other, suburban neighbourhood. Their aging high-rise apartment blocks, diverse immigrant populations, and lower-than-average incomes suggest inner city while their blocks of bungalows, wide roads, and shopping plazas suggest suburbia. A majority of residents of the City of Toronto live in the in-between city, yet their everyday lived experience is marginalized in the branding of Global Toronto. Indeed, their neighbourhoods are most often represented as the least desirable parts of the city. Against this stigmatization, residents of the in-between city struggle to put their issues—jobs, affordable housing, public transit, policing—on the urban policy agenda.

The title of Chapter 8 is inspired by the Broadway musical *Urinetown*, which tells the story of a fictional community in which a severe drought has led to the outlawing of private toilets, and all urination and defecation are controlled by a corporation. While implementing such drastic measures has never been discussed in Toronto, the use of water most certainly has. This chapter investigates water in Toronto through the lens of urban political ecology—in other words, in terms of a hydrosocial cycle made up of the sum of human and physical interrelationships pertaining to water. Two case studies illustrate different aspects of those changing relationships: the near-privatization of Toronto's water system and the critical importance of water to suburban development in the Toronto region.

Like the constant woes of the water infrastructure, Chapter 9's subject of transportation dilemmas have been at the core of the redefinition of urban regionalism in Toronto. Transportation is the bottleneck of regional regulation in Toronto. Looking at issues of moving both goods and people in the GTA and the Greater Golden Horseshoe, this chapter offers insights into the complex problematics of servicing a region of 8 million people that produces a disproportionate amount of wealth in the Canadian economy. Employing a lens that looks at both exchange and use value related issues of transportation and transit, we expose the fissures in the coordination of regional transportation between the long-term global circuits of capital, workers, and goods, and the local capillaries of moving people and things around on a daily basis. This chapter, which is richly illustrated with empirical data, will make an argument for a regional mode of transportation governance. Such a regional transportation authority will have to take into account the specific needs of Toronto's vast transit-dependant community with its issues of social justice and fairness, as well as the demands of a regional sustainability agenda.

Chapter 10, on creative competitiveness, explains how urban prosperity is now framed in Toronto. After the austerity period of the 1990s, strategies for "competitiveness" have shifted hands from dry business attraction guys to cool high-tech, bohemian, artsy folks (Florida 2002). What does this buzz around creativity mean for everyday life in the city? Investing in creativity by promoting the arts, channeling money into urban design, encouraging a café culture and a lively street life, providing tax incentives to high tech industries, or converting an old distillery into a cluster of art galleries will undoubtedly change the everyday mood of certain parts of the city and also empower certain actors previously marginalized, be they artists or drag queens. Yet the not-so-hidden reason behind this creativity talk can be heard in the hallways of City Hall or at Board of Trade meetings: it is to attract the "right type" of residents to Toronto, that is, the young, cool, educated, high value-added worker of the knowledge economy. This chapter asks these questions: what is the effect of this new language of creativity on decision-making processes and on the configuration of power relations, characterized by the rising importance of "new" creative actors? What policies are actually implemented and through what tools? Are these economic development strategies any different from previous business attraction strategies? What is the impact of increasing funding on creative workers' perception of their work? How do the auditing and reporting requirements accompanying funding (and their quantifying and measurable bias) influence self-reflection on the value of creation?

Chapter 11 deals with the new mayoral politics that has entered the City of Toronto. Like a breath of fresh air, David Miller took over City

Hall in November 2003. On election night, he gave his victory speech with a broom in his hand to symbolize his pledge to clean the city (its air, its streets, its management practices). At the provincial level, the Tories had just faced a disgracing defeat, while at the federal level Paul Martin had just taken over. After two terms under Mel Lastman in the post-amalgamation years, the arrival of David Miller signaled the return of reformism or, as we argue, of neoreformism. After the austerity period of the long 1990s, Toronto re-emerged as a progressive city with a neoliberal twist. How is it that neoliberalism evolved in Toronto from an exogenous and ideological force to an endogenous and normalized element of governance is the question we ask in this chapter.

Chapter 12, "Changing Toronto," discusses how Toronto increasingly defies description in the regular terms often used in urban studies texts. It is a city of superlatives, not just in the Canadian context. In recent years, the truisms used to describe Toronto as a "city of neighbourhoods" in the past, a "city that works," "New York run by the Swiss," and "Vienna surrounded by Phoenix" seem to hold less and less. This chapter will extract from the major changes the urban region has been going through, and which have been described in the preceding chapters, new analytical and descriptive narratives of Toronto. It will be argued, in particular, that the hard edges of individual neighbourhoods and the 416/905 divide may have to be softened by distinct social practices and government policy in order to avoid further balkanization and alienation across the urban region.

This final chapter looks at Toronto as a collective regional actor. How do the agendas of elites, and the desires of the workers and residents of the region interact? How do the alleged necessities of sustaining a globally competitive economy intertwine with the needs for the production of creating regional food security? How can the ostensible contradictions between the growth pressures on the region and conservation imperatives be reconciled? How can the dramatic increases of social exclusion and racialized oppression, which the region has experienced, be counteracted by policies of socio-economic redistribution and socio-spatial equity on a regional basis? How can the needs for decisive policy-making be squared with the myriad movements and demands for more democracy?

2
The City that Works (No More): Towards the Crisis of the Mid-1990s

David Harvey (2005) has noted that 1978–80 constituted a major break in the history of world capitalist societies. It was during this period that neoliberalism made the transition from marginal academic theory proposed by semi-clandestine organizations, such as the Mont Pelerin Society, to government policy. The elections of Margaret Thatcher in Britain and Ronald Reagan in the United States, as well as the ascent to power of market reformer Deng Xiaoping in China after the Cultural Revolution, confirmed a trend: ever since Chile's General Augusto Pinochet had solidified his power after the putsch against the Allende government by calling on the Chicago School economists around Milton Friedman to fundamentally overhaul that country's economy, free market neoliberal reforms, built around a structural adjustment program based on monetarist interventions, were put in place. They were designed to, and often did, destroy or push aside Keynesian welfare state institutions such as trade unions, collective agreements, social security, etc. This period of "roll-back neoliberalism" (Peck and Tickell 2002) led to dramatic shifts in the mode of regulation of the affected capitalist core countries and ultimately to a fundamental reorganization of world markets, political camps, and military power around the globe.

As we will see in the following chapters, cities played a significant role in the development of the practices associated with neoliberalization. Deliverers of much social welfare, municipalities first felt the brisk wind of austerity that began to blow hard from the new regimes. In addition to financial belt-tightening—most clearly exemplified by the

New York fiscal crisis of 1976—cities developed new, often real estate driven regeneration programs that produced huge displacement effects, and the terse measures associated with what Neil Smith (1996) called "the revanchist city" were put in place by neoliberal reformers. New York was often seen as the core of the neoliberal revolution, which was linked also to the emergence of right-wing think tanks such as the Manhattan Institute, that targeted the municipal level of government as the place from which to stimulate reforms (Peck 2007). What was then recognizably "neoliberal"—i.e., constructed as a loosening of the state and civic constraints on the market—was often associated with the entrepreneurial city (Lieser and Keil 1988a; Harvey 1989b) and, in particular, with the novel instrument of public-private partnerships. Harvey (2005, 47) goes so far as to say that "inter-urban competition for investment capital transformed government into urban governance through public-private partnerships. City business was increasingly conducted behind closed doors, and the democratic and representational content of local governance diminished."

As these momentous upheavals were put in train, Toronto appeared anchored in a different world. One commentator, primarily thinking of the city's role as a safe haven for Vietnam War draft dodgers, likened the Canadian city to the elven retreat of Rivendell in *The Lord of the Rings* (Thompson 1984 [1971]). The 1970s had been a decade of reform and progress in Toronto as consecutive municipal "reform councils" ostensibly saved the city from being de-cored, as so many American counterparts—with their suburban sprawl and mega-malls—had been in the previous two decades, and as the Canadian metropolis was able to avoid the racialized and violent upheavals of cities south of the border. Enlightened middle-class regimes around two charismatic mayors—conservative David Crombie and liberal John Sewell—between 1972 and 1980 placed conservation over mega-development, kept housing in the inner city, strengthened public transit, recalibrated the education system to meet the needs of an exploding immigrant population, and kept tabs on the still white and regressive police force. All that occurred in the wake of what seems, in hindsight, the rather fortuitous victory by citizens groups led by the urban activist Jane Jacobs of stopping the extension of the Spadina Expressway through the core of the city's inner western downtown in 1971. This made Toronto turn its rebuilding energy

FIGURE 2.1 Industrial landscape, West Toronto. There are only very few classically industrial sites left in Toronto—many of them still along the rail lines—as manufacturing employment has moved out of the city into suburban locations or abroad.

inward, solidifying its urbanity through livable built environments and progressive social institutions. The progressive retrenchment of the inner city during this period did have its dialectic antithesis in the burgeoning suburbanization of the older and later newer suburbs, starting in Don Mills in the 1950s and moving rapidly across the plains of the southern Ontario slopes of the Oak Ridges Moraine and, since the expansion of sewer trunk lines in the 1970s, the fluvial flatlands of the streams that flow into Lake Ontario. Together, the inner city and the emerging suburbs were locked in an embrace of two-tier government between local municipalities Toronto, Etobicoke, York, North York, Scarborough, and East York on the one hand and the Municipality of Metropolitan Toronto on the other. The apparent results of this unique and peculiar regional power-sharing arrangement made Toronto the envy of local governments around the world and served as the backdrop for the now dead metaphor of "the city that works."

The city appeared to remain in this Rivendellian limbo for another decade after neoliberalism had already arrived in New York City and even after the Reaganite federal government of Brian Mulroney took the reigns of power in Ottawa in 1984. A business-oriented mayor, Art

Permeable Fordism

"Canada did not experience a postwar settlement similar to those of other advanced industrial societies after 1945. The Canadian welfare state and other Keynesian-style macroeconomic policies were not sustained by a class-divided party system but implicated, instead, the institutions of federalism. This difference in the politics of Canadian economic policy no longer appears exceptional, as so much of the new Canadian political economy argues, if we bring to bear the theoretical perspective of the French regulation approach and add to that approach the concept of a 'paradigm' which orders the social relations of fordism in Canada. It was this paradigm which entered into crisis along with production-based relations in the 1970s. The crisis of Fordism in Canada, given the particularities of the fordist paradigm, is, then, a crisis of the political arrangements of federalism more than it is one of the party system." (Jenson 1989, 69).

Eggleton, toned down the reform rhetoric of the 1970s considerably during his long reign in the 1980s. While he facilitated an unprecedented economic boom built on speculation in land and money, he handed the backroom keys to power to an elite of determined place entrepreneurs. Among them was newspaper and sports franchise mogul Paul Godfrey, who became the main mover and shaker of city politics until he lost his grip in the 2003 election, of which we will learn more below. While Eggleton championed major growth in business and building activities, he left, for the time being, the local welfare state mostly unharmed. As the 1980s were fuelled by the frantic economic expansion of what we can now recognize as Toronto's global city economy (Todd 1995), little attention was paid to the fact that the weak welfarist institutions of the Fordist period, which had been typical for the class compromises of the "permeable" Fordism of Canada (Jenson 1989), were crumbling. As the bottom fell out from under the economic boom of the decade in 1989, the local welfare rolls eventually swelled to over 200,000, which effectively included more than a tenth of Toronto's population (see Figure 2.1).

Toronto's stealth neoliberalism at the time was mild in comparison with what was to follow, but we would be remiss not to mention another Torontonian invention that was to become the hallmark of an era of urban development and symbolic of the kinds of seismic shifts encountered by many cities in the late twentieth century. This was the emergence of the transnational urban development firm, as exemplified in Toronto companies Cadillac Fairview and Olympia & York (O&Y). The former became a major investor in other global cities' built environments with Los Angeles's spectacular California Plaza development clearly its iconic flagship. The latter was a company based in Toronto from where it became a prime carpetbagger to profit from the selloff of New York City real estate after the 1976 financial crisis. O&Y developed what seemed to be a failsafe business method to reinvigorate investment in dilapidated inner city areas. From its Lake Ontario headquarters at Queen's Quay in the centre of Toronto's Harbourfront, the firm, led by five reclusive brothers, struck a series of high profile real estate deals, the most well known of which was the scandal-stricken development at Canary Wharf on the Isle of Dogs in London's East End.

Locating Toronto

What is Toronto? What is the background for the restructuring of governance in that city in the decade from 1995 to 2005? It is easy to find Toronto on any map and to determine its geographical location just north of the American border, on the shore of Lake Ontario, about equally far away from Detroit in the west and Montreal in the east. It is the capital of Ontario, Canada's most populated and wealthy province, the industrial heartland of the country.

Regionally, Toronto is the centre of southern Ontario which, despite recent upheaval in manufacturing, especially in automotive production, is the economically most powerful and most populated region of the country. Many citizens of the Toronto region are aware of the larger political, economic, statistical, and natural characteristics that define their home such as the creation of the megacity in the late 1990s, the ongoing debates on the Greater Toronto Area (GTA) and the Ontario Greenbelt or Oak Ridges Moraine (ORM), as well as the recent founding of a Greater Toronto Transportation Authority (Metrolinx). First and foremost, however, they tend to define themselves as residents of spatial and social communities, of local neighbourhoods, of the east end or the west end, of the small towns or the inner city. They visit local stores and pubs, school districts tend to be more important than commuter-

FIGURE 2.2 Downtown Toronto, financial district in foreground. This view from the CN Tower shows the classical density gradient of the central business district of the North American city.

sheds, and local parks and ravines are more relevant than the spectacular Niagara Falls, which are only a two-hour drive away from the city and which figure in every advertising brochure the city puts out. These sub-local identities of Torontonians have an increasing significance for the structuring of politics in the area and were the backbones of the anti-Tory citizens revolt of 1996 and 1997. It is only through these myriad and conflicting sub-local identities that a larger Toronto regional consciousness and understanding will be formed.

The social and economic restructuring that characterized Toronto in the 1990s has a number of spatial dimensions. In the larger picture, the Toronto economy experienced a two-pronged process of restructuring. On the one hand, jobs, mostly in manufacturing, have been leaving the urban core—and even Metro—for suburban and exurban locations and other subregions of the province. On the other hand, Toronto's space economy is shifting from an industrial mix that reached from manufacturing to services of all kinds to a more service-based economy.

The move of business to the periphery has been paralleled by demographic tendencies. While the population in the City of Toronto has remained relatively stable with 0.9 per cent growth between 2001 and 2006, the surrounding regions grew between 10 and 22 per cent during

FIGURE 2.3 New development, Vaughan. Despite much talk about New Urbanism and transit-oriented developments in the suburbs, the last two decades saw mostly very conventional low density suburban subdivisions that were carved into the landscape in uneasy proximity to natural features such as ravines, wetlands, streams, and woodlots.

this period (Statistics Canada 2007). A variety of planning reports and government-sponsored studies have dealt with this effect of outer city growth both in business and residential locations. Among them are the Royal Commission on the Future of the Toronto Waterfront headed by former Toronto mayor David Crombie (Royal Commission on the Future of the Toronto Waterfront 1992) and the final report of the Commission on Planning and Development Reform in Ontario headed by former Toronto mayor John Sewell (Commission on Planning and Development Reform in Ontario, 1993). The Office for the GTA, taking note of these various efforts, entered the debate on urban form and land use with a "commentary report" of their own, produced by a consulting firm. This report, called *Shaping Growth in the GTA* (1992), contemplated various scenarios for future developments in the Toronto area and concluded that "some form of concentrated nodal development was preferred and closer cooperation among municipalities across the GTA was necessary" (The Office for the GTA 1992, 9). Finally, the so-called Golden Commission on the future of the GTA published a comprehensive report, well-researched and full of ideas, on how to create regional integration and integration of the region into the global economy (GTA Task Force 1996). A general consensus among planners and politicians seemed to have emerged by the mid-1990s that "urban sprawl" had to be stopped or at least contained. At the same time, differences in opinion about just what this means for the peripheral regions and the central areas became more pronounced.

In terms of the sectoral aspect of spatial restructuring, the core of Toronto has become increasingly more specialized while the outer regions have been urbanized and diversified along sectoral lines with some places developing edge city (Garreau 1991) characteristics. Losing its diversity and regional hegemony in certain sectors has meant that Metro Toronto needed to reassess its role in the larger regional economy. By the early 1990s, it seemed fair to say, as economist Tom McCormack put it, that "Metro's future lies in being an urban core supplying services to outer areas—hospitals, government, business services, consulting, tourism, conventions, communications, print media, and a financial district" (quoted in Little 1994a).

By the middle of the 1990s, large chunks of Toronto sat expectantly waiting to be developed, reused, and recycled in the boom that had started in the real estate industry. The major actors—the real estate and development companies and the local political elite—were waiting in line to put their stamp once again onto the city with huge, mostly office buildings but also increasingly with—conceded under popular and market pressures—mixed use development. Among the largest areas waiting for redevelopment were the Port Industrial Area, the Railway Lands, the Downsview military base, the West Donlands, and the Greenwood racetrack.

The Agony of the Middle Classes

What is the social and political story behind such a complicated and increasingly complex regional reality? Urban and suburban middle classes and a largely internationalized financial and real estate business elite fight over the future character of the urban region mostly at the expense of the diminished working class and most new immigrant communities, as well as the young, the elderly, and the urban poor. The urban middle classes have become statistically and politically more important to the

Toronto Mayors

1966–72	William Dennison
1972–78	David Crombie
1978	Fred Beavis (interim mayor)
1978–80	John Sewell
1980–91	Art Eggleton
1991–94	June Rowlands
1994–97	Barbara Hall
1998–2003	Mel Lastman (previously mayor of North York from 1972–98)
2003–present	David Miller

life of cities as working-class populations and manufacturing industries have been pushed out of the centre. Yet, at the edges of those middle-class communities, gentrification is also a great pressure on their class status and economic security. Many have a largely unfounded fear of crime, are afraid that they will be unable to pay their property taxes, and are worried about the consequences of such developments for the cohesiveness of their community.

On the other hand, the growth of the established urban middle classes during the 1980s and 1990s (at the expense of the traditional working classes and new immigrants) has opened windows of empowerment and opportunity. They inhabit both the new and shiny spaces close to the downtown and the cultural spaces of the postmodern city. They dominate the discourse on urbanity, and they peddle the images that procreate the city through a process that much resembles the notion of a self-fulfilling prophecy. Thus, it can be assumed that professional middle classes now control a larger part of urban life than they used to. Consequently, their political and social weight is felt more strongly due to the decreasing relative presence of other classes in the city. With the decline of the manufacturing sector came the decline of the traditional (male, white, European immigrant) blue-collar working class. Where there is growth in employment, it tends to be in low wage service sectors, such as retail, where much of the workforce has become new immigrant and female. This shift has become more pronounced since the "creative class" has received a large share of attention of politicians and corporate decision-makers (Florida 2002).

Key Dates in Toronto History

1793	Founding of the Town of York
1837	Upper Canada Rebellion
1954	Metropolitan Toronto created
1954	Hurricane Hazel
1954	First subway opens
1976	CN Tower opens
1989	SkyDome opens
1998	Amalgamation and the new City of Toronto

The new middle classes have organized themselves into a novel spectrum of political loyalties, ranging from neo-conservatism to green initiatives. In a variety of ways, they—boosters and reformers alike— funnel and direct global capital flows into distinct downtown political and social communities of young, status-conscious, often neo-conservative professional office workers. However, they also incorporate fractions of new social movements like feminism, gay-rights, anti-racism, and environmentalism, which have gained political clout in City Hall and in the neighbourhoods. These new middle-class sectors coalesce widely with the old reformist regime of Toronto, a social democratic and Red Tory political mixture, which has ruled the core city since the early 1970s.

Civility and Heterogeneity

In a city which has become increasingly globalized both economically and demographically, but which retains an image of itself as mostly a European and even Anglo city, the acceptance of heterogeneity as the starting point for every urban policy has been crucial. Such heterogeneity, however, cannot be a solid ground on which to base an urban society if there is not a degree of civility that comes with it. It is no accident, then, that Barbara Hall, on the night of her election as mayor of Toronto in November 1994, called for "a new civility."

Civility—as understood here and perhaps also by Hall and other politicians and political activists in Toronto—in the words of Mark Kingwell "is not polite behaviour or good manners. It is much more: civility demands that we be open to the claims of others, while at the same time

Ontario Governments

1961–71	John Robarts (PC)
1971–85	Bill Davis (PC)
1985	Frank Miller (PC)
1985–90	David Peterson (Liberal)
1990–95	Bob Rae (NDP)
1995–2002	Mike Harris (PC)
2002–03	Ernie Eves (PC)
2003–present	Dalton McGuinty (Liberal); re-elected 10 October 2007 (Ottawa South)

ISN'T THIS CLASSICAL LIBERALISM? YES, INSOFAR AS KINGWELL IDENTIFIES W. 'ENLIGHTENMENT' PROGRESSIVE ORIENTATION

willing to restrain our own claims, to carry on with our common social project." Kingwell himself conceded that "vigorous dissent" belongs to civility and "implies a commitment to social reform. It is an expression — perhaps the deepest one — of citizenship" (Kingwell 1994, E1). Building civility and civil society out of heterogeneity, rather than out of a circle-the-wagon-mentality of hegemonic groups, is the challenging task before Toronto. *ISN'T THIS ACTUALLY EMANCIPATORY? I.E. OLD REFORMIST REGIME?*

Such an understanding of civility must go beyond the old liberal and new communitarian understanding of the concept. It needs to be infused with a will for socio-economic redistribution and social change. While the civility of the old Toronto was based on the exclusionary culture of a male, English, and Protestant bourgeois elite, the new civility must do away with such privileges and empower those who have been marginalized in the hegemonic structure of the urban region. Such empowerment would add an egalitarian and social justice element to the formal reality of civility Canadian style.

WHY? *How?*

Conclusion

WHAT IS ACTUALLY SAID HERE? THAT THINGS SHOULD BE DIFFERENT THAN THEY WERE HISTORICALLY?

Toronto has been involved for a while in a vivid debate on the right size of urban government. When the Municipality of Metropolitan Toronto was established in 1953, the idea was to have the rich core of the City of Toronto share in the cost of infrastructure and other development in the booming but tax-poor suburbs. This worked well for a generation, and Toronto became something like a model city in North America as far as metropolitan government was concerned. It is believed that this model was meant to be reversed as the tax base of the suburbs grew, yet this never actually happened.[1] By the 1990s, at the latest, the outer city itself grew into urbanized subnodes with their own strong tax base while the centre was still footing the bill for suburban development. Whereas the inhabitants of the City of Toronto particularly questioned the usefulness of the Metro layer of government (Canadian Urban Institute 1994), it was left to the suburban-based "Harris revolution" to finish the job.

Any discussion of urban governance and political regulation includes, by definition, some degree of popular and civil society input into the process of governing. Like in other cities around the world, Toronto has increasingly seen government by non-elected committees of citizens, business, and special interest groups. In Toronto this includes, in the first instance, important public corporations called Special Purpose Bodies such as the public libraries and the zoo. Royal commissions, like the one on the Toronto waterfront headed by David Crombie, have a long tradition in Canada. Newer forms of institutions include development corporations, like the now defunct Toronto Economic Development Corporation (TEDCO), which took much of the power once in the hands of the Harbour Commissioners (later renamed the Port Authority). The Who Does What Panel and the Golden Commission were additional incarnations of the same tradition of governance by citizen committee. Another example is the popularity of roundtables, such as the one on environment and ecology on the provincial level as well as the ones Mayor David Miller introduced after he was elected in 2003. More recently, the Toronto City Summit Alliance led by David Pecaut has captured much of the policy-making energy outside of elected city government. In turn, Mayor Miller, despite his declared goal to concentrate more power in his own office, has been a firm believer in the engagement of influential and knowledgeable individuals, particularly if they ostensibly represent powerful voting blocs or other forms of concentrated power. A case in point is the review panel he established in the fall of 2007, and which reported in the spring of 2008. The panel worked under Chair Blake Hutcheson, the president of commercial real estate giant C.B. Richard Ellis Ltd.; Toronto Community Foundation president and CEO Rahul Bhardwaj;

---

1 We are grateful to one of the anonymous reviewers who pointed this out.

Lorna Marsden, the former president of York University; Chair of Maple Leaf Sports and Entertainment, Larry Tanenbaum; the well-known economist Jim Stanford of the Canadian Auto Workers Union; and Paul Massara of Genesis Capital Corp. One of the stated goals of these special governmental bodies is to cut through bureaucratic red tape and to find more pragmatic and consensus-based approaches to urban planning and governance questions. We will return to these questions of governance later in the book. Before we discuss democratic possibilities further, we will, however, have to dive into a period that has widely been considered a "dark age" for municipal democracy and civil society in urban Ontario: the "Common Sense Revolution" of PC Premier Mike Harris.

3
Tory Toronto: Neoliberalism in the City

The Short Life and Times of Urban Neoliberalism

On September 21, 2001, a by-election for the provincial legislature of Ontario was held in Toronto. The vote in an East Toronto riding carried a social democratic politician—former mayor of the Borough of East York, Michael Prue—to a decisive victory over two high profile contenders from the Liberal and PC parties. The PC candidate, Mac Penney, received only 10 per cent of the popular vote and was humiliated by both the NDP (50 per cent) and Liberal (36 per cent) candidates. Prue's electoral success went almost unnoticed in the midst of the world crisis around him, yet, the next day, local television talk shows began to discuss the sudden demise of neoliberalism and neoconservatism. The neoliberal period—and the provincial PC Mike Harris government, which effected massive cuts to the traditionally more welfarist Ontario state—looked to be near their end. In his acceptance speech, Prue reminded Premier Harris that he had promised to "go after" him three years earlier, when the provincial government amalgamated Prue's hometown of East York with the new City of Toronto.

Three weeks later, on October 16, 2001, Harris resigned. While he was giving a press conference to explain his decision, thousands of demonstrators were assembled in downtown Toronto to protest his government's policies. Planned for months and orchestrated under the leadership of the Ontario Coalition Against Poverty (OCAP), this demonstration aimed at "shutting down" the financial district of Toronto as part of a series of province-wide actions of economic disruption. Whereas some demonstrators claimed—tongue in cheek—that it was their action that brought down the mighty premier, the relationship of the two events was not causally connected. What was remarkable though, and widely commented upon by local observers, was the fact that throughout his premiership, Harris had been a symbol of neoliberal societal restructuring and drew huge protests at every stage of his government's "Common Sense Revolution" (CSR)—so-called after his election rhetoric during the 1995 campaign. This chapter traces some of the steps of this "revolution" as they pertain to the urban scale and particularly to Toronto.

Toronto in the 1990s: Dissociated Governance

The writing was on the wall as early as 1994, long before Mike Harris won the June 1995 provincial election and much longer before "amalgamation" and "megacity" became household words in Canada's largest municipality. When Barbara Hall was elected mayor in the City of Toronto against all odds in November that year, *The Toronto Star* mentioned in an editorial that there were at least two recognizably different approaches to urban governance in Metropolitan Toronto, symbolized by the two largest cities in the region: Toronto and North York. While Toronto seemed to have woken up to the seriousness of the challenge that diversity and heterogeneity had put before a population hit by economic crisis and uncertainty, North York—the instant boomtown north of Highway 401—excelled in self-congratulating righteousness and put blame for home-made problems on outsiders, like those outer cities that allegedly took business away from the centre. These differences were personified by the progressive liberal NDP advocate for the homeless and marginalized, Barbara Hall, who replaced the hapless Tory June Rowlands as mayor, and by the development-oriented parochial tough guy, conservative Mel Lastman, who had been mayor of North York for more than 20 years. The *Star*'s editorial concluded: "Toronto and North York ... share many of the same problems: economic doldrums, declining tax revenues, vacant industrial land, fleeing businesses, and rising crime and other social pathologies. The solutions are elusive. The coming three years will tell which approach, Hall's or Lastman's, works better" (December 10, 1994).

In the fall of 1996, the Tory provincial government—which has sole legislative power over municipal constitutions—took steps to create a so-called "megacity" through the amalgamation of six individual municipalities and Metropolitan Toronto. The product was the merged City of Toronto. The hypothetical and symbolic contrast between Hall and Lastman attained a different reality in the election contest called a year later when amalgamated Toronto had to choose its new mayor. No wonder that the juxtaposition, as suggested by the *Star* three years earlier, was now blown up to full-scale electioneering lore. While Hall was cast as the protector of both the centrality of Toronto urbanity and of the metropolis's marginal populations, Lastman became the popular spokesperson for the small taxpayers in the inner suburbs, as well as the champion of most business interests. The contradistinction was made particularly clear when Lastman professed his conviction that there were no homeless people in his municipality of North York since they all sought services and support in the City of Toronto; Hall had made the homeless issue one of the main pillars of her campaign. The public outcry over Lastman's statement was pronounced—not just because a homeless woman died on the streets of North York the same day—and the candidate suffered his steepest drop in popularity during his entire campaign. Nonetheless, Lastman won the mayoral election by what amounted to a landslide. As expected, he gained about four out of five votes in his North York home base, but he also did better than Hall in the large suburban cities of Etobicoke and Scarborough. Hall won easily in Toronto proper as well as in the smaller communities of York and East York, but she couldn't garner sufficient support to break the early lead Lastman had enjoyed in the polls since the summer. In the end, Lastman put himself over the top with a stunning, though ludicrous promise to freeze local taxes for three and perhaps 10 years. While Hall was proposing a number of innovative ways to deal with the complexities of an internationalized metropolis in both policy and process, Lastman reduced his agenda to the localized sound bites of corporate globalization and to the slogans of a Harrisite populism: free markets and frozen taxes. Former Toronto mayor John Sewell observed at the time:

> Hall's idea of finding consensus and common ground was a hard sell. She
> did well in the older cities of Toronto, York, and East York, where there is a

strong democratic tradition that rewards those who respect the complexity of city life. But in the single-use suburbs, which have been planned to emphasize blandness, Lastman's offer of stupid certainty—can you believe he actually suggested a 10-year tax freeze?—won the day. (Sewell 1997)

Despite his vocal opposition to the Harris government's amalgamation scheme, Lastman became, in the eyes of Sewell and others, the Tory premier's perfect "stand-in." Dramatically displayed disappointment came quickly to Lastman. In the final days of the old Toronto, the mayor-elect claimed he was forced to renege on his election-winning promise when Ontario Finance Minister Ernie Eaves announced that the projected cost of downloading and fiscal restructuring to cities and regional municipalities would cost the new "megacity" $164 million in lost tax income. Just as confidently and boisterously as he had put forward his promise of a tax cut before the election, Lastman now lambasted the Harris government for lying to him about financing local government.

In the weeks before and in the days after the election, local analysts and commentators kept emphasizing the urban-suburban clash for which the two candidates stood. John Barber, in a newspaper column the day after the election, wrote: "This time, the power shift is historic. Mr. Lastman's victory means that the old establishment has finally been deposed. It wielded power through a permanent coalition that joined a reliably Red Tory uptown with a decidedly leftist downtown. Any successful mayor had to manage both flanks; the result was permanently liberal, known by the increasingly obscure codeword 'reform.'" He went on to speculate: "[T]he results of this election will be felt decades hence; individuals win and lose elections, but entire civic regimes rarely ever change" (Barber 1997). Like Sewell and others, Barber seemed to blame the suburbanization of urban politics for the downfall of the civic regime of reform in Toronto. Indeed, the Lastman election signaled the suburban re-regulation of an urban regime.

The urban-suburban political split has long been a subject of debate over the "right" size of a city. Especially in the United States, Progressive reformers had opted for a more "efficient" and "rational" drawing of city boundaries—largely levelled against the "ethnic" working-class regimes of the late nineteenth century—plus a depoliticization of local politics. Moreover, the burgeoning postwar suburbanization process had found its political ideology in the mantra of rational consumer choice and home rule (Tiebout 1956; Peterson 1981; Keil 2000). The results of the de-metropolitanization of the United States are well known: the so-called "donut"-effect of hollowed-out inner cities (no tax base, largely poor, often minority populations) and sugar-coated rings (of large commercial, industrial, and residential tax bases and mostly white, middle-class populations). No other city symbolizes this development as much as Toronto's "neighbour," Detroit, where little has changed since the heyday of suburbanism; in contrast, exurbanization and "edge city" (Garreau 1991) development have tended to increase the metropolitan split. Toronto never experienced this donut-effect, mostly due to a combination of the early institutionalization of Metropolitan Toronto and the lack of an historical pattern of rigid, racially based residential segregation (Frisken et al. 1997).[1] Nevertheless, the emergence of a "blubber belt" of rather well-to-do suburbanites cut off from the problems and spending burdens of the inner city has now materialized in Toronto. Cities like Vaughan, Markham, and Newmarket have become dynamic growth poles of a "flexspec"[2] economy in southern Ontario, often at the expense of the new City of Toronto (Keil and Graham 1998).

What happened in Toronto was not just the replacement of one regime by another, or the defeat of inner city political values by the suburban hordes marching down Yonge Street in a tax rebellion. Rather, the

---

1 While, of course, size and scale are not without consequence for the delivery of services, social well being, local democracy, etc., it would be misleading to take into account only area and population size in assessing the performance of an urban region. While less measurable than tax bases, distribution of transit availability, provision of social housing, etc., the entirety of social relationships constituting governance in cities, and between cities and other scales, are more important for this purpose. Harvey's notion of a "structured coherence" goes a long way in acknowledging the social, spatial, and economic relationships that define an urban region beyond the measure of the provision of collective consumption services alone. An additional important aspect of this debate, which has so far been mostly lacking, is the inclusion of the urban-regional societal relationship with nature as an integral part of the governance system of cities (Keil and Graham 1998). In the largely American-led debate on city size, it seems that the historico-geographical specificity of poor "people of colour–inner cities" surrounded by affluent "white suburbs" has served as the model of much thinking regarding metropolitan government without recognizing its limited value for other circumstances, including the Canadian case.

2 This refers to a shift observed since the 1980s when more rigid Fordist mass production was increasingly replaced by "flexible specialization." Ute Lehrer (1994) has examined the "flexspace" created in this period.

political regime in Toronto experienced a bifurcation into a discourse on democracy and civicness on one hand and a discourse (or rather non-discourse) on development and growth on the other. While Hall's Toronto had stood for economic growth with a cash dispenser for social and environmental concerns, Lastman's North York had epitomized having one without much of the other. The new megacity regime voted in on November 10, 1997 sanctioned a situation that had been in the making for some time: the existence of a virulent discourse on democratic rights and process alongside, but unconnected to, a dramatic new wave of megalomaniacal urban growth.

The Common Sense Revolution in Ontario

In Ontario, an uncompromisingly neoliberal provincial government under PC Premier Mike Harris—and his successor, Ernie Eaves—from 1995 to 2003 created a political environment reminiscent of Thatcherism and Reaganism. The Tories came to power in a rather surprising victory based on their CSR election platform. Populist in its appellations, the Tory program was a textbook case of a neoliberal policy strategy and project. It contained many internal contradictions. While espousing a rhetoric of small government, the Harris government became, in effect, perhaps the most interventionist government this province and city has ever seen. It preached market liberalism but lived out authoritarian and classist fantasies that were intended to create long-term societal change in the province. Instead of just dismantling the state, the provincial government entered the lives of many groups in Ontario society in a recognizable, tangible way. Teachers and school boards, universities, nurses and other health care professionals, government workers, homeless people, welfare recipients, urban residents, and many other groups were adversely affected by job cuts, welfare cuts, re-regulation, boundary redrawing of municipal government, and restrictive legislation. In fact, amalgamation created new and bigger state apparatuses; in Toronto, for instance, the number of municipal employees has grown since amalgamation. Moreover, the government implemented new regulatory modes that have caused many problems; for example, in education, teaching professionals in schools and universities were reeling under the quotidian effects of changing workloads, stagnating salaries, increased class sizes, shifting curricula, altered governance, and reduced budgets.

The seductive simplicity of the CSR led to dramatic incisions into the everyday life of many people in the province. Overall, the neoliberal project in Toronto appeared as a mix of half-hearted market reforms (including the privatization of Toronto's collective consumption, a lean local state, etc.) and frontal attacks on the poor, the Left, Labour, etc. Among the provincial policies implemented post-1995 that affected the urban were:

- drastic welfare cuts (starting with a 21 per cent cut in benefits in September of that year),
- the *Safe Street Act* (directed against squeegee kids and panhandlers),
- the reduction and redesign of local government (Boudreau 2000; Keil 2000),
- the amalgamation of hundreds of local governments (Sancton 2000),
- the reduction of the number of provincial full-time social service positions by 21,000 (Mallan 2001),
- the introduction of workfare, the legalization of the 60-hour work week (based on total intransigence towards public and private sector unions and their concerns and demands),
- the loosening of planning restrictions and the pursuit of an aggressive (sub)urban growth strategy (only recently reigned in through a "smart growth" strategy with doubtful credentials),
- the elimination of all public housing programs and downloading of responsibilities to the local level (Urquhart 2001),
- the de-regulation of the province's environmental regime (Winfield and Jenish 1998),
- strategic attacks on public worker unions,
- the dismantling and systematic underfunding of the education system, including the curtailing of school boards and their rights,
- the monitoring and harassment of civil society organizations.

During the roll-back phase alone, the Tories rescinded the *Planning Act* (just reformed under the previous NDP provincial government) and killed anti-scab legislation and other sparse progressive regulations created by the NDP or earlier.

Deregulation and Drinking Water

In May 2000, E. coli contaminated drinking water in the community of Walkerton, two hours north of Toronto, killed seven people, and made thousands of residents violently sick. Blame for this incident was partly put on the deregulation of water monitoring and other environmental services under the Harris government. It led to major reform of the drinking water system in Ontario.

Some aspects of the Tory agenda can be explained by the sociology of power. The inner circles of Mike Harris's regime tended to be mostly white Anglo males, who were non-urban small entrepreneurs (such as car salesmen and resort owners) and who displayed an anti-urban bias. They were supported by aggressively neoliberal young, right-wing intellectuals and practitioners, who were ideologically tied to ideas of market liberalism and state retrenchment. The modernizing global appeal of their "reforms" blended in well with the more reactionary, socially conservative, non-urban, or even anti-urban agenda of the provincial PC Party. Yet, rather than separating themselves from the masses, these "common sense" revolutionaries walked a fine populist line and constructed a carefully guarded centrist hegemony that tried to capture the spirit of middle Ontario (Dale 1999). Only after the Walkerton water debacle (see box above) did this populist strategy unravel in the face of mounting evidence that this state was no good for the people and that this government was associated with the notion of "death" (Salutin 2001, A13).

Urban Neoliberalism in Toronto

In what follows, urban neoliberalism is viewed through six lenses.

1. Changing the Space of Politics

The CSR has had severe spatial effects. Amalgamation was the main venue through which the Harris Tories "revolutionized" state-society relationships in Ontario. Since the province has sole constitutional jurisdiction over urban affairs in Canada, the shift towards a radical neoliberal agenda has had severe impacts on the province's cities, most notably Toronto. First, the provincial government amalgamated seven local governments in Toronto into one municipality. Second, it downloaded social welfare and transit costs to the city and caused a painful budget crunch at the municipal level. Third, it continued to cut—rather than expand—the powers of local government to tax or otherwise raise funds in order to meet the growing needs of an expanding world city reality.

The top-down approach to amalgamation of mostly large urban regions was designed with a glance at the regional political landscape in Ontario. The Tory victories—the original in 1995 and the repeat in 1999 for their second term—were mostly built on that party's strong support in rural and exurban areas. Mostly white—and relatively wealthy—voters determined the political fate of the entire province and its major cities. It is significant to note, though, that like other neoconservative and neoliberal governments before them (see box, p. 24–25), the Harris Tories did the "political splits," resting one foot of their platform on a rhetoric of small town conservatism while placing the other on a radical modernization strategy.

2. The Reluctant Global City Strategy

The same kind of political gymnastics were present in the Tories' relationship to Toronto as an international city. While widely considered ignorant of urban issues and uncomfortable with—if not antagonistic towards—Toronto's multiculturalism and diversity, the Harris government consistently pushed Toronto as a location for international capital accumulation. This was nowhere as visible as in the period of the (unsuccessful) bid process for the 2008 Summer Olympics.

3. Bourgeois Urbanism

Reminiscent of their counterparts in Europe, Canadian elites are increasingly presenting themselves as "urban." This is a reversal from earlier North American trends of middle-class flight to the suburbs, which admittedly was never as strong in Toronto as elsewhere. The new urbanity of certain elite factions is quite compatible with the continued colonization of the rural countryside through wealthy urban fugitives. The "re-embourgoisement" of the city goes hand in hand with the continued tendency of Canadian capital to reinvest its resource-based superprofits into real estate and the built environment. This tendency also corresponds well with the increased movement to sanitize, control, and suburbanize inner city spaces as they become the site for the staging of global elite culture and spectacle. The Harris government's policies of

TABLE 3.1 **Six Perspectives on Neoliberalism in Ontario**

	Political economy	Technologies of power	Everyday urbanism and resistance
Changing space of politics	Amalgamation, lean government	Downloading, fewer politicians; Bill 46 (Public Sector Accountability) brings all public sector organizations under strict auditing controls	Suburbanization of the city, but fierce resistance to amalgamation
The reluctant global city strategy	Waterfront plan, Olympic bid, and the "competitive city"	Urban revanchism (*Safe Streets Act*) and entrepreneurialism; Toronto Competes and the new general plan	Diversity as public relations strategy, but continued racism in institutions and on the street; new political force in immigrant politics
Bourgeois urbanism	Condominium boom, high end culture	Gated communities, private policing; quit public housing programs; 60,000 Ontario families evicted in 2000; growth in provincial eviction rate; end of rent control (Walkom 2001)	Priority of housing property in the public mind; renters fight back; homeless activism soars
Re-scaling of urban imaginary	The global region; the learning region; the auto region; leisure economy, sprawl, suburban subdivisions	Re-regulation of the city and the countryside; no development controls; lately: "smart growth"	The reversal of the downtown-centred imaginary brings in new urban actors; struggle over development of the Oak Ridges Moraine

liberalization of urban development regimes and policing of urban space strongly supported these general trends.

4. The Re-scaling of the Urban Imaginary

The claim for Toronto's global prominence—or at least competitiveness—is now built on the larger region in which the old core is

TABLE 3.1 **Six Perspectives on Neoliberalism in Ontario (continued)**

	Political economy	Technologies of power	Everyday urbanism and resistance
Ecological modernization	Development with nature, privatization of natural resources and services (water, sewers, etc.)	De- and re-regulation of everything environmental; ecological citizenship becomes defined through markets	The Tory heartland, the "905" telephone region around Toronto gears up for protest as their suburban exclusivity is threatened by out-of-control development
New social disparities	The new economy; continentalization, Americanization, globalization	Cuts to welfare, workfare programs; no public housing, labour standards lowered, working time has increased; health care for marginal groups has worsened; Bill 57 weakens workers' right to refuse unsafe work; Bill 147 introduces potential 60-hour work week	Redefined social norms: welfarism stigmatized, poverty made invisible; strong anti-Tory resistance throughout their mandate; days of action, anti-globalization movement localized in OCAP protests

considered only one among possibly many growth poles of economic and residential development. Rather than viewing Toronto as the core of a regionally or nationally constructed hinterland, it now appears as an almost de-nationalized switching station of a global economy, whose flows of capital, people, and information dissolve the traditional spatial arrangements of the urban region. On one level, neoliberalism appeared as a mode of re-regulation of the city and the countryside, town, and suburbs. The Harris government killed extensive planning reform measures just implemented under the previous NDP government and created the conditions for continued sprawl in the province. Only late in their second mandate did the Tories feebly voice a "smart growth agenda," which — at close inspection — was little more than a stepped-up and rationalized road building program.

FIGURE 3.1 Dundas Square: sanitized and spectacularized public space. This symbolic intervention in the core of the downtown commercial area was inspired by the Times Square redevelopment in New York in the 1990s but has gone further: it did not just gentrify space considered blighted with digital storefronts and entertainment venues but also tied in educational functions (Ryerson University is nearby and shares spaces with a movie theatre) under a comprehensive security concept.

5. Ecological Modernization

The Harris Tories fundamentally affected societal relationships with nature in the province. De-regulation of the environment and cutbacks in the Ministry of the Environment proved deadly in Walkerton, where seven people died in 2000 as a result of water contamination (see box, p. 60). Harris also instituted new and more relaxed regulations for forestry, hunting, the land use process, and conservation, to name just a few. The result, again, was confusion, government retreat, ecological modernization, and outright regulatory interventionism in favour of mostly privileged social groups, such as suburban homeowners. The exurban strategy of development with, rather than against, "nature" has its urban counterpart in all manner of "green" strategies for the waterfront, urban wetlands, and a golf course next to the CN Tower in the city's downtown core. With few exceptions, these strategies were apt to increase the role of the neoliberal project in the restructuring of the relationship with nature, particularly through marketization and privatization of land, services, and resources.

6. New Social Disparities

As the social is now increasingly redefined in cultural terms, difference is also marked more or less in cultural terms. During the 1990s, there was certainly a "growing gap"—i.e., a rising inequality in income distribution, debt and wealth, and mounting rifts in labour markets—between "good," well-paid, and relatively secure managerial and (selected) professional jobs, and a rapidly increasing number of "bad," low-paid, non-unionized, and "casual" (part-time, temporary, or contract) jobs. The growing gap was mostly attributed to economic restructuring (layoffs, downsizing); neoliberal policies (tax cuts, cuts to social programs, reduced public employment, financial deregulation, high real interest rates, etc.); the heightened influence of aggressive corporate interests in public policy; and the role of finance and speculative business horizons in accelerating economic restructuring, prolonging economic stagnation, and pushing corporate interests into neoliberal directions. In virtually all these domains, the Harris Tories played a decisive role in redefining the norms of poverty, welfarism, workfarism, housing, etc.

Conclusion: From Defense to Resistance

Our main argument has been that throughout this chain of restructuring and rescaling of spatialized political economies, neoliberal ideological advances, and new technologies of power, a new urban everyday was formed that dramatically redefined the social and territorial compromise, the mode of regulation, and the experiences—the perceived, conceived, and lived spaces—of the city. The Tory CSR transformed the horizon of individual and collective expectation and altered urban subjectivity. The premier and his ministers repeatedly commented on what they expected to be normal and on what they expected others—like poor people, workers, or mothers—to view as normal. Remarks on the low price of tuna fish in the face of cuts to welfare, propagating the value of a warm breakfast cooked by stay-at-home mothers in reaction to cuts to school funding, and expounding the virtues of home ownership in an age of non-existent funding for rental or social housing characterized the government's tenacity in making their policy reforms stick in the minds and practices of people in Ontario.

Yet the hegemony of the CSR waned after a few years. What began with the dynamic and contested spirit of its program for a new "post-socialist" everyday after five years of social democratic government ended in a politics of fatigue and even failure. For a few short years, Harris—at least in the eyes of his supporters—appeared to have the Midas touch: his policies turned around a floundering economy, stabilized the provincial budget, rid the cities of bloated governments, reduced crime, displaced street people and squeegee kids, broke trade union power in the public sector, etc. After 2001 his government was haunted by a series of deadly incidents, which affected regular people in their normal everyday lives: rural citizens died of water contamination, a highly pregnant woman under house arrest for welfare fraud passed away in unbearable summer heat, and an Aboriginal protester was killed by police with the knowledge of—or even orders from—the premier's office (see Edwards 2003).

The fundamental redesign of social values under the Tory regime has led to entirely new ways of living life in Toronto. It is interesting to note that the CSR represented both "roll-back" and "roll-out" neoliberalism (Peck and Tickell 2002). The speed with which the Tories destroyed and replaced time-honoured and engrained institutions of the welfarist local state took many by surprise. The "Red" Tory-Liberal social welfarism, as well as feeble attempts at social democracy during the second half of the twentieth century, gave way to a workfarist, revanchist regime; ideologies of municipal service and public government were substituted by neoliberal governance models and market-driven development schemes. As a result, the local state has diversified into a complex web of governance functions spread out over all parts of civil society but tied to the logic and technologies of rule one finds in the marketplace. The willful subjection of people to ethical laws and norms that demand sacrifices plays an important role in a regime that pretends to have all opportunities open for all people (Harris gave himself a pay raise while cutting back welfare and not hiking the minimum wage). The CSR ultimately posed some fundamental questions about the meaning of democratic theory. As substantive neoliberal reforms took shape, they impacted on the very understanding of the process of politics as public and democratic. Harris governed on the basis of what one critic in a different context once called "the streamlined, focus-grouped responsiveness of the marketplace" (quoted in Drainie 1998, 80).

The Tory-led neoliberalization of Toronto was largely coincident with a new form of urban development politics which introduced an increasing dissociation within urban political economy and a disengagement of urban development politics from other political sectors, especially from social and environmental politics as well as from questions of local democracy, citizenship, and governance. While urban development is indeed often articulated in connection with culture and nature for reasons of legitimization, it withdraws itself at the same time from public political processes. The set of demands of civil society in regards to urban politics, which is not only restricted to economic growth and the critique of it, is separated from urban development politics and reconstructed as a realm of secondary relevance to municipal governance.

4
Making the Megacity

For some reason, many people think that bigger is better. Names such as "The World's Biggest Bookstore," slogans such as "Mega Sale," or fantasies of owning ever bigger SUVs are examples of the fascination for bigness as a means of becoming winners in the competition for everything.

However, the 1990s were the decade of smallness: small and lean governments; bringing power down to the community in order to break out of the big bureaucratic structures of nation-wide fiscal solidarity; fighting obesity and individualizing responsibility for health; and cultivating lean and clean bodies, small and efficient families, productive and competitive communities.

The rationale for Mike Harris's amalgamation of Metro Toronto and its six local municipalities was about both bigness and smallness, competitiveness and individualization. It was, in other words, a concretization of that government's mixed ideology of neoliberalism and neoconservatism. Under Harris, the provincial PC Party underwent an important ideological transformation, drifting from a tradition of Red Toryism characterized by big government spending that supported values of traditional family life and heterosexual morality to an emphasis on individual performance and a retraction of state monies.

Amalgamation came to be seen across Canada as a magic solution to streamline municipal governance. Beginning with Winnipeg, Halifax, Toronto, then Montreal, Ottawa, Quebec City, and many other smaller agglomerations, it became a Canadian cultural trait when compared to

Consolidation, Merger, and Amalgamation

Consolidation, merger, and amalgamation refer to the process of redrawing administrative and political boundaries by eliminating smaller units and bundling them in a larger entity. The choice of one term or the other generally depends on the local political culture. Merger is the preferred term in Montreal as it is a direct translation of the French term *fusion*. In Toronto, the debate was initiated by the Harris government with the term amalgamation. The term consolidation is common in the United States and in academic literature. It does not necessarily lead to amalgamation; sometimes two-tiered structures are preferred. It refers to the "consolidation-fragmentation debate," which dates back to the late 1920s but which intensified in the 1950s and 1960s.

In general terms, consolidation was thought to be an excellent way to produce economies of scale, efficiency, and cost savings while equalizing the provision of services throughout the metropolitan area (Studenski 1930; Jones 1942; Committee for Economic Development 1966). Some regionalists argued also that it creates stronger democratic institutions because it gives more power and functional competence at the city-regional level and thus provides more autonomy from state/provincial legislatures (as summarized by Keating 1995). Other arguments in favour of regional consolidation are the fact that it facilitates long-term comprehensive planning while enhancing the competitive advantage of the region as a whole. It is also argued that it provides the institutional scaffolding to resist class and racial segregation by installing redistribution mechanisms.

In reaction to the strength of the regionalist movement, a group of scholars centered at Indiana University gained prominence in the 1960s by making the case for jurisdictional fragmentation (Tiebout 1956; Ostrom, Tiebout, *et al.* 1961; Bish 1971). By enhancing competition between local states, jurisdictional fragmentation was thought to offer individuals a wider choice of tax/service packages to respond to their preferences. Local cities, they argued, compete with one another to attract residents, who "vote with their feet" if the balance between taxes and services do not satisfy them anymore (Tiebout 1956). This market-based rationale relies on deeply held American beliefs in citizen choices and on the fear of big government, big businesses, and monopolies (Bish and Warren 1972). It is thought that smaller units are more responsive to local preferences and that the addition of various functional arrangements (such as special-purpose bodies) will provide citizens more opportunities to participate in the "coproduction" of services (Ostrom, Tiebout, *et al.* 1961).

the continuous fragmentation solutions south of the border. Interestingly, both amalgamation and fragmentation were solutions implemented in the name of fiscal austerity and neoliberalism. This is why they did not happen without resistance.

The New Deal for Cities and Communities

What came to be known as the New Deal was officially announced in Paul Martin's first Throne Speech in February 2004. Building on the report published in November 2002, by Jean Chrétien's Caucus Task Force on Urban Issues, "Canada's Urban Strategy: A Blueprint for Action" (led by Judy Sgro), the New Deal focuses on coordinating federal departments in order to foster a coherent urban strategy and coordinating urban actions with provincial and municipal governments. This is necessary given that the federal government does not have constitutional jurisdiction over municipal affairs. However, it can act on affordable housing, transportation, infrastructure, and immigration.

In February 2004, Paul Martin promised municipalities a full rebate on the GST they pay when buying goods and services, and a share of gas tax, in order to stimulate infrastructure renewal. This money is slowly coming down into municipal revenues. Public transit has been given special funding from the federal government. Arts and cultural institutions in Toronto are receiving funding for renovation. In certain provinces the New Deal became more of a reality, with, for example, the Vancouver tripartite agreement. In Ontario, the new *City of Toronto Act* (Bill 53) resulted from a joint city-province task force.

In the meantime, the Toronto City Summit Alliance and the Big City Mayors Caucus of the Federation of Canadian Municipalities continued to work behind the scene to concretize the New Deal, even after Paul Martin's defeat and the election of Stephen Harper as prime minister. Harper has remained largely silent on urban issues. The newest struggle led by New Deal advocates is to be systematically consulted by the federal government on urban issues and to receive a portion of sales tax.

The Story of Amalgamation

Although never explicitly announced, two of Harris's promises during the 1995 electoral campaign led to the government's decision to merge local municipalities in the former Metro Toronto. The promise to cut income taxes by 30 per cent, while balancing the provincial budget at the same time, meant that $6 billion needed to be cut out of the $56 billion of annual government spending. Thus, the new Harris government initiated a series of trimming measures through deep reforms of the education and welfare systems, which had important impacts on the relationship between the province and its municipalities. First, municipalities were now responsible for a considerably heavier burden of social services, from day care to housing and welfare costs. Second, a reform of property taxes meant that owners in the central city had to

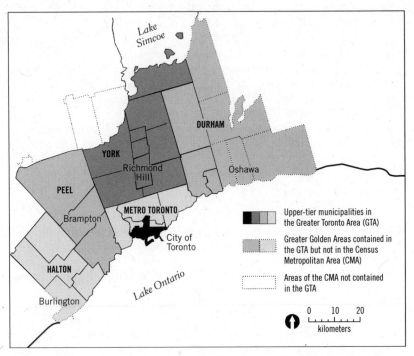

FIGURE 4.1 The Toronto city-region before amalgamation. Metro Toronto and its six constituent lower-tier municipalities (including the pre-amalgamation City of Toronto) were merged to create the new City of Toronto. Halton, Peel, York, and Durham remain as two-tier regional governments.

face huge jumps in the amounts they owed, which meant that local politicians could hardly increase taxes to cover the increased expenses they were required to assume. This led to reduced services, much public discontent, and immense uncertainty in a period of transition from the pre-amalgamated Toronto to a completely new administrative, political, and fiscal structure.

Why did the Harris government decide to amalgamate? It was, in their view, the only way Toronto could assume its new responsibility for welfare and social costs. Of course, the government did not explicitly put it this way. Instead, they argued that amalgamation was good for all municipalities, not only to fulfill the special needs of Toronto: "It is clear to Ontario taxpayers that maintaining 815 municipalities in the province's current fiscal climate is simply unrealistic. Taxpayers want a smaller, more efficient public sector, and fewer levels of government. Those municipalities that remain reluctant to look at restructuring must realize that there is more belt-tightening to come" (A note from Al Leach accompanying the report from the Ministry of Municipal Affairs and Housing 1996).

But Toronto (followed, later, by other municipalities such as Ottawa) was the first to taste forced mergers in order to make the fiscal rearrangement plan known as "downloading" work. The official objectives for the *City of Toronto Act*, first announced in December 1996, were to "bring in lower taxes, [...] better services and [...] deliver services closer to the people" (Leach 1996). The rationale was that amalgamation would eliminate the duplication of services

FIGURE 4.2 No-mega-cd. Produced as a fundraiser for Citizens for Local Democracy, the CD contains speeches given during C4LD meetings as well as songs composed by local music bands in support of the struggle against amalgamation.

and competition between municipalities, thus fuelling economic growth; furthermore, it would increase accountability to taxpayers by disentangling the current complex two-tiered structure.

Despite many reports proposing to enlarge Metro Toronto to incorporate the GTA, amalgamation of the central core appeared to the Harris government as the most seductive solution to the fiscal crisis looming over Toronto after downloading. Beyond this pragmatic reason, it had a strong political appeal, as it was seen as a means to weaken Toronto's tradition of left-of-centre reformism by merging it with more conservative-friendly suburban municipalities. Harris's electoral base was indeed in small-town Ontario, where resentment towards cosmopolitan Toronto has traditionally been strong.

Initially, amalgamation had the support of the Board of Trade, the Urban Development Institute, the Greater Toronto Home Builders Association, the staff at the Metro government level, and Metro Toronto Council. On the other side, the reformist and urban middle-class actors of the central city were fiercely opposed. Former Toronto reformist mayor John Sewell (1978–80) initiated a movement called Citizens for Local Democracy (C4LD). Structured around a steering committee of about 15 people, C4LD organized actions such as weekly public meetings. Ideas and actions were conveyed through a strong communication system of

TABLE 4.1 **Chronology of Events Leading to Amalgamation**

April 1996	Appointment of the Who Does What panel headed by David Crombie (to give advice on downloading)
Summer 1996	Publication of a guide to (voluntary) municipal restructuring
October 17, 1996	*Better Local Government Act* Toronto is given 30 days to come up with a restructuring plan
December 11, 1996	Creation of Citizens for Local Democracy (C4LD), led by John Sewell
December 16, 1996	Release of a KPMG report on "savings" to be made by amalgamation
December 17, 1996	Official statement on the government's intention to amalgamate Toronto
January 13–17, 1997	Mega-week announcement of "disentanglement" measures: reduction of number of school boards from 129 to 66; removal of education costs from property taxes; downloading of 50% of welfare costs and their full administration onto municipalities; municipal proportion of day care costs were to rise from 20 to 50; housing, public transit, and public health were transferred in totality to municipalities; grants for community policing and libraries were abolished; provincial share of long-term health care services reduced from 80 to 50%; property tax reform based on actual value assessment announced.
January 29, 1997	End of Second Reading of Bill 103 at Queen's Park
February 3, 1997	Public hearings begin and last for weeks
February 15, 1997	Street demonstration against Bill 103

newsletters, a web page, three e-mail list serves, a telephone tree, and a hotline. C4LD did not have paid staff and received no government funding; it was entirely financed by individual contributions mostly gathered during the weekly Monday night meetings. Information, updates, action coordination, and entertainment by prominent artists, academics, and public figures were consistently part of the agenda.

Two main arguments opposing the amalgamation bill were at the core of C4LD: first, it was a threat to local democracy; and, second, despite the province's constitutional power to impose municipal restructuring, it lost legitimacy because it was rushed through the legislature without prior public consultations.

C4LD was a dynamic movement that enjoyed extensive media attention. It had the support of municipal and provincial politicians who had many electoral points to gain by opposing the Harris government. In early

TABLE 4.1 Chronology of Events Leading to Amalgamation (continued)

End of February	Mr. Justice Lloyd Brenan ruled that Trustees' appointments were made without authority. Yet, Toronto Citizen's Legal Challenge is eventually defeated by Mr. Justice Stephen Borins
March 3, 1997	Municipal referenda on amalgamation: 76% say no
March 27, 1997	Modifications to Bill 103: Trustees are replaced by a Financial Advisory Board; adoption of the federal riding system for council elections; 56 (instead of 44) councillors; neighbourhood committees are no longer compulsory
April 2, 1997	Legislative assembly resumes with filibuster
April 21, 2007	Bill 103 is voted into law
Spring 1997	Introduction of *Fair Property Tax Act*
Fall 1997	Major province-wide teachers' strike
November 10, 1997	First megacity elections
January 1, 1998	Incorporation of the new City of Toronto
October 1998	Establishment of community councils with limited powers upon recommendation from David Miller's committee on neighbourhood councils
March 4, 1998	Creation of a Task Force on Community Access and Equity
Fall 1999	Debate around city-state status for Toronto
December 15, 1999	Adoption of recommendations by the task force

February 1997, up to 15 meetings a night were held across Metro Toronto, indicating citizens' concern about the issue. On February 15, different organizations, citizens, political parties, mayors, councillors, artists, and musicians marched on Yonge Street. The carnivalesque march prominently featured a great symbol of Canadian democracy: William Lyon Mackenzie (1795–1861). Mackenzie, first mayor of Toronto, was a democracy advocate struggling against aristocratic control. The march re-staged his attempted insurrection of 1837, which occurred on the same street. Thousands

FIGURE 4.3 "Say No to Megacity," produced by Citizens for Local Democracy.

of people attended the protest. "It started out so very slick, with their deficit arithmetic," sang Moxy Früvous, a Toronto rock group, "but today's the day that we fight back!" Energy was high, but on April 21, 1997, Bill 103 was voted into law, and Toronto was ordered amalgamated, effective January 1, 1998.

The Transition and Early Growing Pains

The Harris government still faced resistance to its plans. Fall 1997 came with a province-wide strike of teachers who were struggling against the education reform. The streets of Toronto were filled with protests. In this climate, the first municipal elections for the amalgamated city took place. People sensed the importance of the moment. For elections that usually gather from 28–38 per cent of voters' participation, the turnout that fall hit 50 per cent in many areas across the new megacity. The day following the elections, the media gorged itself on headlines such as "Birth of a City" (*Toronto Star*), "Lastman makes megacity history" (*Globe and Mail*), or "The mourning after" (*NOW Magazine*).

Two frontrunners dominated the landscape: Mel Lastman, populist mayor of the former North York for 25 years, and Barbara Hall, liberal progressive mayor of the former Toronto. As a result of this election, the right-leaning new megacouncil had twice more suburban councillors than their urban counterparts and less than a quarter of left-leaning representatives. Mel Lastman won the mayoralty. C4LD had lost not only the fight against amalgamation but the struggle to keep reformist Barbara Hall in power in order to mitigate the effects of restructuring.

The new council sat for the first time shortly after January 1, 1998, when the new city was officially incorporated. It was cacophonous, immense, and confusing. The amalgamation act left the question of community councils open. Left-leaning councillor David Miller was appointed head of a special committee to review the Transition Team Report, which had recommended that community councils should "listen to the community, monitor its well-being, and bring community priorities and concerns forward to City Council." The report is filled with the language of democracy and citizen involvement. Miller tried to reconcile different views, some hoping to recreate with community councils the former local municipalities, others preferring to endow them only with advisory powers. In the end, community councils were given a mandate over local planning, development control, local transportation and recreation, and neighbourhood matters. Currently, alongside six other committees (Policy and Finance, Administration, Planning and Transportation, Economic Development and Parks, Works, and Community Services), community councils are accountable directly to City Council and the mayor. They play an advisory role and can conduct hearings on behalf of City Council. They are composed of city councillors elected in the area and are not an additional layer of government. Basically, they are top-down local bodies that act merely as administrative units.

The feeling of starting anew and the nervousness of city staff amidst the changing structure did not help newly elected Mayor Lastman when he faced a budget crisis. The new megacity was threatened by a deficit of $163.5 million (a figure later revised to $151 million) — $84.1 million from increased responsibilities and $79.4 million from the loss of provincial grants. The province finally offered Toronto a two-year $200 million interest-free loan and a one-time $50 million grant to ease the transition. In addition, the new *Fair Property Tax Act* introduced by Harris — the basis of which was a reassessment of the market value of homes as of June 1996 — meant that some people were faced with huge increases because many properties in the former City of Toronto had not been reassessed for over 40 years. The new system fixed residential taxes at approximately 1.26 per cent of the property's market value, to be reassessed every three years. Astonishing tax fluctuation stories filled the media with figures: small retail stores would be consumed by tax hikes of up to 10,000 per cent, while bank towers would pocket million-dollar refunds. Given the urgency of the situation, Lastman later asked Harris for a three-year cap on commercial and industrial property tax to 2.5 per cent (up or down). Council ultimately decided on a 7.5-year phase-in period.

This climate of budget crisis and fiscal austerity, combined with residents' dissatisfaction and political uncertainty had important impacts on the morale of city employees. Many projects were stalled for years until the arrival of Mayor Miller in the fall of 2003 (and, as we will see in Chapter 10, the growing influence of Richard Florida and his creativity mantra on public discourse).

From a Struggle Against Amalgamation to Mobilization For a City-region

How did amalgamation and the fierce struggle against it affect the political dynamics in Toronto? Did the suburbs win over downtown, as many opponents of amalgamation feared? What happened to social mobilization during the struggle against amalgamation and after? How did the megacity saga shape Toronto's self-identity?

Transition to the new city faded into a well-functioning administrative structure of 50,000 public employees, a council with 44 councillors, and a populist mayor with a strong personality. C4LDers gradually abandoned weekly meetings and channelled their mobilizing energies towards a new, but closely related struggle: Toronto's self-determination. Despite skirmishes and growing pains, amalgamated Toronto did not become divisive and dysfunctional. C4LDers, business owners, intellectuals, city employees, and local politicians converged (with varying degrees of intensity and conviction) around the project of ensuring Toronto's central role in Canada and the world. Yes, the old metropolitan core was amalgamated, but the GTA wanted to be recognized as Canada's leading city-region.

Despite apparent agreement on the need to fight for Toronto's autonomy, the strategies people devised to get there differed. Lastman began the process in the fall of 1999, when he declared, while on vacation in Florida, that Toronto should be its own province. He later pulled back from this position, but the comments had already unleashed waves of comments back in the city. A *Toronto Star* editorial (*Toronto Star* 2000) pointed to the fact that, with a population larger than that of Newfoundland, Prince Edward Island, Nova Scotia, New Brunswick, Manitoba, and Saskatchewan combined, Toronto still could not collect sales, gas, or tobacco taxes. Proposals varied from the creation of a Province of Southern Ontario to the creation of a new designation of city-states that could also include Montreal and Vancouver. John Sewell started a website exploring how to ensure local self-government in Canada, while a Committee for the Province of Toronto was formed in order to seek provincial status for Toronto by changing the Canadian Constitution. Main arguments in support of such a special designation relied on the imbalance of power between the urban region and mainly rural provinces, as well as the importance of the urban regional economy in the global world.

To compete in the world, it was argued that Toronto needed the same resource and power as other global cities such as London, Paris, or Berlin. Some in Toronto saw the city headed for a grim future of increasing homelessness, traffic gridlock, service cuts, and steeply increasing user fees. Citizens and experts alike debated how to change this situation. However, the idea of a Province of Toronto or a change in the Canadian Constitution to create a new city-state status seemed too far-fetched.

One possible solution, embraced by a wide variety of individuals and organizations, was a city charter that would be granted by the province. Such charters already existed in Vancouver, Winnipeg, Montreal, and Saint John (www.canadiancities.ca). A charter would provide Toronto with new and inalienable rights and powers with respect to how it could raise certain revenues and conduct business and deliver services, as well as determine the sorts of direct relationships it could enter into with the federal government (or other governments), the private sector, and non-profit sectors.

A number of state, business, and civic groups made proposals for enhanced municipal autonomy for Toronto:

- *The Greater Toronto Charter* was the product of a group headed by Alan Broadbent, corporate philanthropist and chair of Avana Capital Corporation in Toronto (Avana Capital Corporation 2000). Broadbent's efforts were supported by the publication of a small book called *Toronto: Considering Self-Government* (Rowe 2000).
- *Towards a New Relationship with Ontario and Canada*. This report, dated June 2000, from the City of Toronto's Chief Administrator's Office, requested that Toronto be granted a charter (City of Toronto 2000a).
- *Ontario Charter: A Proposed Bill of Rights for Local Government* was published in 1994 by the Association of Municipalities of Ontario (AMO 1994) and promoted local self-government.
- *Local Self Government* was (and is) a web-based newsletter on issues pertaining to local self-government, published by John Sewell (Sewell 2005).
- *Towards a Greater Toronto Charter and the Environment* was published in 2000 by Toronto's most influential urban environmental group, the Toronto Environmental Alliance (TEA) (Corbett 2000).

· The Toronto Board of Trade strongly supported the main themes of
the charter debate (The Toronto Board of Trade 2001b).

The debate paved the way to the Canada-wide New Deal for Cities.
Yet, two lines of conflict were already apparent. There was disagreement
on whether a Toronto Charter should include the GTA or the amalgamated city only. At the Canadian scale, there were important tensions
between those who argued for special privileges to big cities because of
their specific economic and cultural role and social responsibilities, and
those, such as the Federation of Canadian Municipalities (FCM), who
argued that all municipalities, irrespective of size, should benefit from
the New Deal.

The New Deal for Cities was announced by Paul Martin when he
became prime minister in 2003. As an integral part of the Liberal Party's
electoral platform, and central to its first Throne Speech, the New Deal
reflected many of the concerns that had been expressed by big city mayors
across Canada after the 1990s wave of municipal amalgamation. Urbanist
and Toronto resident Jane Jacobs had called a meeting of the five big city
mayors in 1999, with the help of Glenn Murray, who was then mayor of
Winnipeg. Known as the C5, they intensively lobbied the federal and
their respective provincial governments. They got some response at the
federal level from the NDP (which had elected former Toronto councillor and FCM president Jack Layton as federal party leader) and from the
Liberal Party. When Paul Martin became the new leader of the Liberal
Party after the departure of Jean Chrétien, he appointed John Godfrey as
the Minister of State Responsible for Infrastructure and Communities in
order to implement this new urban agenda.

The New Deal for Cities also concerned provincial governments,
because the Canadian Constitution puts municipal affairs strictly under
their jurisdiction. It was fraught with tensions not only between levels of
government (which are particularly acute in Quebec) but also between
large cities and other towns in Canada. Because of the necessity to create
intergovernmental cooperation in order to implement the new urban
agenda, the Liberal federal government slowly drifted from an "urban"
agenda, conceived as a new regionalist philosophy encouraging winning
city-regions on the global market, to a "cities" then "communities" agenda,
destined to rethink the division of labour between levels of government

and to provide more autonomy to all municipalities. The FCM made an important breakthrough in this respect during the constitutional debates of 1988–92 (the Meech Lake and the Charlottetown Accords), but they were unable to capture the attention of federal leaders or win the public debate. With the hype around global cities and the new regionalism, Paul Martin and his Liberal Party were more receptive in 2003.

A provincial-municipal joint interim report for a new *City of Toronto Act* was published in May 2005, proposing important advances in providing Toronto with specific powers. Most importantly, Toronto was to be granted "permissive powers," that is, legislative power that other municipalities would not have (they can pass bylaws only on issues predetermined by the province). Municipalities in Ontario can act solely on issues listed in the provincial municipal act. With permissive powers, the City of Toronto could take the initiative to pass bylaws on issues they deem important, even if they are not explicitly listed in the municipal act. The report also suggested that the city could levy a new hotel tax and taxes on parking lot spaces, but it could not get a share of income or sales taxes.

Based on this report, Bill 53—the new legislation for Toronto—was finally released on December 14, 2005 with great fanfare. "It is the dawning of a new era in municipal affairs in this province," announced John Gerretsen, Minister of Municipal Affairs and Housing. Vancouver lawyer Donald Lidstone, an advocate of stronger municipalities, commented: "Toronto and the Ontario government are now 156 years ahead of the rest of urban Canada in terms of the City's empowerment and self-determination. That makes Toronto's citizens gifted and it happens to make Toronto more of an international player. This constitutional milestone will help cities in the rest of Canada in their quest for palpable recognition as an order of government under our constitutional regime" (Local Government Bulletin 2005).

The new legislation was called *The Stronger City of Toronto for a Stronger Ontario Act*. The city could now set opening hours and closing hours for bars and businesses. It gained more control over the appearance and design of buildings, particularly the power to establish green roofs, i.e. roofs covered with vegetation that make use of precipitation and provide natural insulation for the building below. It expanded powers to license and regulate businesses. Its existing powers to establish a lobbyist registry and an integrity commissioner were expanded, and it got the power to change ward boundaries. The bill also allowed the city for the first time to impose taxes on alcohol, tobacco, and entertainment. It was estimated that the tax revenue generated from these services might reach as high as $50 million. By comparison, the amount the city raised in 2006 from parking tickets was approximately $70 million. Thus, this new taxing authority does not amount to much, particularly since the city's current budget is over $7 billion.

Moreover, the act is hamstrung by Sections 151–54, which give the provincial government power to dictate exactly what the city can and cannot do, including regulations "imposing conditions and limitations on the powers of the city" (Section 152). In the face of this provincial power, it is not easy to say that the act will make the city a self-governing body. Even the current province-wide *Municipal Act* does not allow the provincial government to intervene in such a gross manner into city affairs. Worse, Section 151 specifically gives the provincial cabinet the ability to pass regulations

- requiring the mayor to appoint the chairs of committees,
- requiring that the mayor (rather than City Council, as is now the case) appoint the chief administrative officer (thus making staff political),
- requiring that City Council appoint an executive committee and determining who will be on that committee,
- and controlling various other matters that have always been seen as under the control of City Council.

This explains why City Council was in such a hurry two days before the bill was released to agree to exactly those provisions without public hearings and in the face of a strong presentation by former mayor David Crombie against them. City Council pretended to make its own decision although it was acting under duress, knowing the province would force this system of a muscular mayor on Toronto regardless of whether the people or the council wanted it. The existence of these sections made a mockery of any notion that this legislation empowers the city.

Another curious aspect to Bill 53 is its length — over 300 pages of text. It is full of detailed prescriptions on what the council can do and cannot do on virtually every power that it is given. A quick review of the *Municipal*

Act, passed by the PC government of Mike Harris in 2001, provides a clue to the length. Bill 53 is modeled, part by part, and section by section, on the 2001 legislation. A comparison of the two documents shows that more than 90 per cent of Bill 53 is taken word for word from the *Municipal Act*. Many have noted that the 2001 legislation was not a step forward for municipalities in Ontario, and many would have preferred to live with the 1849 *Municipal Act*.

This is hardly a reasonable way to embody the hopes of those who saw the new legislation as a serious attempt to empower Toronto. It freezes the city under provincial control and the straightjacket of the current *Municipal Act*. Of course, there are some differences. The 2001 *Municipal Act* permitted municipalities (Section 11) to enact by-laws in specified "spheres of jurisdictions," and Bill 53 proposes (Section 8) that the city can pass bylaws respecting a broader range of activities—of course subject to provincial intervention (Sections 151–54) and provincial and federal law (Section 11). Is that a difference of substance? As we will see below, the *City of Toronto Act* created much conflict in City Council and among various groups in the urban region. It has meant empowering the city to take control of its own affairs, but it has also devolved conflict over scarce resources onto the city itself. Mayor David Miller learned that lesson in 2007.

Neither the new *City of Toronto Act*, nor most other proposals for more autonomy, made any concrete and believable proposals for increasing the influence of urban civil society on the institutionalized metropolitan governance process. To the contrary, the new *City of Toronto Act* gives the mayor more powers while imposing an executive committee structure in council. All proposals were concentrated on the functional efficiency and effectiveness of local—as opposed to supra-local—*governments* instead of demanding broadened bottom-up govern*ance*.

Conclusion

In the end, these were years of institutional turmoil during which city, regional, and provincial actors sought to realign power relations to their advantage. While the provincial government of Mike Harris sought to displace reformists at City Hall, urban left-leaning actors realigned within the new megacity and, soon after the election of David Miller, regained visibility. A new alliance was then struck between city and suburban actors in order to create a regional force aimed at giving Toronto more powers *vis-à-vis* the provincial and federal governments. Were they successful in this interscalar dance? Yes, to a certain degree. As a city-region, Toronto has gained some institutional and political autonomy. What remains far from being assured, however, is whether such autonomy will necessarily benefit all citizens, for autonomy does not guarantee justice and equality. Indeed, as we will see in later chapters, city-regionalism in Toronto has largely been a proxy for implementing a neoliberal agenda.

5
Diverse-City

Toronto's official doctrine is diversity. About 40 per cent of the nation's immigrants settle here. More than half of its population belong to "visible minorities." Roughly half are immigrants. These well-known figures describe an urban centre of a new type: the transnational metropolis.

The transnationalization of the urban experience in Toronto reflects its increasing relationship with international and global inter-urban economic and cultural networks, which are characterized by new forms of migration and settlement. Regardless of whether they are poor or wealthy, newcomers are tied into far-reaching diasporic, transnational relationships. Canadian cities have always been immigrant cities, but what that means has been fundamentally transformed since changes to its immigration policy in the 1960s. Previously, immigration was mostly restricted to European, typically white individuals; now, more newcomers come from all parts of the world. This has led to the formation of non-white majority neighbourhoods in the city. Due to the class and gender specific bias of immigration policy in favour of male experts and investors, immigrants are either formally well-educated and skilled migrants, whose credentials are honoured in Canada and are mostly from Europe and the United States (though also from other regions), or they are poor refugees or immigrants, whose educational record is not acknowledged here. For many of these immigrants, settlement in Canada means taking a job below their educational standard. Often, it is only the second generation—the children of these immigrants—who attend university and change their status.

This discrimination against many immigrant groups on the labour market is matched by the systemic disadvantage that racialized immigrant groups experience on the housing market, both as tenants and as buyers. Family poverty is clearly correlated with the immigrants' origins: about one-third of non-Europeans living in Toronto live below the poverty line and—although they make up only 36.9 per cent of all families in Toronto—account for 58.9 per cent of all poor families in the city (Ornstein 2000, i). In the past, Toronto lived off its reputation of being a "city of neighbourhoods" in which loosely grouped immigrant communities provided a folkloric mosaic—defying the more segregated patterns observed elsewhere, especially in the United States. But more recent tendencies—combining new forms of socio-economic stratification with social space—challenge the voluntary aspect of this enclaving of urban residential communities. In fact, new immigrant and visible minority status is becoming an indicator for location of residence in the city (Hulchanski 2007). Since most of the poorer, more diverse immigrant neighbourhoods tend to be in the old suburbs of the metropolitan region, a new challenge arises: how can the integration mechanisms—which have historically been identified with the old inner city—be replicated in the suburbs? This is of particular importance as social difference is now increasingly marked by the appearance of cultural differentiation.

Thus, Toronto has the image of a multicultural mosaic, where diversity serves as a defining character and source of pride for its residents, as well as a marketable asset. In the 1990s, an urban legend circulated and became entrenched in the city's self-image that the United Nations had designated Toronto as the most multicultural city in the world. Michael J. Doucet traced back this appellation: "from somewhere in the race relations area of the municipal bureaucracy to the speeches of municipal politicians and local media reports of those speeches to press releases from the Metropolitan Toronto Convention and Visitors Association to stories by American travel and business writers and back to the Toronto media" (Doucet 2001). However, it was never officially proclaimed by the United Nations.

Since the end of the 1970s, various task forces have examined ethnocultural tensions in Toronto. Indeed, under the control of reformists between 1972 and amalgamation, the old City of Toronto had developed a well-known participatory culture. When John Sewell won the

FIGURE 5.1 African Video Rental Store, West Toronto. Globalization and immigration are processes that work through the capillaries of neighbourhoods and communities where shops and services reflect a mix of cultures, fashions, and traditions tailored to specific immigrant groups.

mayoralty in 1978, one year after Prime Minister Pierre Elliot Trudeau proclaimed the country's policy of multiculturalism, diversity was slowly becoming a defining character of Canadian—and Toronto's—identity. The Urban Alliance on Race Relations led to the city's first employment equity policy in 1977. A year later, the Municipality of Metropolitan Toronto adopted an official multicultural policy. Today, federal and provincial governments spend considerable amounts of money promoting multiculturalism every year. But, as Croucher argues, over the years this symbolic celebration of multiculturalism has erased the need for really understanding the material conditions of minorities: "the Canadian state, by embracing and managing multiculturalism has, in effect, co-opted political space available to minority groups for mobilization or resistance along ethnic and racial lines" (Croucher 1997, 335).

Toronto the Good: Multicultural Policies and Identity

The name Toronto is a derivative from "Turuntu," the Huron word for meeting place (Croucher 1997, 324). Toronto capitalizes on this image: the amalgamated city's motto is "Diversity, our strength." The city is said to be home to residents who speak 160 languages. Nearly half (48.4 per cent) of the population was foreign-born in 1996, and 14.6 per cent of its residents arrived in Canada after 1976 (Ornstein 2000, 22). Immigrants do not settle only in the central city but also in the postwar suburbs of York, East York, North York, Scarborough, and Etobicoke. Others decide to live in the outer suburbs of Markham, Brampton, Richmond Hill, and Mississauga. In fact, the amalgamated City of Toronto is home to 80 per cent of the GTA's recent immigrants (those who arrived in the 1990s), and for nearly 25 per cent of all new arrivals in Canada (Garrett 2001, 2).

Pursuing the reformist tradition, the amalgamated city initiated a number of "diversity actions." In March 1998, a Task Force on Community Access and Equity was mandated to organize public consultations and to make recommendations on how the new council could "ensure the voices of the City's diverse communities continue to be heard." The mandate was to reinforce civil society, eliminate barriers to participation, reinforce community input into decision-making, and continue to be a model employer with a civil service that reflected the city's diversity. The task force's final recommendations ranged from supporting community organizations to engaging in a more proactive role by convincing private employers and other levels of government to eliminate discrimination in employment practices that ranged from affirmative action policies to protection against sexual harassment and translating municipal documents into several languages to support ethnic media coverage of municipal affairs.

On December 15, 1999, Council adopted all recommendations proposed by the task force and created five Community Advisory Committees (not to be confused with Community Councils) to address Aboriginal affairs; access for disabled persons; the status of women; ethnic and racial relations; and homosexual, lesbian, bisexual, and transgendered affairs. These advisory committees established a formal mechanism, through which Council could seek community advice on a given policy. They formalized certain of the former City of Toronto's procedures. For many

FIGURE 5.2 Pacific Mall, Markham. This commercial establishment at the northwestern edge of Toronto in the south of the municipality of Markham is the most spectacular example of a so-called "Chinese theme mall," where vendors offer their wares in narrow and diverse stalls on several levels.

activists, however, they were a meager compromise in comparison to their original demand: to establish a permanent committee on council to address equity issues, as well as to create an Equity Commission within the bureaucracy (Community Social Planning Council of Toronto 2000, 1).

In December, 2000, the city nominated its first Diversity Advocate (a councillor appointed by City Council), who was mandated to coordinate all diversity-related activities between council and Community Advisory Committees. The advocate was further responsible for raising awareness on equity issues among private employers and non-municipal institutions. In nominating a councillor to this function, Council officially declared that Toronto was working towards eliminating "violence, racism, homophobia, homelessness, hate crimes, hunger, illiteracy, and all barriers to human rights," further recognizing that "the City of Toronto is increasingly becoming known as a city of diversity and that this very diversity creates unique challenges" (Toronto City Council Policy and Finance Committee 2001). The Diversity Advocate's mandate was later transferred to the Chair of the Roundtable on Access, Equity, and Human Rights (2003–06). The Roundtable is currently under review by the Mayor's Office.

Hence, in its preparatory report for the city's participation in the .United Nations World Conference against Racism (UN-WCAR), held in Durban, South Africa in August 2001, its anti-racist initiatives were listed as follows:

- nomination of a Diversity Advocate;
- adoption of an action plan on access, equity, and human rights, based on the recommendations of the Task Force on Community Access and Equity;
- creation of five Community Advisory Committees;
- creation of task forces to address linguistic equity and illiteracy, immigration and refugees, elimination of hate crimes, and equity in salaries;
- adoption of a policy on non-discrimination;
- affirmation of the necessity to adopt such policy for all municipal subcontractors;
- adoption of a policy against workplace sexual harassment;
- adoption of a policy on the elimination of hate crimes;
- adoption of an employment policy;
- support for access and equity programs;
- a response to federal government proposals for reforming Canadian immigration laws; and
- support for diverse awareness-raising and education programs against intolerance (City of Toronto 2001a).

When Toronto delegates returned from Durban at the end of the conference, the city adopted an action plan for the elimination of racism and discrimination, its main objective being to ease the participation of all residents in its civic, economic, social, cultural, political, and recreational life (City of Toronto 2002a).

However, in political terms, visible minorities still have low representation at City Hall. In Canada there is no redistricting policy equivalent to the US *Fair Voting Act*, which helps facilitate the election of people of colour. Here, anti-racism politics in the areas of employment, land use (location of mosques and cultural centres), police, education, and environmental racism are still important but not yet fully achieved goals. Many social movement organizations—such as the Metro Network for

Social Justice (MNSJ), the Ontario Coalition against Poverty (OCAP), and the labour movement, which has undergone an interesting transformation of focus to include the unemployed—have been mobilizing to change this (Conway 2000).

Reality Check: The Racialization of Poverty

It is not our objective in this chapter to debate on what is the "best" practice in terms of managing diversity (assimilation, interculturalism, and multiculturalism) nor to enter the philosophical debate surrounding the virtues of multiculturalism versus other models (see, for instance, Tully 1995; Martiniello 1997; Amselle 1996; and Kymlicka 1995). What is striking, however, is that racism remains pervasive. Multiculturalism is meant to regulate demographic diversity by celebrating cultural differences rather than asking minorities to deny their cultural origins. Yet, in the context of neoliberal market-regulated everyday life, cultural differences are being commodified. Multiculturalism is reduced to the celebration of ethnic foods as something to be added to the marketing image of the city. It becomes, in other words, a new form of "differentialist racism" (Goonewardena and Kipfer 2005).

Official multiculturalism perpetuates the myth of an immigrant society in which there is no class difference. However, discrimination on housing and labour markets is pervasive. The first major study demonstrating this with Toronto figures was based on 1996 census data (Ornstein 2000). Though numbers may have changed slightly since then, the study is still relevant in that it proves how people of colour are confined to lower skilled jobs whatever their level of education. In 1996, unemployment hit 18 per cent for Arabs and West Asians, while remaining less than 7 per cent for British, Northern European, and Scandinavian residents in Metro Toronto. Consequently, almost half of Arabs, West Asians, Africans, blacks, and Caribbeans, and a little over 40 per cent of Latin Americans, have a family income lower than the Statistics Canada low-income cut-off. More recent figures for the whole of Canada show that in 2000 immigrant men earned 63.1 cents for every dollar earned by a native-born Canadian with the same education level (Helly 2003).

In the meantime, research by Punam Khosla (2003) has shown that immigrant women of colour, in particular, bear the brunt of the city's complex socio-economic restructuring, as they are systemically excluded from jobs and housing on the basis of gender and ethnicity. Even more recently, the Colour of Poverty campaign, self-described as an "Ontario community-based effort to help raise public awareness about poverty within racialized communities" (Colour of Poverty 2008), has created a set of fact sheets in order to educate communities, activists, and policy-makers about the incidence of racialization and poverty. These fact sheets address "different aspects of racialized poverty and its negative impacts on education and learning, health and well-being, employment, income levels, justice and policing, immigration and settlement, housing and homelessness, and food security in Ontario" (Colour of Poverty 2008). Though not focused on Toronto alone, this campaign points to grave injustices that are linked directly to the city's growing socio-demographic diversity. In another study, Toronto has been described as a metropolis divided into three distinctive cities, driven apart by dramatic income polarization. This polarization, the authors contend, gives a clear disadvantage to immigrants (not entirely, but strongly correlated with visible minorities) who are concentrated in low income neighbourhoods (Hulchanski 2007).

Multiculturalism, in other words, has not prevented the racialization of poverty but has led to inequalities in the well-being of visible minority populations: "such documented characteristics of racialized poverty as labour market segregation and low occupation status, high and frequent unemployment status, substandard housing combined with violent or distressed neighbourhoods, homelessness, poor working conditions, extended hours of work or multiple jobs, experience with everyday forms of racism and sexism, lead to unequal health service utilization, and differential health status" (Galabuzi 2004, 235). This spiral of inequalities is described in Chapter 7, where we discuss the Jane and Finch neighbourhood.

Crisis of Multiculturalism

During the SARS crisis of 2003, the official policy and everyday practice of multiculturalism were both put to the test in Toronto. At the time, the infectious disease, introduced to Toronto by a visitor from Hong Kong, was the trigger for many reported acts of racism, which linked the infection to people of Asian origin (Keil and Ali 2006). The usually harmonious tone of public discourse between hospitals, the community, and the media declined rapidly, Chinatown's restaurants emptied, and Asian-Canadians experienced exclusion due to their ethnic profile. When the virus was ultimately brought under control, some mopping up still had to be done as cracks could be observed in the veneer of the multicultural city. Perhaps the much-praised multiculturalism model—the very basis of Toronto's identity—is vulnerable to racist conflicts and racialized poverty, and may not be not as resilient as we had hoped in times of crisis.

It is possible to use as an example the pervasive association of violence and "race" in the public debate since 2001 and to argue that it legitimizes repressive actions based on institutionalized discrimination. Ironically, multiculturalism serves as a powerful symbolic resource that is used to legitimize state and civic actions that are doing the very opposite of what multiculturalism is supposed to do. Indeed, as a set of policies, multiculturalism originally meant that the government established programs aiming to socialize Canadians towards diversity—i.e., aiming to redefine Canadian identity as being flexible and shaped by successive waves of immigration. Concretely, the federal and provincial governments, as well as the City of Toronto, crafted advertising campaigns, imposed affirmative action in public sector employment, designed diversity education program for their employees, and funded ethnic organizations in order to help them organize and defend their rights. In the neoliberal 1990s, these programs were severely cut by the federal government in its cost-saving, balanced budget measures. In Toronto, as we have seen, . diversity programs remain and anti-racism efforts are real. Yet, despite these municipal actions, multiculturalism is endangered on the one hand by security measures and police actions that are racially marked and on the other by the commodification of multiculturalism.

In August 2005, *The Globe and Mail* reported that Toronto councillor Michael Thompson had suggested that the police should be allowed to use racial profiling techniques and stop young black males randomly to check if they had a gun (Canadian Press 2005). A few hours later, an update was posted on *The Globe and Mail* web site to say that the police and the mayor had ruled racial profiling as "completely unacceptable." It was and still is publicly impossible for the police and the mayor to openly support racial profiling, not to say that it is legally reprehensible according to the Charter of Rights and Freedoms. However, police practice often reflects the reality of discrimination, not the hope of multiculturalism.

Institutionally, it is prohibited to discriminate by intentionally denying certain people from the enjoyment of a right that is recognized to others; however, new security tools implemented since 9/11 have tempered this and have, in fact, legalized certain forms of individual rights curtailment. The federal anti-terrorism law (C-36) has led to modifications of the Criminal Code and of the law regulating the protection of personal information and access to information, as well as many other pieces of legislation. Simultaneously, C-36 created new criminal offenses: facilitating and inciting terrorist acts, affiliating with organizations that are suspected of being involved, and financially supporting a terrorist entity. In our cities, this is concretely translated into increased power for the police, giving them the right to conduct secret searches; to hold people in custody for 72 hours without charge; to conduct inquiries without warrant; to oblige detainees to undergo interrogation in front of a judge under the penalty of a year's imprisonment; to expand the six-month period of electronic eavesdropping; to listen to a person's overseas communications on a decision by the Minister of National Defence, without judicial oversight; and to track air travels and keep the records for six years. As Denise Helly writes:

> Law C-36 erodes the freedoms of all Canadians through procedures that undermine the rights of an accused to remain silent and to know the charges against him/her. But, in fact, it targets directly people of Muslim heritage and has two particular consequences for them. The first is their profiling by the security forces, especially at the borders (Hurst 2001; Makin 2003). The second is the Canadian Security Intelligence Service (CSIS) and RCMP attempts to collect intelligence from people who are active within the Muslim community or from Muslims who have precarious immigration status (foreign students, asylum seekers whose files are under examination by the authorities). These attempts are justified by the need for intelligence on the possible existence of Islamist networks in Canada, and are extremely harmful for Muslims. They create suspicion in people's minds about an important presence of Islamist extremists in Canada and the Muslim population's failure to report their existence to the authorities. Law C-36 is the most serious infringement on the rights of Canadian Muslims, and is highly criticized by their representatives. (Helly 2004)

Clearly, racial profiling is an existing practice, protected by anti-terrorist federal laws. On the ground, while fighting gang violence has nothing to do with terrorism, the new legal framework influences the debate and, arguably, police practices. Moreover, public perceptions of crime are dangerously and—more and more—openly linking violence and race. This is a serious threat to multiculturalism as a way of life.

A second development is worrisome. Multiculturalism is being increasingly commodified. We have seen how the Toronto tourism sector sells itself as multicultural and capitalizes on this positive image. For instance, Doucet points out that "[f]or more than two decades, multiculturalism has been one of Toronto's best tourist magnets, especially through the CHIN International Picnic at Exhibition Place, Caribana, and the annual week-long, multi-pavilion Metro International Caravan festivals" (Doucet 2001). Diversity has become so central to Toronto's identity that any threat to this harmonious image is silenced. Racialized poverty is simplified in the public debate as a problem regarding professional immigrants' access to the labour market. The Toronto Region Immigrant Employment Council (TRIEC) is a very vocal actor on this. Comprising members from big businesses and foundations, its aim is to improve immigrants' access to employment. TRIEC has been successful in bringing together all three levels of government to reflect on the barriers to professional jobs that are faced by new immigrants. The result is the Career Bridge program—offering paid internships for skilled immigrants—to help them gain Canadian experience, as well as a Mentoring Partnership and a website, offering employers resources to better assess immigrants' skills and experience.

These programs have provided interesting changes for skilled immigrants. However, TRIEC has been so successful in dominating public discourse on the issue of access to the labour market that it has relegated the concerns of lower skilled immigrants to the back burner. TRIEC justifies its mandate in these words:

> Toronto's community and business leaders recognize that the future success of the region is tied to its ability to take full advantage of immigrant skills. Removing obstacles to immigrant employment requires a collaborative and coordinated approach from government, business, and the community. The immigrant employment council offers a unique and exciting opportunity to get all the players together and ensure that the Toronto Region realizes the

benefit of immigration, and immigrants are able to realize their potential. (www.triec.ca/index.asp?pageid=5).

This instrumentalizing language, and the reduction of racism and discrimination to the question of access to higher skilled jobs, is problematic. Can Toronto's diversity be something else than a marketing asset?

Multiculturalism is not only commodified through marketing techniques but also through its instrumentalization as a political strategy. In the campaign for a New Deal for Toronto, political and economic elites used immigration settlement as a key negotiating argument. The city's diversity measures described above follow the tradition of the 1978 and 1988 federal *Multicultural Act*. However, multiculturalism is also played out as an argument to attract more revenue to the city and more authority to speak on traditionally non-municipal issues—immigration being the prime example. This strategy was successful, given that the new *Canada-Ontario Immigration Agreement* (2005) increased funding for immigrant settlement services while formally establishing a partnership with municipalities.

Multiculturalism, we argue, is more than an intergovernmental negotiating instrument or a marketing tool; it has to be a worldview translated into anti-racism practices. Rather than simply selling the image of the diversity of passengers riding the subway, to use one example, multiculturalist Toronto will focus on building anti-racist sociability in those "spaces of mediation between private lives and experiences, and their public roles as residents and citizens," write Wood and Gilbert. They continue:

> The fact that people assembled on a sidewalk or shared a subway train certainly does not automatically translate into engaging with each other or with the state; but it is nevertheless the initial contact (made of silence, brief conversations, and even conflicts) blurring our private conceptions and public affirmations of multicultural politics. These public spaces are not only important because they are the site of representation of a multicultural society, but rather because they test the relationships between the members of such society. (Wood and Gilbert 2005, 687)

The Challenge Ahead:
Afro-centred Schools and the Threat of Re-segregation

"This black school thing—no, it ain't right. ... Don't propose it—Martin
Luther King thought we could sit at the front of the bus together."
—Loreen Small (mother of Jordan Manners, killed at a Toronto high
school in 2007) (quoted in Alcoba 2008).

"I don't know what it's like to be a black parent, but I do know pain when I
see it and recognize despair when I hear it, from the deepest part of the soul
of those who believe time is running out." —Sheila Ward, Toronto School
Board Trustee (quoted in Brown and Popplewell 2008)

On January 29, 2008, the Toronto District School Board (TDSB) approved
a proposal to create an Afrocentric Alternative School in September 2009
in the city. This proposal, one of four strategies ostensibly aimed at helping black students in the public school system to perform better, has
become the most hotly debated item on the diversity policy agenda of the
city in years. Fearing the introduction of publicly sanctioned segregation,
many critics of the move by TDSB came out with strong statements opt-
ing for a unified school system. Rebuttals from proponents pointed out
that the unusual move actually replaced de facto segregation in the city's
schools by providing a new and hopeful beginning. Besides, supporters
of the move argued, there are already many other alternative schools,
so why should this one be treated any differently? Well-resourced and
well-planned, black schools could be an important basis for educational
success in Toronto's disadvantaged black communities.

The introduction of black schools followed a divisive provincial
election campaign in the autumn of 2007, when John Tory, the leader
of the PCs, opted for funding for faith-based schools, a policy that was
staunchly opposed by most Liberals and NDPers. Not only did the PCs
lose the election on October 10, 2007, but Tory lost his constituency race
against Liberal Education Minister Kathleen Wynne.

Both these education-related issues in Ontario and Toronto are typical weathervanes of public opinion around issues of multiculturalism,
religion, immigration, and "race." Ideas about universalism and cultural relativism are prominent in this debate in which identity politics
dominates the discourse. As has been the case in previous such public

conversations, the culturalization of differences is the prime default option for all involved. As policies are to be found for protracted urban problems, categorizations along ethnic lines are easier to come by than complex social solutions. In Ulrich Beck's (2007) terms, this situation has increased human insecurity around some basic human rights, linked to the education and integration of immigration on one hand and to the sedimentations of racialized divisions on the other.

Conclusion

While both sides of this problematic of immigration and racialization meet in the reality of settlement and urban restructuring in Toronto, the economic prosperity of the metropolis evades many of the city's racialized immigrant groups, as wealth and prosperity are increasingly concentrated amongst the white upper middle classes in the central core of the city and in certain suburbs. Diversity as a good-weather motto for a multi-ethnic metropolis is beginning to wear thin as a strategy for togetherness, in a city divided geographically and socio-economically along class and racialized lines.

6

Official Planning

"[O]ne vision
one city
one plan" (City of Toronto 1999, 6).

With this motto, the City of Toronto embarked on an ambitious project—the preparation of a new Official Plan to replace the seven Official Plans of the municipalities that were amalgamated to create the new city. Planners and politicians viewed the new plan, called *TorontoPlan,* as an opportunity to change both the policy direction and the process of planning in Toronto. Their objective was to produce a focused and strategic document that would assist the City of Toronto to succeed in what was perceived to be a global competition among urban regions. Their overarching goal was to change planning so that planning could help change Toronto.

At the same time, separate and parallel exercises were underway to reshape planning at the regional scale to devise a vision and method of planning for the urban region that stretches far beyond the boundaries of the City of Toronto. Those regional planning exercises culminated in 2005 with the passing of two important pieces of provincial legislation that, together, redefined the scale of the region and attempted to change the pattern of development within it. The *Greenbelt Act* declares a large territory of land to be off limits to property developers, and the *Places to Grow Act* serves as a land use and transportation master plan. Both pieces of legislation refer to the region as the Greater Golden Horseshoe and define it as an area that extends far beyond the GTA to include the Niagara Peninsula and much of Central Ontario.

During the period 1995–2005, several significant changes occurred to planning in Toronto at the scale of both the city and the region. To an extent, those changes reflected general trends in urban governance that were apparent in urban regions around the world, but at the same time they were also reflective of the particular politics of development and the institutional arrangements of governance in Toronto. Most fundamentally, they reveal to us now the inherently political nature of planning. While planning may be considered, in very general terms, a collective attempt at shaping the "good city," and while many planners may believe that they serve the (unitary and identifiable) public interest, planning is continually rent by conflict over who will play what role in the planning process, over who will get to define the "good city," and over what steps can or should be taken to create it. Such conflict was readily apparent in Toronto at the turn of the twenty-first century.

A New Official Plan: Getting Started

One of the challenges posed by amalgamation in Toronto was shaping new bureaucratic structures to devise and implement city-wide policies. In the realm of planning, seven Planning Departments—each of which had a Commissioner of Planning and a unique departmental culture— were merged. Dramatic cuts were made to the overall complement of planning staff: seven Commissioners of Planning were reduced to one Chief Planner; 26 Directors were reduced to seven; 75 Managers were reduced to 16; many planners and administrative support staff left voluntarily. These shakeups within the newly created Planning Division led to a sense that institutional memory was being lost. There was also tension between planners who had worked in the former City of Toronto and those who had worked in the former suburban cities within Metro, with some in the suburbs viewing the spreading out of staff from the centre as an attempt to take control of planning in the new city. Those tensions played out against the background of an increase in applications for planning approval fuelled by an upswing in the economy. It was in this context of staff upheaval and overwork that the process of writing a new Official Plan was launched.

Each of the seven municipalities that had been part of the Metro Toronto federation (Metro itself plus the six lower tier municipalities)

What is an Official Plan?

An Official Plan can be thought of as a Master Plan of a municipality or region. It is a legally binding document that sets out a city's long-term planning policy. As such, an Official Plan provides a framework for decision-making by city councils. Its time frame is usually 20 to 30 years and, generally, it is subject to review every five years or so to determine if its policies are still relevant or in need of updating. In Ontario, city-wide Official Plans can be supplemented by Secondary Plans (also called Neighbourhood Plans or Part II Plans) that look more closely at districts within the city. Secondary plans take legal precedence over city-wide plans.

Generally, Official Plans describe in words and maps an idealized urban structure of the city. It is possible that the picture they paint is very different from the city of the present day. In such a case, the municipality is indicating that it encourages dramatic change to the urban environment. On the other hand, if the picture is not much different from what currently exists, the municipality is discouraging change. The urban structure described in Official Plans is comprised of a pattern of land uses and a transportation system (both roads and transit). They can also further shape the desired urban structure by including density and height limits.

Another important function of Official Plans is that they guide public sector and private sector investment. So, for example, a town's Official Plan might have policy regarding minimum amounts of park space to be created in every neighbourhood. Such policy would guide the town in purchasing property to create parkland in park-deficient areas. Similarly, private businesses and individuals make decisions about buying property and undertaking developments based on what the Plan says is the future direction of land use and transportation in the municipality.

While it is possible for municipalities to individually tailor the policy direction of their Official Plans, all must operate within the broad parameters of a planning process set by the Province of Ontario's *Planning Act*. The province also has the authority to dictate planning policy to municipalities if it so wishes.

had an Official Plan. After amalgamation, they remained statutory plans for their respective portions of the new City of Toronto. It was relatively easy to make a case that it was illogical and inefficient to maintain seven Official Plans in what had become one municipality—it was pointed out, for example, that together they totaled 2,000 pages in length and weighed 34 pounds. The Interim Chief Planner at the time of amalgamation, Lorne Ross, promised a new Official Plan by June 1999, based on his assumption that a simple technical consolidation of the seven plans was possible. However, Paul Bedford, the first permanent Chief Planner, decided upon his appointment that it would be impossible to stitch the 2,000 pages into a workable document. The plans were simply too diverse in policy direction and degree of flexibility and restrictiveness. For example, Metro Toronto's Official Plan, *The Liveable Region*, was guided by the concept of sustainable development (Municipality of Metropolitan Toronto 1994) while, on the other hand, the Official Plans of the former Cities of Scarborough and North York were documents with extremely restrictive development controls more typically found in zoning by-laws. Thus, Bedford concluded that an entirely new Official Plan should be prepared. In April 1998, City Council endorsed the preparation of a new Official Plan, and in December of that year Budget Committee allocated $700,000 for the project. A draft of the new plan was expected in the spring of 2000. An Official Plan team of nine was created within the Policy and Research section of the Planning Division. It is worth noting that roughly five times that number of people had worked on *City Plan 91*, the pre-amalgamation City of Toronto's Official Plan Review undertaken in the late 1980s and early 1990s.[1]

The New Plan

TorontoPlan was seen by planners and politicians as an opportunity to change planning in Toronto, to move beyond what they considered the constraints and inadequacies of a traditional approach to land use planning. Instead of a detailed description or cataloguing of what is and what has been (i.e., of the present and the past), the new Official Plan, they thought, could be a much more visionary document that clearly looked to the future. It should do so without detailed development controls like building densities[2] and heights, which they felt could be covered in the zoning by-laws, and instead focus on painting a future vision of the city and the policies that would lead to the realization of that vision.

---

1 The former City of Toronto's population of about 700,000 was roughly 28 per cent that of post-amalgamation Toronto (2.4 million in 1998). Pro-rating the number of staff who worked on *CityPlan 91* to the post-amalgamation city would have generated a staff of 180 to work on *TorontoPlan*.

2 While land use refers, literally, to the uses that may be incurred on a parcel of land, density refers to how much of that use may be placed on a lot. Density is usually expressed as a ratio of building floor area to lot area. So, for example, a density of 1.0 means that for every 1.0 square metre of land area, 1.0 square metre of building floor area is permitted.

TorontoPlan and the early policy direction statements that preceded it appear to be based on an understanding of globalization as a competition between cities around the world. Cities, it is believed, can choose to be winners or losers in this zero sum game, and planning can be enlisted to help a city be a winner. This perception underlies the key policies of the new Official Plan, one of the most dramatic of which is that the population of the City of Toronto should increase by between 500,000 and 1 million (from a population of 2.5 million in 2001) over a 20- to 30-year period. The desire for continued growth can also be understood, at least in part, as a continuation of a decades-old tradition of civic boosterism, which considers all growth good, and an absence of growth as a crisis. Setting a target of a 20–40 per cent increase in population can also be understood as a reaction by the city to its being outpaced in population and employment growth by the 905 municipalities that surround it. Thus, the City of Toronto can be seen to be competing both locally and globally.

Promoting property development and population growth is part of a long tradition of civic boosterism on the part of local growth coalitions or growth machines in Canadian cities (Magnusson and Sancton 1983). Growth machines try to build as wide a base of support as possible for the concept of "value-free development" and to "connect civic pride to the growth goal.... The overall ideological thrust is to deemphasize the connection between growth and exchange values and to reinforce the link between growth goals and better lives for the majority" (Logan and Molotch 1987, 32, 60, 62).

However, citizens are not always amenable to the growth coalition's point of view and sometimes stage "use revolts" (Logan and Molotch 1987, 14) in defense of the use value of their neighbourhoods. The challenge facing planners, politicians, and developers in Toronto is one of avoiding use revolts that might arise in opposition to the scale of intensification that is promoted in the new Official Plan.

The target of substantial population growth leads to a second key policy, which is to identify areas where the massive amount of development required to support the growth targets (200,000 to 400,000 new dwellings) could be built. This is sketched out in a proposed urban structure that views the city through three "lenses": areas suitable for large-scale, intense development; areas suitable for substantial change and development, though not as much as in the "big-change" areas; and

FIGURE 6.1 North York Centre, viewed from the south. The extensive downtown development north of Sheppard Avenue was deliberately furthered by former North York Mayor Mel Lastman and his allies in the development industry. It has been struggling to attract more than disconnected businesses and residents and to become a true civic centre of public services, commercial establishments, culture, and exchange.

other areas where change would be very modest and gradual. There are five "big-change" areas, where the most intensive development and redevelopment would occur: downtown and the waterfront, where so many hopes of building an image of a dynamic world city are pinned, and four subcentres or "mini-downtowns"—Yonge-Eglinton, Etobicoke Centre, North York Centre, and Scarborough Centre. These areas have been chosen to avoid, as much as possible, conflict with existing low-density residential neighbourhoods. One of the legacies of the Reform Era of the late 1960s and early 1970s in Toronto is a very protective stance regarding the built pattern in such neighbourhoods. The pre-amalgamation City of Toronto's 1969 Official Plan had identified many such neighbourhoods as suitable for redevelopment as high-rise areas and was subsequently viewed as a "hunting license" for developers (Caulfield 1974). The wave of "creative destruction" for which it set the stage in the central city led directly to the growth of a reform movement that was hostile to large-

AN APPROACH
TO DENSIFICATION — MAIN STREET!

scale redevelopment. Thirty years later, Toronto's planners did not want to repeat that mistake with the new Official Plan.

The "medium-change" areas are the major roads in the city that are deemed suitable for redevelopment to accommodate tens of thousands of new dwelling units. These roads are generally lined with low-rise buildings (one to three storeys) and parking lots and are designated "Avenues" in the proposed urban structure. To a certain extent, this can be seen as a risky policy. In the late 1980s, a Main Streets Strategy was proposed as a way of accomplishing essentially the same goal—the redevelopment of properties on the city's main roads to accommodate thousands of new dwellings. Main Streets died in the face of hostility from abutting homeowners who feared overshadowing and traffic congestion. Finally, the areas slated for only minimal change in the plan are the many existing low-rise, low-density residential neighbourhoods that comprise, in total, about 75 per cent of the land area of the city. Given the history of politics and planning in Toronto, the low-rise neighbourhoods of the city are "untouchable"; to suggest more than incremental change in them would be a planning non-starter and political suicide for elected officials.

To facilitate the massive amount of development encouraged by the plan, the planning process and overall regulatory framework was made less restrictive and more flexible. Making planning regulations more flexible is in keeping with the general neoliberalization of urban governance that is meant to create attractive supply-side conditions for global capital. Toronto's planners achieve the desired flexibility in two ways. First, density and height limits are removed from the Official Plan. Whereas in the past a developer's request for density above the limit set in the zoning by-law would have been considered against the usually higher limit set in the Official Plan, now no such upper bracket exists. Of course, developers were always able to request densities above the maximums in the old Official Plans; however, such requests were considered to represent major deviations from established policy and required a strong rationale that argued their benefit to the city. With those limits out of the way, the link between the mass of a building and "good planning" has been largely severed. Secondly, the new Official Plan simplifies land use designation categories to a total of eight. These are very broadly defined in order to make the plan less restrictive.

TRUE +/- - ACTUALLY OMIB CHALLENGE
TO 2, B, LEVEL ONLY
(MORE POLITICALLY FLEXIBLE?
MORE RESPONSIVE TO OPPORTUNITY?)

FIGURE 6.2 Point tower residential building in central Toronto. Tall and slender buildings like this one have become the building type most favoured by planners and condominium builders alike.

The final stage in the process of changing planning in Toronto was a shift in planning discourse that makes the massive scale of development the plan encourages not only palatable but desirable. Brooks and Miljan define discourse as "an unfolding tapestry of words and symbols that structures thinking and action" (Brooks and Miljan 2003, 8). In the 1970s, reformists in Toronto had shifted planning discourse to the point that low-rise development came to be thought of as preferable to high-rise and incremental change to the built urban environment preferable to dramatic change. Undoing that discursive legacy of the reform era was a major task for planners 30 years later. Maarten Hajer defines discourse as "a more or less coherent set of ideas and concepts used to define the meaning of specific empirical phenomena" (Hajer, quoted in Hajer and Reijndorp 1995, 15). In the context of Toronto's new Official Plan, this means that what was required was a planning discourse that would frame how Toronto's citizens would respond to the many new high-rise buildings that it encourages.

The discursive shift has two foundational arguments. The first is that building height and density don't matter; what is more important

FIGURE 6.3 1960s-era slab residential building in central Toronto. About 50 per cent of Toronto's population are renters, a substantial number of them in high rise buildings built since World War II. Many of these towers are now under consideration for fundamental retrofits and renovations under a process called Tower Renewal.

is whether or not a building "fits" into its surrounding context. It is also argued that people are most affected by building design close to the ground—how a building looks and functions at street level and for the first few storeys. Once it heads skyward, it is claimed, whether a building is 25-storeys or 50-storeys tall is not of great consequence to passersby. In favour among planners and developers in Toronto in the early twenty-first century is the slim and very tall point tower. The new discourse argues that this is an elegant shape of building and one that ameliorates shadow impacts relative to a lower and squatter slab-shaped high-rise building. Thus, the discursive shift is towards an overall aestheticization of planning and development that supports the removal of density and height limits from the plan. Such limits, it is claimed, cannot guarantee contextual fit or beautiful buildings—indeed, they may even act as straightjackets to architectural creativity—so why not eliminate them?

The second foundational argument in support of loosening the regulatory framework of planning is that intensification of development in the city is necessary as an antidote to sprawl. The choice facing Torontonians is painted as a stark one—intensify in the city or face the dire consequences of continued regional low density expansion in the suburbs (Bunce 2004). Thus, if we apply Hajer's definition of discourse to the sight of 30-, 40-, and 50-storey condo towers being built at locations across the city, Torontonians should appreciate them as buildings that represent sustainable urbanization. These very tall and very dense buildings will not only be considered beautiful but an antidote to sprawl as well.

Removing density limits from the plan completely changes the way planning debates are framed. The consideration of what constitutes good buildings and good planning shifts from numbers to the more elusive and subjective realm of aesthetics. In a debate over whether a proposed development fits its surroundings or is beautiful, the ordinary citizen will be at a serious disadvantage against the opinion of the expert architect in the employ of the property developer. Removing density limits from the Official Plan clearly facilitates the construction of buildings at densities and heights far in excess of what would have been considered good planning just a few years earlier. It can also result in public discussion of planning in Toronto becoming increasingly expert-led.

De-Democratization of Planning

→ JAB is leading ↱ point here; shift is leading to consideration of 70's reformists and earlier.

The new Official Plan has, arguably, made planning in Toronto less democratic. Indeed, the de-democratization of planning can be seen in the process of preparing the Plan itself. This represents a significant turning away from another of the legacies of Toronto's reform era of the early 1970s, namely, a commitment to participatory and democratic planning. While public participation in the planning process has been institutionalized in Ontario, clearly—as seen in the preparation of *TorontoPlan*—there are many different ideas about what constitutes meaningful participation. Bramley and Lambert have noted that

> [A] critical element of any New Right programme for planning must be to reduce excessive and unnecessary planning regulation affecting new ... development, including possible delays and costs imposed by procedures and by negotiations with planning authorities. The whole force of New Right thinking is to be critical of bureaucratic or professionally based regulation of the market, perhaps particularly when this is allied to local democratic control through the suspect institution of local government. (Bramley and Lambert 1998, 92; emphasis in original)

The approach taken by Toronto's planners was to focus on facilitating the participation of so-called community leaders and to limit widespread participation to a few general information sessions. For example, a public launch for *TorontoPlan* was held on April 7, 1999 at Toronto City Hall with international figures offering their thoughts as to how Toronto should proceed on its new planning venture. Technically, this was a public event; however, only invited community leaders were allowed to attend; all other interested members of the public were sent to Metro Hall, a kilometre away, to watch the proceedings on a large screen.

A series of open house information sessions was held in each of the six former city halls, but consultation with the general public did not take place on a finer scale than that (i.e., an average of one open house per 400,000 residents). Planning staff also prepared newsletters outlining their ideas, and the public were invited to email their comments to a project website. In place of facilitating widespread public debate about the plan, staff assembled teams of experts and gathered their ideas about urban issues facing the city. Sector-based focus groups were established on housing, tenants, small business, heritage, the arts, multiculturalism, transportation, and the environment. In November 1999, a series of "visioning" workshops was held with the different focus groups. The city contracted out the undertaking of the workshops to a high-profile private firm of planning consultants, Urban Strategies.

The visioning exercise was called SWOTS, an acronym for strengths, weaknesses, opportunities, and threats. Some 300 invitations were sent out to community leaders representing business (manufacturing, retail, property development); major institutions (universities, museums); social, cultural, and ethnic agencies; special interest groups (heritage, environment); and youth (university student councils and organizations). About 200 people attended sessions organized into nine groups of about 25 each. Each group met for a three-hour session facilitated by two partners from Urban Strategies.

As noted above, the formal commitment to public participation in planning in Toronto is an important legacy of the 1960s and 1970s. It stands as an acknowledgement in the realm of urban planning of the importance of "people's need and right to participate in decisions affecting their daily lives in cities and communities" (Sandercock 1998, 29). But, as Sherry Arnstein points out in her classic article, "A Ladder of Citizen Participation," there are many degrees of participation ranging from non-participation all the way to power shared by government and citizens. Much so-called participation is little more than a token gesture of informing without actually involving the citizenry in any significant way in decision-making (Arnstein 1969). Certainly, that appears to be an accurate characterization of the public consultation process of *Toronto-Plan*. It compares very unfavourably, for example, to the *CityPlan 91* exercise, when public outreach included mailing 300,000 questionnaires, one to every household in the former City of Toronto. To be fair, the understaffed and underfunded planning team was faced with the logistical challenge of preparing a city-wide plan for a municipality in which 2.5 million people lived, spread over 622 square kilometres. Nevertheless, the public participation process during the preparation of *TorontoPlan* can be seen as setting the stage for the de-democratization of planning in Toronto.

Beauty and the Growth Machine

In globalizing Toronto, beauty has been adopted as the strategy for both promoting growth and muting opposition to that growth. Beauty is instrumentalized in the interests of building the image of a global city and, in turn, attracting footloose capital and knowledge workers, whom Torontonians are told are essential if the city is not to "fall behind." At the same time, beauty is hailed for its intrinsic qualities that, it is argued, will enhance the lives of all citizens. Torontonians are told that they will benefit from a massive wave of development if that development is beautiful, and if citizens are unable themselves to recognize beauty, experts will identify it for them. Just as planners once claimed a privileged position in the planning process based on their self-professed expertise in rational comprehensive planning, today "starchitects" now claim the unique ability to identify beauty.

Minto Midtown

Minto Midtown is the name of a large residential development at 2195 Yonge Street, about five kilometres (three miles) north of downtown Toronto in the Yonge-Eglinton neighbourhood. The developer, Minto Development, received approval of densities and building heights significantly higher than those allowed by the old Official Plan and zoning bylaw. This project clearly illustrates the successful instrumentalization of beauty in support of growth. Minto Development's initial application was for planning permission to build two apartment towers containing a total of 1,030 apartment units (a mixture of condominium and rental) and a small component of retail space. The Yonge-Eglinton Part II Official Plan (then in effect) permitted residential development on the subject site to a maximum density of 3.0, commercial development to a maximum density of 4.0, and mixed-use development to a maximum density of 5.0 times lot area. The proposed development was to have a density of 12.6 times the lot area or slightly more than two and a half times the maximum density that was allowed at the time (City of Toronto 2002b). The buildings, as originally proposed, were 54 and 47 storeys tall; the former would have been the tallest residential building in Canada. In January 2002, Minto submitted a revised proposal of 954 units, with a density of 11.9, and building heights reduced to 54- and 39-storeys.

The city planners initially adopted a cautious position regarding the development, noting on the one hand that "[t]he density and height of the proposed development are dramatically in excess of current zoning and Official Plan limits" (City of Toronto 2001b, 6), but, on the other, they recommended further study and public discussion of the project rather than outright rejection. The residents of the adjacent neighbourhood were unequivocal in their feeling that the project was too big and staged an all-out use revolt. Twelve residents' groups formed the Confederation of North Toronto Ratepayers' Association (CONTRA) to fight the proposal (Warson 2001).

The Minto project would appear to have had two key ingredients in its favour, given the new planning discourse in Toronto around beauty, growth, image construction, and intensification. First was the proposal to provide over 900 new dwelling units at a site identified in previous official plans as a regional sub-centre and in the new Official Plan as a suitable location for big change (City of Toronto 2000b; 2000c). Second was the use of a "starchitect" who provided the scheme with a design pedigree and who speaks the current language of beauty.

The star in this case was Peter Ellis, partner in the Chicago office of Skidmore, Owings & Merrill (SOM), who designed the project in conjunction with the Toronto firm Young & Wright Architects Inc. In May 2001, Ellis spoke at the Royal Ontario Museum in Toronto as part of a series of lectures by architects called Conversations with the World's Great Practitioners. He stated his belief that the Yonge-Eglinton intersection "*needs* very tall, very slender buildings that will be landmarks on the skyline" (quoted in Warson 2001; emphasis added). In his opinion, this project would produce "architectural drama" in Toronto. In effect, he was playing the role of expert (or more specifically Great Practitioner), telling the residents of the Yonge-Eglinton neighbourhood, and the city at large, that his project was beautiful and that it would therefore be in the public interest to approve it. His thoughts were echoed by local architecture critic Christopher Hume, who noted that "urban drama has been conspicuous in its absence from the Toronto skyline" (Hume 2001). Hume went on to ask, in reference to the Minto project, "What's wrong with being spectacular and remarkable?" It should be noted that the City of Toronto itself contributed to Ellis's celebrity by appointing him one of three jurors to select the recipients of the city's 2001 Urban Design Awards.

In February 2002, Toronto's planning staff recommended refusal of the Minto proposal, arguing that it "represents an overly aggressive and inappropriate approach to intensification." The report notes that "[p]art of the rationale put forward by Minto to justify the scale of their proposal is architectural excellence. Specifically, because the proposed buildings are of high architectural quality, an increase in height and density is said to be required to offset the associated costs." The planners rejected that argument stating that "[a]rchitectural excellence should not be achieved at the expense of good planning" (City of Toronto 2002b, 17). The planners indicated that they could support a density of 8.0 times the lot area

FIGURE 6.4 Minto Midtown in background, early twentieth-century streetscape and 1960s-era apartment building in foreground. This image shows a typical gentrified Toronto streetscape now punctuated by denser developments at subway nodes.

which, while being much less than what Minto proposed, nevertheless is an increase of 60 per cent over the allowable maximum. The planners also indicated that they could support a maximum building height of 118 metres which, while representing a significant reduction from Minto's proposed 187 metres, is still roughly double the allowable maximum of 61 metres (City of Toronto 2002b, Attachment 4).

In April 2002, City Council instructed planning staff to negotiate with Minto. As a result, the developers made further reductions to the size of their proposal: the building heights were reduced to 160 and 118 metres (51 and 37 storeys respectively), the number of units to 908, and the total density to 11.3. At the ensuing Ontario Municipal Board (OMB) hearing,[3] the City of Toronto appeared in support of the Minto proposal. The city's planners, however, maintained their position that the buildings were too tall and were summonsed by the residents of the neighbourhood to give evidence against Minto. The OMB approved the development, clearly agreeing with the developer's position that "the proposal will constitute 'world-class architecture,' in essence it will be a landmark and the design

---

3 The Ontario Municipal Board (OMB) is a quasi-judicial body appointed by the provincial government to hear appeals of planning decisions taken by municipalities.

will be memorable"; in the opinion of the Board, "the end product, re-gardless of density, properly addresses built form principles of the Official Plan and addresses potential impacts through bold, thoughtful design" (OMB 2002, 2, 19). In the winter of 2003, Minto began clearing the site in preparation for construction. SOM, the starchitectural firm that "has been very helpful to Minto" (Hume 2003), was replaced by the well-known Toronto office of Zeidler Grinnell Partnership.

Resisting the Aestheticization of Planning

We argued in Chapter 4 that the Toronto growth machine has success-fully dissociated or disconnected development from politics. The current planning discourse in Toronto is founded on an ideological belief in the unquestioned necessity of, and the universal value of, growth—now framed in terms of global competition among urban regions. Growth per se is sheltered from political and planning debate. Planners in Toronto have become active champions of "beauty through growth" and part-ners in a campaign to sell Toronto to the world. On the home front, the campaign is to sell to Torontonians the selling of Toronto to the world. Citizens are told by their planners that if Toronto is to be a great city, it "has to invest in design excellence" because "in the new knowledge-based economy, a city has to look good to entrepreneurs and workers who can locate anywhere in the world" (City of Toronto 2000b, 11).

Will Torontonians be able to resist the idea of living in a beautiful city, especially when told that the reward for being beautiful is global economic success? The Minto Midtown case study suggests that at least some will stage use revolts and resist the expert-driven, imposed-from-the-top-down discourse that links beauty and growth. They will attempt to define the good city in their own terms. If they are to successfully challenge the alliance of beauty and the growth machine, Torontonians face two tasks. First, they will have to *disconnect* beauty and growth in the current discourse about planning for Toronto's future and challenge the idea that the former can only be achieved by the latter. They will also have to resist elitist definitions of beauty and redefine good design in their own terms, based on their everyday lived experiences. They will have to insist that the city look good to *them*, not just to footloose entrepreneurs and new-economy knowledge workers. The second task they will have to undertake is to *reconnect* development and politics and to politicize growth. Underlying both of these challenges to current planning policy in Toronto—that is, of de-aestheticizing and re-politicizing planning—is an explicit recognition of the distributive impacts of different types and forms of growth and development. It is exactly these impacts that the beauty turn disguises. Some observers, like Christopher Hume, may opt for architectural drama and the spectacular. Others, like those in CON-TRA, likely will not and instead will insist on pointing out that growth is not value-free.

Re-planning the Region

While City of Toronto planners were working on the new Official Plan for the megacity, attempts to change planning at a regional scale were also underway. In fact, the search for the appropriate scale at which to address important regional issues like land use, transport, and waste has been underway in the Toronto area since the 1940s. After 1953, the newly created Metropolitan Planning Board was given planning authority over an area three times the size of the municipality itself. A second and lower tier of municipalities (originally 12, later reduced to six) dealt with local matters including local planning. The Metro model was considered by many to have successfully combined the practical necessity of regional scale planning and provision of infrastructure with the political desire for local difference.

In 1966, the Ontario provincial government launched a province-wide regional planning exercise called Design for Development. In 1970, it produced a plan for the Toronto-Centred Region, a large area that stretched roughly 120 kilometres to the west, north, and east of the city. Key regional planning policies attempted to shift more growth to the east of Metro and to severely limit growth to the north. The intention of the province had been to make the Toronto-Centred Region Plan legally binding; however, after nearly losing the provincial election in 1975, and in the face of stiff opposition from municipalities to the north of Metro, the government backed off from such an interventionist stance.

The province did alter the boundaries of local government in the area surrounding Metro (the area now referred to as the outer ring of the GTA). In the early 1970s, it created four new regional governments—Halton, Peel, York, and Durham—based on the admired Metro Toronto two-tier model. Each of these four regions was given regional planning authority for the territory within its boundaries. At the same time, Metro's planning authority was shrunk to the area within its own boundaries. No over-arching, super-regional planning authority was created; instead, Metro and each of the four surrounding regional governments were allowed to develop their own planning policies independently. By the late 1980s, there was a general consensus that the lack of coordination in planning and development in the GTA was a problem. The province created an Office for the Greater Toronto Area, which encouraged discussion among the four regions and Metro; however, once again it chose not to impose a legally binding super-regional plan on the GTA.

In the early 1990s, the provincial government appointed a task force to consider the question of urban governance reform in the GTA. As noted in Chapter 4, the provincial government chose to ignore the recommendations of this task force, instead deciding to leave the existing structures of local government in place outside of Metro and to implement changes within Metro. They proceeded with the amalgamation of Metropolitan Toronto and its six constituent lower tier municipalities into the new City of Toronto (Isin and Wolfson 1998).

Since then the province has initiated a number of regional planning exercises. Following amalgamation, it established a non-elected (and ultimately short-lived) body, called the Greater Toronto Services Board (GTSB). Before its demise, and before it acquired real decision-making authority, the GTSB began to issue policy documents on regional issues such as land use in the GTA's countryside (Greater Toronto Services Board 2000). The GTSB was followed by the Central Ontario Smart Growth Council (COSMC), another provincially appointed body that lacked actual planning authority. COSMC was noteworthy in that its territorial reach went far beyond the GTA—in that regard it was reminiscent of the Toronto-Centred Region Plan—and because of the relative under-representation of the City of Toronto on it. COSMC reflected the growing interest in governance by partnerships in that it was made up of representatives of business and non-governmental organizations as well as government. In April 2003, it issued a final report called *Shape the Future*.

In 2005, the province passed two pieces of legislation that covered a large area referred to as the Greater Golden Horseshoe.[4] One piece of legislation, building on the earlier creation of the Niagara Escarpment Plan in 1973 and the Oak Ridges Moraine Plan of 2002, created a large greenbelt stretching through central Ontario. The *Greenbelt Act* and the *Places to Grow Act* argue a virtuous circle of economic and population growth, preservation of open space including prime agricultural land, and quality of life. It is too early to determine how interventionist this provincial government intends to be in the area of regional growth management; however, we are inclined to believe it will not be as radical in this regard as perhaps some environmentalist groups would like. For example, while Places to Grow encourages intensification within existing urban areas, it also accepts as given all areas currently designated in area official plans for development and goes on to suggest areas where growth beyond those limits could take place. It is also reluctant to impose a binding plan on area municipalities and considers legislation a last-resort implementation tool. *Toward a Golden Horseshoe Greenbelt* appears promising in that it includes agricultural lands and not just prestige natural areas as lands worth declaring off-limits to property developers. However, creating a greenbelt that is physically extensive and supported by tough legislation could well prove extremely difficult, given the pressure exerted by property developers geared towards churning out tens of thousands of detached houses every year, the apparent strong cultural preference for that form of housing, and the desire among farmers to cash in on the development boom (Walkom 2004).

Places to Grow is a development plan that is intended to guide where and how growth will take place on either side of the greenbelt. Reaction to both pieces of legislation was mixed. Environmentalists were pleased that the provincial government exercised its constitutional authority over municipal government and established, in effect, some key regional planning directives. They were critical, however, of the plan for not being tough enough. For example, the inner boundary of the greenbelt was set so far beyond the current edge of developed land in the GTA that sprawl can continue for several decades before bumping into it; some districts that are experiencing intense development pressure—such as

---

4 The Greater Golden Horseshoe is roughly the same territory as that covered by the Toronto-Centred Region Plan and COSGC's *Shape the Future*.

the southern part of Simcoe County—were not included. Some development (critics argue too much) is permitted in sections of the greenbelt; and while the province promises the greenbelt will never shrink in total area, its boundaries can be redrawn. The harshest criticism came from the house-building industry and farmers. Developers were unhappy with the decision to take thousands of hectares of land out of the development equation and also with the suggestion that they would have to explore alternatives to the single-family detached dwelling. Farmers in the greenbelt lost the opportunity of selling the family farm to developers as the way to a financially comfortable retirement.

Conclusion

As noted in the introduction to this chapter, significant changes were made to the policies and processes of planning in Toronto during the decade 1995–2005. Within the City of Toronto, planning regulations were loosened in order to facilitate massive scale intensification and population growth, and beauty was enlisted as a key prop in a discursive shift necessary to convince Torontonians that such dramatic intensification was in their best interest. In contrast to that approach, at the regional scale there was a tightening of the planning regulatory framework in the form of the *Greenbelt Act* and the *Places to Grow Act*.

At first glance, it would appear that the City of Toronto's new Official Plan opens the door wide to property developers while the province has done the opposite at the regional scale. On the other hand, both sets of actions—those of the city and of the province—can be viewed as working together to build a competitive city region. Both are premised on a fundamental belief that growth is inevitable and good, and neither suggests that attempts should be made to put the brakes on growth or to steer it away from the Toronto region. The city's actions can be seen as those of a government worried that there isn't enough growth taking place within the municipality's boundaries, while the province can be seen as providing some planning order to a region that has been growing out of control.

7
The In-between City

Most of the attention in urban debates in Canada today is on the inner city, the new culturally enhanced downtowns where office towers, condominiums, entertainment districts, sports stadia, and lavish public spaces have created a gentrified ambience that sets the standards for urban development and discourse. Much is also made of the exurban residential neighbourhoods—the endless sprawl where city folk park their cars at night after a good day's work in the employment centres of the urban region. Sandwiched between these extremes and largely eclipsed by their shadow is what we call "the in-between city," those rather undefined areas that surround the old core of Toronto from west to east. From Mississauga and Brampton, through the airport and Rexdale, the Steeles corridor from Vaughan to Markham, and large parts of Scarborough is a huge swathe of mixed uses containing postwar suburbs, extensive high-rise housing projects, carpets of bungalows and monster homes, oil tank farms, real farms, a major university, Canada's only urban national park, a major theme park, a freight rail terminal, a burgeoning immigrant Jewish community, a high tech belt, an Asian-Canadian commercial and residential area with North America's largest Asian theme mall, a restructured Golden Mile, major green spaces between the Humber, Don, and Rouge rivers, and kilometers of infrastructures of all kinds. One finds some of the most pronounced urban contradictions in these areas: poor reside next to rich, a university with 50,000 students is neighbour to one of Canada's most troubled quarters, and the desires of the suburbs meet the necessities of the inner city.

FIGURE 7.1 Downsview Park, an urban national park. An ongoing object of restructuring and planners' desires, Downsview Park has become a focal point of linking the in-between city of the old suburbs with the denser developments of the old downtown. Complex socio-natural relationships are overlaid with transportation, transit, and housing investments that are going to be changing the area in the next generation.

At the heart of Toronto's in-between city lie the once-modern suburbs of the 1950s and 1960s that are located, literally, in between the fashionable downtown and waterfront and the booming edge cities of the 905. These places defy conventional urbanism also in another sense—they fall in between traditional perceptions of inner city on the one hand and of suburban neighbourhood on the other. Their aging high-rise apartment blocks, diverse immigrant populations, and lower-than-average incomes suggest inner city, while their wide roads, shopping plazas, and blocks of tidy bungalows evoke suburbia. Many southern Ontarians live in the in-between city, yet their everyday lived experience is marginalized in the branding of Global Toronto. Indeed, their neighbourhoods are most often represented as the least desirable parts of the city, as "problems" in need of "solutions." Against this stigmatization, residents of the in-between city struggle to put their issues—jobs, affordable housing, public transit, policing—on the urban policy agenda.

In looking closely at the Jane and Finch neighbourhood in the municipality of Toronto, we borrow and build upon the work of German urban scholar Thomas Sieverts. Sieverts studied what he called, in

FIGURE 7.2 View looking east on Finch Avenue to the intersection of Jane Street. A typical landscape in the in-between city: the wide streets and gas bars suggest suburbia, while the high rise, high density apartment towers suggest inner city.

German, *die Zwischenstadt* (literally "intermediate city" or the "city-in-between"), which we translate as the "in-between city." In the English language version of his book, *Cities Without Cities: An Interpretation of the Zwischenstadt* (2003), Sieverts argues that the idealized model of the compact pre-modern city in Europe clouds an appreciation of the fact that the majority of urban citizens in many urban regions live and work in a very different kind of environment. His particular study was of German urban regions in which, typically, a compact urban core is surrounded by a much larger territory characterized by a very scattered pattern of built and unbuilt areas. The reality of the *Zwischenstadt*, according to Sieverts, calls for a debunking of the myth of the ideal compact city and the development of new analytical and practical methods of planning in the in-between city. His work can be seen as contributing to an international conversation about emerging patterns of urban development that has been ongoing over the last two decades and that includes concepts such as Joel Garreau's edge city (1991), Robert Fishman's technoburb (1987), and Ed Soja's exopolis (1996). It is important to note that Sieverts's work is not meant to be an apologia for suburban sprawl. Rather, his intent is to provoke an acknowledgement of the reality of existing patterns of urban development and to encourage policy responses to the problems and the potential that they embody. In particular, he argues against policy that merely attempts to create simulacra of historic urban design set-pieces while simultaneously devaluing all other urban spatial types.

A Case Study of the In-between City in Toronto: Jane-Finch

Jane and Finch is the intersection of two arterial roads in the northwest part of the City of Toronto—Jane Street and Finch Avenue West. In physical terms, it appears as an unremarkable place in the overall context of the city: gas bars and shopping malls on three corners; a 33-storey apartment building on the fourth. But "Jane and Finch" is an idea as much as it is a physical place. The intersection lies 16 kilometres northwest of downtown Toronto, but many Torontonians perceive it to be somewhere at the distant margins of Toronto society. As an idea in the collective imagination of many Torontonians—in its "mythic geography"—Jane-Finch is an unattractive and unsafe part of the city, "a place of violence, poverty, and foreboding suburban design" (Cash 2006). Its boundaries, both as a physical place and idea, are not easily pinned down. Reference is often made to the Jane-Finch "corridor," comprised of the lands on either side of Jane Street from Highway 400 on the west to Black Creek on the east and from Highway 401 in the south as far north as Steeles Avenue, which is the boundary between the City of Toronto and the City of Vaughan. Home to more than 60,000 people, it is about six kilometres from north to south and two kilometres from east to west in size.

Jane-Finch was created in the 1950s, 1960s, and 1970s by a combination of the Fordist social welfare state's vision of modern urbanism and the methods of modernization utilized as part of an overall mode of governance. That particular combination—of a modern vision and methods of modernization—marked Jane-Finch from its inception as different from other districts in Toronto. It was different in terms of the large scale at which it was conceived, planned, and developed, as well as in terms of its built form, its type of housing, and its resident population. Moreover, Jane-Finch has always been portrayed as an unattractive and undesirable district in the city.

We argue that, rather than considering Jane-Finch to be a failed modern city, as many do, a fairer and potentially more productive perception

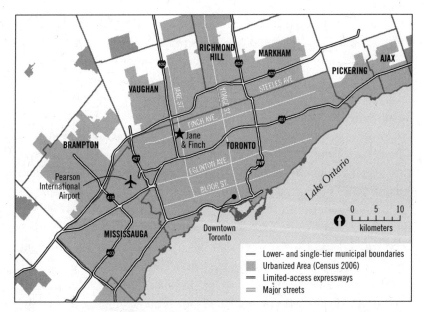

FIGURE 7.3 Jane and Finch in the Toronto urban region. When first developed in the 1960s and 1970s, Jane-Finch was at the periphery of the built-up city; today suburban development spreads for many kilometres beyond it.

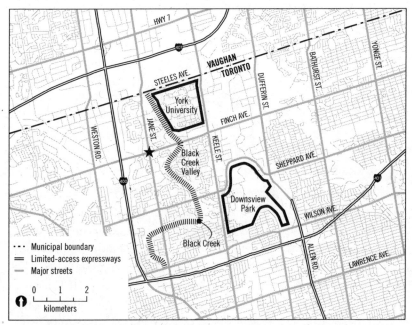

FIGURE 7.4 Map of Jane and Finch and surrounding districts. The proximity of Jane-Finch to York University is evident in this map.

of the district is to see it as an in-between city. Such a perception has the potential to turn around the concept of failure. It suggests that it is not modernism that has failed at Jane-Finch, nor have the people of Jane-Finch failed by not living in one of the glamour zones downtown or in the exurbs. Rather, the failure is on the part of traditional methods of urban analysis employed by many scholars, planners, politicians, and the press to acknowledge the vision of the progressive urbanism upon which Jane-Finch was founded and the important contribution which that vision—now embodied in the lived modernity of the neighbourhood—could make in the present-day consideration of social problems in Toronto's older suburbs. "In-between city" is a relatively neutral term that describes an area in need of some rebuilding—of buildings, physical infrastructure, and social infrastructure—some 40 years after its initial creation. At the same time, however, it acknowledges the potential of this dense and diverse district as well as its relatively central geographical location in the Greater Golden Horseshoe urban region.

In-between Modernity and Post-modernity

Jane-Finch is founded on three modern ideas that were made real in the 1950s, 1960s, and 1970s: the large-scale production of public housing, experimentation in urban planning and urban design, and the de-racialization of Canadian immigration policy. In the post- and/or after-modern era of the early twenty-first century, these ideas are widely discredited along with places like Jane-Finch, where they are so strongly evident. In that sense, Jane-Finch is in-between modernity and post-modernity.

Modern Idea #1: Public Housing

Amendments to the *National Housing Act* (NHA) in 1964 facilitated the large-scale production of public housing across Canada. As David Hulchanski (2004, 180–81) has noted, whereas only 12,000 units of public housing were built in Canada between 1949 and 1963, almost 200,000 units were built between 1964 and 1973. In Ontario, public housing was owned and operated by the Ontario Housing Corporation (OHC), which was established in 1964 to coincide with the NHA amendments. OHC was attracted to the green fields of the Jane and Finch area, and the pro-development North York Council welcomed them. By 1975, 22.5 per cent

The Athens Charter

The Athens Charter is a statement of principles, developed in 1933, at the 4th Congress of CIAM (the Congrès Internationaux d'Architecture Moderne or International Congress of Modern Architecture). The theme of the Congress was "The Functional City." The architects and planners in attendance concluded that all cities could be reduced to four essential functions—dwelling, leisure, work, and circulation—each of which has distinct functional requirements. They argued that a good city would be a functional city divided into separate land use zones, all linked by a hierarchical network of circulation routes. The Swiss-born architect, Charles Édouard Jeanneret-Gris (better known as Le Corbusier), published the conclusions of CIAM IV as *The Athens Charter* in 1942 (Jeanneret-Gris 1973). The functionalist approach to urban planning and urban design prescribed by the book came to dominate modernist thinking about the city for several decades.

of all dwellings in North York's Ward 3 (the Jane-Finch corridor) were public housing units developed by the OHC. In contrast, about 10 per cent of all dwellings in the post-amalgamation City of Toronto and only 5 per cent nationwide are social housing.

Modern Idea #2: Experimentation in Planning and Urban Design

In 1962, Metro Toronto planners produced a District Plan for the area bounded by Dufferin Street, the Humber River, Highway 401, and Steeles Avenue—the area that includes the Jane-Finch district. While it was never adopted as a legally binding Official Plan (see Chapter 6), it provided the basis for a similar legal document adopted by North York Council in 1969. Most striking about that plan is its recommendation that more than 50 per cent of all dwellings be provided in high-rise buildings. This represented a new and experimental modern vision of a more urban suburban community.

The clearest example of the modernist planning experimentation of the 1960s in Jane-Finch is the plan prepared by the Central (now Canada) Mortgage and Housing Corporation (CMHC) in 1964–65 for lands on the east side of Jane, south of Steeles. Edgely Village, as it was called, was designed by Irving Grossman, one of Canada's leading architects. Edgely's mix of high-rise buildings and townhouses, and of private and public sector housing, was groundbreaking in 1960s Toronto. Its total separation of pedestrian and vehicular routes and its abundant open space conformed to then-popular ideas of the Ideal City, derived from the 1933 Athens Charter (see box, p. 125).

Modern Idea #3: Immigration Policy

In the mid-1960s, the federal government de-racialized immigration policy by introducing a merit-based point system to determine admissibility to the country. This meant that immigrants from previously excluded parts of the world—Africa, Asia, and Latin America—were able to come to Toronto. Jane-Finch, newly developed with a lot of affordable housing, came to house a proportionately large number of new immigrants, many of whom were people of colour.

The Branding of Jane-Finch

As noted above, three modern ideas—large-scale production of public housing, experimentation in planning and urban design, and the de-racialization of immigration policy—coincided in time and space to produce the Jane-Finch district. It was a district that looked different from other parts of Toronto, due to its many high-rise apartment buildings and experimental site plan layouts. It also housed people who, in the 1960s and 1970s, were different from the majority of people in other Toronto neighbourhoods, in that many were recent immigrants from non-European countries and a significant number were of low income, living in public housing.

Jane-Finch became an easy target of the social, cultural, and racial biases of mainstream Toronto society. In a city where the ideal home was considered to be a detached and privately owned dwelling, the high-rise, rental, and public sector aspect of housing in Jane-Finch branded it as inferior. Discomfort at the changing demographics of the city could be focused on Jane-Finch and linked to the social and cultural devaluation of the built environment. And, to Jane Jacobs-inspired urban reformers in 1970s Toronto, Jane-Finch—with its tall slab apartment buildings, pedestrian-only rowhouse neighbourhoods, curving collector roads for cars with grade-separated pedestrian bridge crossings, and segregated land uses—came to be seen as a physical representation of out-dated and disreputable concepts of planning and urban design.

"If your family name is Finch, you can do something really rotten, such as christening your daughter Jane" (Needham 1974). This quotation from a

Toronto newspaper column indicates how widespread was the perception of Jane-Finch as a terrible place. "Jane-Finch" was branded very early in the process of its development as a poorly planned, ugly, dangerous, and undesirable place in the city—a suburban ghetto. This branding—i.e., the construction of what the area represents—has been continually renewed over the last several decades by repeated representations of the district in the mass media as a troubled and dangerous area. It is almost impossible to find reference to it in present-day mass media other than as the "crime-ridden and impoverished Jane-Finch corridor."[1]

The perception that Jane-Finch has "too much" social housing was established very early in its history and still prevails several decades later among local politicians. The anti-social housing sentiment was expressed by a journalist in *The Globe and Mail* in December 2005, who opined that social housing projects themselves were to blame for "[t]he riots in France…, the emergence of Islamic terrorism in England…, the angry return to authoritarianism in eastern Germany…, [and] the surprising spate of gun crime in Toronto" (Saunders 2005).

Who Lives in the In-between City of Jane-Finch?

Several demographic characteristics distinguish the Jane-Finch area from the City of Toronto as a whole: incomes are substantially lower as are post-secondary education levels; the population is younger; there are many more lone-parent families, more immigrants, and more recent immigrants; and more people of colour (Table 7.1). It is also clear that there is demographic variation within Jane-Finch, with the Black Creek neighbourhood being less similar to Toronto as a whole than the Glenfield-Jane Heights neighbourhood (See Figures 7.5 and 7.6, and Tables 7.1, 7.2, 7.3, and 7.4).[2] For example, in the Black Creek neighbourhood,

---

1 In fact, a search for articles about Jane-Finch in two Toronto newspapers for all of the 1970s and 1980s found only negative coverage. One Toronto newspaper, *The Globe and Mail*, began a series of positive articles about the area in 2005.

2 Black Creek is the neighbourhood name given by the City of Toronto to the area bounded by Steeles Avenue West, Black Creek, Finch Avenue West, and Highway 400. Glenfield-Jane Heights is the area to the south and is bounded by Highway 400, Finch Avenue West, Black Creek, and Sheppard Avenue West. Together, Black Creek and Glenfield-Jane Heights correspond to the old North York Ward 3 boundaries.

approximately 75 per cent of the population is non-white compared to approximately 65 per cent in Glenfield-Jane Heights and 43 per cent in the city. North of Finch Avenue, 62.1 per cent of dwellings are in buildings with five or more floors, whereas south of Finch, only 36.4 per cent of dwellings are in such buildings.

Issues faced by residents of Jane-Finch of poverty, racism, access to education, and employment opportunities are well-documented in reports such as *If Low Income Women of Colour Counted in Toronto* (Khosla 2003) and *Poverty by Postal Code* (United Way of Greater Toronto 2004). In her report, Khosla connects gender to the increasing racialization of poverty in Toronto and highlights problems faced by low income women of colour related to housing, public transit, policing and justice, childcare, recreation programs, and health services. *Poverty by Postal Code* documents the increasing impoverishment of inner suburban neighbourhoods in post-amalgamation Toronto. In it, both Black Creek and Glenfield-Jane Heights are identified as neighbourhoods with "very high" poverty rates of 40 per cent or more. While poverty levels increased in many parts of the former City of North York, "[t]he most prominent is the Jane-Finch area, where formerly 'high' poverty neighbourhoods evolved into four 'very high' poverty areas, and where others that had 'lower' or 'moderate' levels now have 'high' poverty" (United Way of Greater Toronto 2004, 29, 34).

Perception of Crime

During the summer of 2005, a spate of shootings in Toronto led to a renewed focus on, and portrayal of, Jane-Finch as a high-crime area in the city. In one incident in early August 2005, a four-year-old and three adults were shot on Driftwood Avenue in what *The Toronto Star* repeatedly referred to in its coverage of the story as "the Jane-Finch corridor" (Edwards and Grossman 2005; Edwards and Siddiqui 2005).[3] In response to this incident, one Jane-Finch area city councillor, Giorgio Mammoliti, proposed a city-wide curfew for everyone under the age of 16. His proposal was widely criticized as being discriminatory, unenforceable, and ineffectual. While unorthodox crime fighting strategies were being floated by municipal politicians, the Police Service launched a special task force to

---

3 Referring to Jane-Finch as a "corridor" rather than as a neighbourhood or district contributes to its negative portrayal.

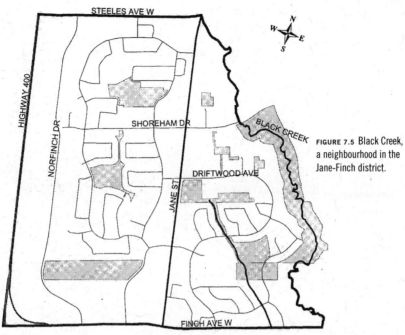

FIGURE 7.5 Black Creek, a neighbourhood in the Jane-Finch district.

FIGURE 7.6 Glenfield-Jane Heights, the neighbourhood immediately to the south of Black Creek.

TABLE 7.1 **Demographic Profile of Jane-Finch**

	Black Creek	Glenfield-Jane Heights	Combined	City of Toronto
Number of households	7,330	10,500	17,830	943,080
Population	24,355	33,340	57,695	2,481,560
Average household size	3.32	3.17	3.23	2.63
Population age 0–14	27%	23%	24.5%	17.5%
15–24	15%	14.1%	14.6%	12.4%
25–64	50%	50.5%	50.4%	56.5%
65+	8%	12.4%	10.4%	13.6%
Lone parent families as percentage of all families	34.6%			19.7%
Median household income	$37,081	$41,632		$49,345
Visible minority population	18,220 or 74.8%	21,860 or 65.4%	40,080 or 69.5%	1,051,125 or 42.8%
Immigrants as percentage of total population	62.6	63.0	62.9	49.5
Recent immigrants as percentage of total population	14.4	11.1	12.6	11.4
Dwellings: single, semi, or rowhouse as percentage of total	36.4	56.1	47.8	48.1
In apartment buildings: 5 floors or more as percentage of total	62.1	36.4	47.7	37.6
Percentage of population with university education	7.4	4.7	5.8	25.3

Tables 7.1, 7.2, 7.3, and 7.4 are based on data from the 2001 Canada Census.

address crime in selected areas of the city. Its goal was to reduce crime by increasing the number of officers patrolling at night. In the Jane-Finch area, *The Toronto Star* reported that "[f]our trouble zones—housing complexes along Jane St.—will be the focus" (Huffman 2005).

Social Housing

One of the consequences of the municipal amalgamation that created the new City of Toronto in 1998 was the restructuring and rescaling of the administration of social housing within the boundaries of the new city. A new housing authority, the Toronto Community Housing Company (TCHC), began operations on January 1, 2002. It was created by merging the pre-existing housing corporations that originated in the Toronto Housing Authority (which operated Regent Park), the Metropolitan Housing Company (which operated public housing throughout Metro Toronto), and the former City of Toronto's housing company, Cityhome. Ontario's neoliberal PC government (1995–2003) transferred, as part of its general downloading of social service responsibilities to municipalities, ownership of and ongoing responsibility for all of its social housing in Toronto to the city (Toronto Community Housing 2002, 13). With 58,000 units[4] and 164,000 tenants, TCHC is the one of the largest landlords in North America (Toronto Community Housing 2004, 8). It houses 6 per cent of the City of Toronto's residents and 12 per cent of its tenants; their median annual income is $13,200 (Ballantyne 2004), well below the City average of about $49,000 (Statistics Canada 2002).[5] The estimated value of its real estate portfolio is between $4.5 and $5 billion (Toronto Community Housing 2004, 13).

TABLE 7.2 **Recent Immigrants, Country of Origin**

Black Creek	Glenfield-Jane Heights
Iraq	India
Sri Lanka	Guyana
Guyana	Ghana
Jamaica	Jamaica
Ghana	Vietnam
China	Pakistan
Pakistan	China
India	Iraq
Vietnam	Afghanistan
Ukraine	Sri Lanka

The average age of TCHC buildings is almost 40 years (Toronto Community Housing 2002, 27). The age of the buildings, coupled with years of under-funded maintenance and repairs, has resulted in an enormous backlog of building work to be done. TCHC acknowledges that limited funds have forced it to focus spending on maintaining fire safety, structural, and mechanical systems, as well as roofs at the expense of upgrading building interiors and renovating dwelling units (Toronto Community Housing Company 2006). It estimates that it needs to spend an immediate $224 million on building repairs and a total of $1 billion over the next ten years (Toronto Community Housing 2002, 27). At the same time, it is severely restrained financially. Roughly half of its revenue

---

4 TCHC's portfolio consists of 2,800 buildings in 350 developments across the city (Toronto Community Housing 2004, 8).

5 2001 Census data.

comes from rent paid by its tenants (Toronto Community Housing Company 2002, 16), which is calculated on a rent-geared-to-income basis in 93 per cent of its units; therefore, rent is not a growing source of revenue. The other revenue source is operating subsidies provided by government (Toronto Community Housing 2004, 3). Given the general climate of fiscal constraint practiced by all governments in Canada today, those levels of subsidy are unlikely

TABLE 7.3 **Language (English plus Top 10)**

Black Creek	Glenfield-Jane Heights
English	English
Vietnamese	Italian
Arabic	Vietnamese
Italian	Spanish
Tamil	Chinese
Spanish	Punjabi
Chinese	Tamil
Punjabi	Gujurati
Urdu	Arabic
Russian	Persian (Farsi)
Turkish	Khmer (Cambodian)

to grow. TCHC also faces the bureaucratic operational challenge of addressing tenant concerns within such a huge portfolio, especially given the very diverse cultural makeup of its residents.

In 2003, TCHC adopted a Community Management Plan that divided its portfolio into 27 Community Housing Units (CHUs), each with a manager who has budgetary control over that CHU. CHUs range in size from 1,600 to 2,500 dwellings (Toronto Community Housing 2004, 9). The TCHC developments in the Jane-Finch area are divided among three CHUs, the central one of which—CHU 18—is relatively small in territory, reflecting the concentration of social housing units. The manager and community health worker attached to each CHU are also charged with devising a "community engagement and development strategy" (Ballantyne 2004). Each building within a CHU elects a tenant representative who sits on a CHU Tenant Council. Tenant Councils are given control over a small budget to be applied to capital projects; for example, in the spring of 2004, tenant councils across the city decided how to spend $9 million.[6]

At a public event organized by TCHC that was held one weekend in November 2004, visitors from Brazil described the experience of Porto Alegre, the self-proclaimed "Capital of Participatory Budgeting" (TCHC

---

6 $5.4 million was allocated on the basis of numbers of rentable rooms; $1.8 million was divided equally between the 27 CHUs; a further $1.8 million was allocated to special projects as decided by representatives of all 27 CHU Tenant Councils.

Meeting, 26 November 2004)[7] to an audience of several hundred in a large auditorium at the Ontario Institute for Studies in Education in downtown Toronto. The following day a similar session, including a representative of the Brazilian Federal Ministry of Cities, a Porto Alegre city councillor, and the director of the Porto Alegre Housing Department, was held at the National Trade Centre for tenant representatives of the 27

TABLE 7.4 **Ethnicity (total responses, i.e., single and multiple responses combined)**

Black Creek	Glenfield-Jane Heights
Jamaican	Italian
East Indian	East Indian
Italian	Jamaican
Canadian	Chinese
Vietnamese	Vietnamese
Chinese	Canadian
English	Spanish
Guyanese	English
Spanish	Guyanese
African Black	West Indian

CHUs (TCHC Meeting, 27 November 2004). This weekend event seems remarkable for a number of reasons—the jumping of scales to look for global models of participatory budgeting; the transfer of knowledge from south to north, rather than the more typical north to south; and the admiration expressed for a model developed by a Workers Party[8] municipal administration, given the general neoliberal climate of politics in Ontario in 2004. The only discordant note in the entire event was sounded by an attendee at the large public session who asked if the TCHC Tenant Council exercise wasn't just an attempt to co-opt tenants. In other words, he suggested, TCHC had pre-empted any organizing that tenants might undertake on their own and created a model that they must fit into.

This criticism implies that TCHC is attempting to diffuse tenant frustration with its tight fiscal restraints. Having tenants prioritize budget items—in effect asking them to choose only a few items from a long tenant-generated wish list—can, perhaps, be interpreted as a way of limiting tenant expectations. At the same time, the Community Management Plan does appear to be an opening, however small, to a more democratic administration of the housing projects. It is simply too early to evaluate its outcome.

---

7 See Abers 1998 for a discussion of Porto Alegre's participatory experiments.
8 The Workers Party, or PT, is a socialist political party.

Black Creek West Community Capacity Building Project

The community-initiated rebuilding of Jane-Finch has culminated in the Black Creek West Community Capacity Building Project (BCWCCBP) and its Action Plan. The BCWCCBP was one of three responses by the City of Toronto and the Jane-Finch community to the fatal shooting of a three-year-old area resident, Breanna Davy, in June 1999. The first was to create a memorial to her, which has taken the form of an outdoor art installation at Driftwood Community Centre. The second was a commitment to undertake major physical changes to the built environment;[9] however, that idea has not been seriously pursued. The third was to undertake a needs assessment of the district bounded by Steeles Avenue, Black Creek, Highway 401, and Highway 400.[10] Soon after work began on the needs assessment, community members involved in the process "turned it around" so that, instead of focusing negatively on the area's weaknesses, it described how to build on the area's strengths (Rieder interview 2005). The needs assessment became the BCWCCBP, which was undertaken in three phases.

Phase I, completed in 2003, produced a demographic profile of the area and also included a survey of 39 community agencies, highlighting the problems they face in doing their work. Phase II was a series of consultations with different sectors in the community and was carried out by a private consulting firm with funding provided by TD Bank Financial Group. Phase III is an Action Plan based on the findings of the Phase II consultations. The Action Plan was presented at a public forum in February 2005 and was subsequently approved by City Council.[11] An Action Plan Coordinating Committee was established in the summer of 2005,

---

9 Planning staff focused on the Yorkwoods TCHC community, located in CHU 18.

10 It is significant that the name of the project is "Black Creek West" and not "Jane-Finch." Partly, this reflects a desire to move away from the negative connotations of Jane-Finch, but it also reflects the fact that some parts of the project area are quite far from the intersection of Jane and Finch. Neighbourhoods at Jane and Wilson, for example, are four kilometres south of Finch.

11 The Action Plan proposes six strategic directions: economic independence and stability; development of services; showcasing the Black Creek West Community; healthy, safe, and aesthetic space and facilities; enhancement of information and services; and involvement in decision-making. Of the six, the first four are deemed to be "specifically task oriented," while the last two are considered to be guiding principles (Joyette Consulting Services 2005).

and subsequent Working Group subcommittees were set up for each of the four task-oriented strategic directions that had been identified.

The mandate of the Coordinating Committee is to work for the benefit of the entire Black Creek West community rather than advocating on behalf of particular groups or projects within the community. Thus, a key role it plays is information sharing and general advocacy in the interest of the community as a whole. The limit to its involvement in specific issues was highlighted by the case of a proposal to redevelop the property at 1900 Sheppard Avenue West, just east of Jane Street. For several years the site was occupied by a vacant building that had previously been the Toronto Police Services 31 Division station. TCHC proposed to build 27 units of supportive housing for young mothers and their children in a three-and-a-half storey building, plus a separate one-storey building that would house a branch of the Toronto Public Library. The residential building would be managed by Humewood House, an agency that supports young single mothers. The proposal to add new social housing to the area met with strong opposition from area homeowners and Maria Augimeri, the local councillor. The Space Working Group identified the debate over the redevelopment proposal as being fundamentally about socio-spatial justice and wanted to intervene to help secure the right of low-income young mothers and their children to live in the area. The Working Group found itself constrained, however, in terms of how directly engaged in the debate it could be, given the mandate of the Coordinating Committee to advocate on behalf of the Black Creek West community in general, rather than support particular projects. In the end, the Working Group decided that it could not send a representative to speak at the North York Community Council meeting at which the project was considered. It did, nevertheless, play an important role in monitoring the planning approval process and in keeping the wider community of supporters of the development proposal informed.[12]

12 North York Community Council voted in favour of the proposal on July 11, 2006 after a debate that lasted several hours. City of Toronto Council subsequently approved it at its meeting in late July. Area residents have appealed Council's decision to the OMB.

Strong Neighbourhoods/Neighbourhood Action

The local state has also become a key initiator of activities intended to contribute to the rebuilding of Jane-Finch. The underlying motivation and strategy of state action is succinctly captured in a 2005 document published by the United Way of Greater Toronto, in conjunction with the City of Toronto, called *Strong Neighbourhoods: A Call to Action* (United Way 2005). This report outlines the recommendations of a Strong Neighbourhoods Task Force, made up of municipal and provincial government officials and representatives from community groups, labour, and business. The task force built on the work of the earlier *Poverty by Postal Code Report* (United Way 2004). Its focus was to develop a strategy to address the twin trends of "growing neighbourhood poverty and inadequate community infrastructure" (United Way 2005, 3). It identified nine neighbourhoods (later expanded to 13) in the City of Toronto that are most in need of "immediate investment." Two of these neighbourhoods are in Jane-Finch: Black Creek and Glenfield-Jane Heights. The task force's vision of rebuilding is laid out in the following:

> We call on all governments to respond quickly to our proposed *Toronto Strong Neighbourhoods Strategy*. We urge them to implement the key components of the strategy: an intergovernmental agreement to ensure coordinated investment; a commitment for new targeted resources and mechanisms to support local resident leadership and participation.
>
> Strong neighbourhoods mean safer streets, engaged, active residents, and ultimately, a more prosperous economy. This benefits everyone in Toronto. The responsibility to strengthen Toronto neighbourhoods does not rest exclusively with governments. Business, organized labour, and community agencies all make important contributions to building a stronger city, neighbourhood by neighbourhood.
>
> The neighbourhood strategy we are recommending addresses one of the most deeply troubling developments in Toronto: patterns of social exclusion based on geography that constitute a threat to the health, well being, and prosperity of everyone in our City. We are driven by an ultimate vision of Toronto neighbourhoods where no one is disadvantaged by where they live. We must all work in partnership to make this vision a reality. (United Way 2005, 3)

This excerpt clearly establishes the contours of what we characterize as the "return of the state" and what Neil Brenner (2004) describes as neighbourhood-based policy initiatives, which attempt to address regulatory deficits and crisis management caused by uneven development. They have the following characteristics:

- Toronto's new neighbourhood strategy is to involve "all governments"—local, provincial, and federal—acting in a coordinated manner.
- Referring to money to be spent as an "investment," rather than viewing it as supporting social entitlements of citizens, underscores the entrepreneurial mode that characterizes urban governance in Toronto in the early twenty-first century.
- Investments are targeted and strategic, aimed at only 13 out of a total of 140 neighbourhoods in the city. They are intended not only to achieve safety and economic growth as much as to overcome social disadvantage, but also to eliminate "a threat" posed by the 13 neighbourhoods to the city as a whole.
- Initiatives are to be undertaken by a partnership of governmental and non-governmental actors. This can be interpreted in two ways. On the one hand, it seems desirable to tap resources in the business community, especially if business has not, to date, been an enthusiastic investor in Toronto's most socially troubled neighbourhoods. It also seems desirable to support the ongoing work of community agencies and to strengthen their capacity, financial and otherwise, to do that work with as many resources as possible. On the other hand, involvement of private sector partners could suggest an unwillingness of government to break the neoliberal taboo of tax increases as a way of generously funding urban initiatives. Governments can limit their investment by calling on the private sector to match their contribution. Private sector involvement could also have the impact of "de-radicalizing" community-based initiatives.
- While geographic patterns of social exclusion are explicitly acknowledged, it is the geography itself that is seen as the basis of the exclusion and not systemic problems within capitalist society. This framing of the discourse facilitates state intervention that targets geography—i.e., specific neighbourhood territories within the city—rather than broad city-wide problems such as racism and poverty. As Brenner notes, because such policy initiatives do not address the supra-local causes of social problems, they could simply

result in a shift in the geography of uneven development and social exclusion within Toronto (Brenner 2004).

Parallel to the work of the Strong Neighbourhoods Task Force and also of the Black Creek West Coordinating Committee, the City of Toronto has established a Neighbourhood Action Program to coordinate and implement strategic state intervention in the 13 identified neighbourhoods in need. Two city-wide entities, an Investment Board and Intergovernmental Table, oversee the program and facilitate the involvement of provincial and federal state institutions. Each of the 13 neighbourhoods will be served by a Neighbourhood Action Team of city staff headed by a director; all of the Neighbourhood Team Directors report to a Deputy City Manager. In each of the 13 neighbourhoods, a Local Neighbourhood Partnership (LNP) is to be established with broad representation of community-based groups, local institutions, business, the city, and city agencies, boards, and commissions.

The highly targeted and strategic approach of local state institutions was made apparent in the unfolding of funding announcements in late 2005 and early 2006. For example, in the summer of 2005, the Black Creek West Coordinating Committee was encouraged to apply to the city's Service Development Investment Program (SDIP) for money to hire a project coordinator. SDIP had a total of $250,000 to invest in five to eight organizations in the neighbourhoods targeted by the Strong Neighbourhoods report. Black Creek West applied for funds to hire a full-time coordinator and was partially successful, receiving sufficient funds for a part-time hire. The case of SDIP is exemplary of the return of the state. The city can claim to be an activist caring state as it spends the relatively tiny amount of $250,000 in the targeted neighbourhoods. In the spirit of entrepreneurialism, community groups across the city are made to compete for funds with only a handful being selected. The funding they receive is not guaranteed beyond one year.

An example of targeted investment by the provincial government is the Youth Challenge Fund announced in February 2006. This program will provide money for a variety of projects for at-risk youth in the 13 Toronto targeted neighbourhoods. The initial provincial funding commitment is for $15 million, with up to $15 million more over the next three years as matching funds to contributions from the private sector.

Thus, the total amount of funding could be anywhere from $15-45 million over three years. The province appointed a popular Toronto sports figure—Mike "Pinball" Clemons, then coach of the Toronto Argonauts football team—to launch the venture. He chairs a Board of Directors selected from the community, government, sports, and business. The board receives administrative support from the United Way of Greater Toronto, and staff at the University of Toronto are involved in assessing its ongoing work.

The Youth Challenge Fund is another clear example of the strategic character of the return of the state. The provincial government is firmly committing only $15 million to the program; additional funds will be forthcoming only if the private sector also contributes. This approach is not without its critics. One member of Toronto's Youth Cabinet[13] said that the premier in effect "has come out and said it's not the government's responsibility to prevent crime. It's now up to corporate Canada." The same critic described the amount promised by the province as "crumbs...what we actually need are several loaves of bread" (Gillespie 2006). Two other critics of the program were the chairs of the TDSB and the Toronto Catholic District School Board, neither of whom had been consulted prior to the announcement of the program. According to the TDSB chair, "To have a program without involving the school boards, when you're talking about youth seems a little silly" (Gillespie 2006).

The widespread perception in the Toronto area of a dramatic escalation in gun crime in 2005 has played a significant role in prompting local state action on urban issues. For example, in August 2005, Police Services deployed additional officers in certain areas of the city, including Jane-Finch, in the belief that more cops on the beat would lead to a reduction in crime. Not all residents believe this is a good idea. They suggest that a better use of resources would be directing them towards social policies and programs that would prevent people from turning to crime. What is especially needed are employment opportunities. For example, Paul Nguyen—an area resident, graduate of York University's film program, and creator of a community-based website (www.Jane-Finch.com)—has suggested creating a recording studio in the area: "There's no point in

---

13 The Youth Cabinet was established by the City of Toronto to advocate on behalf of youth, in particular those from marginalized communities. Its volunteer members are all teenagers and young adults.

having programs where no one's going to show up. Yeah, basketball is still in, but what skills does it teach you besides dribbling a ball? Recording time will be highly coveted, and you learn life skills that you can keep" (Paul Nguyen quoted in Gandhi 2005, A8).

The fatal shooting on Boxing Day 2005 of a teenaged girl who was shopping on Yonge Street in the heart of downtown Toronto brought the three levels of government together to act on urban issues in the Toronto area under the guise of a Community Safety Plan (BCWAPCC meeting, 31 January 2006). The federal government agreed to consider changes to criminal legislation, the provincial government to fund specialized police activity, and the municipal government to fund program enhancement targeted especially at youth. The Community Safety Plan will complement the city's Neighbourhood Action Plan. The 2005 shootings in Toronto have, in effect, prompted governments to open their purses (Thomas interview 2005).

Conclusion

Hundreds of thousands of people live in Toronto's in-between cities, those unglamourous and ordinary districts that possess neither the fashionable cachet of gentrified central city neighbourhoods nor the shiny newness of exurban development. These often-overlooked parts of the city have recently become the focus of increasing concern on the part of urban policy-makers, who perceive the evidence of social exclusion of their residents as a potential threat to the region as a whole. That concern has prompted strategic interventions by state institutions together with business community partners; however, those interventions only reach 13 neighbourhoods identified as priorities. Even in those cases, the funding is scarce and time-limited. Clearly the new programs are not intended to improve the quality of everyday life of all citizens of the in-between city. What is not at all certain, however, is the possibility of a different urban politics in Toronto, one that would de-marginalize the in-between city and reshape the perception of it as something other than a social and economic threat. Such a politics would allow a different definition of problems faced by residents of the in-between city and would point in the direction of different policy solutions. More likely, the in-between city will remain in the shadow of Toronto's glamour zones.

8
Urinetown or Morainetown?

The offbeat Broadway musical *Urinetown*, written by Mark Hollmann and Greg Kotis, tells the story of a fictional town where urinating and defecating is strictly controlled by a private corporation, the Urine Good Company (UCG), put into power at the tail end of a major drought that necessitated the regulation of water and led to the outlawing of all private water closets. As a consequence, "it is a privilege to pee" in Urinetown, and a classical power struggle ensues over UGC and its lackey state. The story told in the musical, as some characters sing in the beginning, is "the oldest story—masses are oppressed, faces, clothes, and bladders, all distressed. Rich folks get the good life, poor folks get the woe. In the end, it's nothing you don't know" (Hollman and Kotis 2001). The story may be old, but it is also new: it reflects the seemingly unstoppable dynamics of the current, neoliberalizing period of global capitalism. In this period, more than in any other in modern capitalism, privatization and marketization of social relations, production, and service delivery has taken hold. This has also strongly affected certain aspects of societal relationships with nature, especially those that involve water. Looked at this way, *Urinetown* can be seen to capture the *zeitgeist* quite well. As water is being privatized, can the total marketization of our water-related bodily functions be far behind? Toronto is no Urinetown. In fact, a coalition of environmentalists, social justice activists, and progressive politicians undermined a municipal foray into re-regulating the city's water supply and potentially opening up the possibility of privatized water services (Debbané and Keil 2004). Still, the city and its region are built on extensive privatization of space and nature and on the capitalist exploitation of natural functions.

Cities are sustained by a web of metabolic processes established through socio-technical processes at the heart of modern urbanism. Parts of this metabolism are the urban hydrosocial cycles—the sum of the human and physical interrelationships pertaining to water in cities— that are regulated by complex social, economic, political, planning, and ecological processes (Bakker 2000; Gandy 2002; Swyngedouw 1996). The intertwined nature of these processes forces us to look at water as a "thing" that can be studied from a variety of perspectives.

We begin with the notion of "metabolism" and the "interwoven knots of *social process, material metabolism,* and *spatial form* that go into the formation of contemporary urban socionatural landscapes ... [I]t is on the terrain of the urban that [the] accelerating metabolic transformation of nature becomes most visible, both in its physical form and its socio-ecological consequences" (Swyngedouw and Heynen 2003, 906–07). The concept of urban metabolism has been present at least since the 1960s, following the seminal article by Abel Wolman "The Metabolism of Cities" (1965). Environmentalist Herbert Girardet (1992) revived the concept as a principle to understand the position of urban regions in a larger world, and the "ecological footprint" basically denotes the same thing (Wackernagel and Rees 1996). Cities depend on inflows and out-flows of materials, energy, and so on, but a full empirical study of such processes is complicated and rarely undertaken. A study of Toronto, for example, claims that it "presents the first urban metabolism of a Can-adian urban region, and possibly the first for a North American city. It also makes a first attempt at comparing the urban metabolism models of a few cities worldwide" (Sahely, Dudding, and Kennedy 2003, 469). It concludes:

> The most noticeable feature of the GTA metabolism is that inputs have generally increased at higher rates than outputs over the study years [1987–99]. The inputs of water and electricity have increased marginally less than the rate of population growth (25.6 per cent), and estimated inputs for food and gasoline have increased by marginally greater percentages than the population with the exception of diesel fuel. With the exception of CO_2 emissions, the measured output parameters are growing slower than the population. The outflows of residential waste and wastewater loadings have even reduced in absolute terms. (Sahely, Dudding, and Kennedy 2003, 478)

Metabolism is a powerful concept in the urban studies toolbox if one keeps in mind a few important caveats. First, it is necessary to pay attention to the political changes in cities; second, the use of the term metabolism must be resonant of a perspective that is critical of current market liberalism; third, social factors (modes of regulation, habits of consumption, social justice, etc.) must be factored into the equation; and fourth, nature must be seen as dynamic and not just an object of engineering ingenuity.

Water, in the sense of being part of complex urban metabolisms, is a prism through which we can look at urbanization processes, social power, economic transactions, cultural habits, etc. This conception of urban hydrosocial cycles deals with a set of relationships we build with non-human nature, which in turn are shaped by how we understand and act upon the city's external nature . Critical urban political ecology (Biro and Keil, 2000; Keil 2003, 2005; Swyngedouw *et al.* 2002; Swyngedouw and Heynen 2003; Bakker 2003a, 2003b) attempts to integrate into political economy the notion that nature or the environment—materially and discursively—always need to be present in radical societal analysis. "The *urban* is a particularly important space and scale where the production of nature/water occurs. As a consequence, urban political ecology helps us understand the relationships of globalization, urbanization, and nature" (Keil 2003).

In Toronto, water issues have come to occupy centre stage of the regional development discourse: from waterfront development and the idea of using deep lake water to cool downtown buildings to the exurban ravines of the Oak Ridges Moraine (Desfor *et al.* 2006).[1] Both development and the regulation of the region's water are now strongly influenced by the neoliberalization of Toronto's political economy (Keil 2002; Kipfer and Keil 2002; more generally, Brenner and Theodore 2002). In this chapter we link urban/regional development, water/nature, and neoliberalization in Toronto. We explore the ways in which the regulation of water intersects with the growth of the city and the urban region's increased neoliberalization. How, we ask, do neoliberalized regimes of urban regions intersect with water regimes?

---

1 The Oak Ridges Moraine, a headwaters region to the north of Toronto, is under intense development pressure.

Neoliberalization, Globalization, and the Urban Environment

Neoliberalization and globalization intersect with nature typically in one of two ways (or in any combination of the two): rabid exploitation of natural resources and of "the commons" (always under threat of privatization) and/or ecological modernization—i.e., production, trade, and consumption that ostensibly takes place *with* rather than *against* nature (as an option mostly reserved for the most developed and hence most ecologically threatening Western societies). This is a somewhat surprising turn because, as Swyngedouw has correctly pointed out, "Nature itself has long resisted full commodification." But, he continues, "in recent years, nature and its waters have become an increasingly vital component in the relentless quest of capital for new sources of accumulation" (Swyngedouw 2003). At the same time, struggles over the commodification and privatization of water have frequently altered the course of the neoliberalization of water management in global and local contexts (Bond 2003, 2004; Heynen *et al.*, 2007).

The often trumpeted virtues of neoliberalism—efficiency, market accountability, personal responsibility, etc.—have been transferred into the regulation of nonhuman nature. The result has been a wave of privatization, conservation, water management, and other socio-ecological practices and the marketization of natural assets (even dirty air) to save the environment. In the 1990s, the inclusion of nature (or rather of societal relationships with nature) into the core of the accumulation process was achieved—more or less successfully and in more or less sustainable and benign ways—through countless ecological modernization schemes (Desfor and Keil 2004; York and Rosa 2003). Whether the current push towards even more total subsumption of nature (and of its societal relations) under capital is a new phase or an extension of ecological modernization remains to be seen.

Neoliberalization and Nature in Ontario

In the Province of Ontario in the 1990s, neoliberalization of nature came first as a moderate program of ecological modernization under the social democratic NDP government (Stewart 1999); in the latter half of the decade, the election of the Mike Harris Tories brought to power an exploitative, resourcist regime under the leadership of an ideologically committed group of neoconservative Common Sense Revolutionaries, who ruled Ontario between 1995 and 2003. Judith McKenzie observes: "There appears to be little question that Ontario's environmental policies have been very much influenced by an ideology that is pro-business, anti-regulation, and grey. Environmentalists have been cast as enemies of economic growth and regulation as barriers to investment" (McKenzie 1998; Winfield and Jenish 1998). The Tories both de- and re-regulated environmental matters in water, forestry, hunting, land use, conservation, and other domains. This entailed the facilitation of specific accumulation processes, such as suburban growth, and tended to redistribute social wealth to the middle classes whose "natures" were privileged (Keil 2002; see also Ali 2004 and Prudham 2004).

Toronto geographer Scott Prudham noted that Harris's "Common Sense Revolution was a remarkably nature-centred project," wreaking havoc in the field of regulation of air, water, agriculture, forestry, and energy (Prudham 2004). Since the defeat of the Tories and their replacement by a Liberal government in 2003, a return to the more moderate policies of ecological modernization favoured by the previous NDP government has begun. The Liberals moved quickly on a number of fronts: the preparation of a growth management plan for a large territory referred to as the Greater Golden Horseshoe, the creation of a large greenbelt around Greater Toronto (as discussed in more detail in Chapter 6), and the establishment of an infrastructure funding program intended to address what the government considers to be the province's $100 billion dollar infrastructure deficit, especially in the areas of transportation and water (Ministry of Municipal Affairs and Housing 2008).

Histories of (Sub-)Urbanization and Water

The water-development nexus has had a long history in Toronto and, for that matter, in Canada. When Canadian cities entered their first waves of large-scale suburbanization in the postwar decades, providing water infrastructure was seen as one of the major pillars of modernization and urbanization. In fact, the explosive expansion of major metro areas like Toronto was based on the extension of supply systems for water and sewage. The growth in the urbanized territory of metropolitan regions was considered itself a major leap in societal modernization. We have come a long way since the heyday of this first wave of—largely automobile-

FIGURE 8.1 Toronto's waterfront viewed from the air. At the lower left corner of the photo waterfront condominium towers can be seen near the CN Tower. Just off-shore is the controversial Toronto City Centre Airport.

driven—suburbanization. Although, currently, development continues in leaps and bounds across the exurban landscapes around Toronto and there is talk of adding 2 million people to thè GTA over the next generation, the discourse accompanying such growth has changed significantly (Keil and Graham 1998). Not only has rapid development bred its polar opposite, a strong anti-growth movement in the rural periphery, it has also changed its discursive dimension considerably: growth now seems to occur in direct (and seemingly) positive reference to nature and rural landscapes. In many instances, growth discourse has co-opted its critics and has taken on a green face: developers talk eloquently of watersheds, wetlands, ravines, ground water, and woodlots when making their sales pitch to the masses of suburban home buyers that flood the suburban marketplace.

On the city's southern development frontier, its waterfront, where 800 hectares of land have been identified for redevelopment, Lake Ontario, the potentially marshy mouths of the Don, Humber, and Rouge rivers, and the body of water called "Toronto Bay" between the downtown and the city's islands, have been rediscovered as a values-producing "nature."

The environment seems safely inscribed into a process of ecological modernization (Keil and Desfor 2004). Simultaneously though, technical, planning, and political modes of regulating the suburban hydrosocial cycle have been cast into crisis as subdivisions continue to eat into rural or wild lands north of the city. As exemplified by the current struggles over development on the Oak Ridges Moraine, citizens are beginning to question the urbanization-modernization nexus which undergirded suburban residential and business development in earlier decades (Desfor *et al.* 2006). The "big (sewer) pipe," once considered a sign of progress, has now become to many a symbol of the evil of sprawl (McMahon 2000).

Water and Privatization in Canada

The abundance of water is one of the founding myths of Canada and part of the national imagination so much so that an ostensibly progressive campaign to keep water resources in the country and under national control can unabashedly use the highly problematic nationalist appellation "They're coming to take our water" as a slogan.[2] In Ontario water has been on the public agenda at least since the Walkerton E. coli deaths in 2000. Much of the blame in that particular case was attributed to the de-regulation and privatization of water inspection in the province under the governing Tories. Water has also loomed large as a regional issue and was inscribed into the collective imagination of the GTA as a consequence of the fierce battle between environmentalists and developers about further encroachment of sprawl on the Oak Ridges Moraine.

As Karen Bakker recalls, the first water networks in industrialized cities were often built by private companies: "The poor had to rely on public taps, wells, rivers or, in the most desperate cases, stolen water. The terrible cholera and typhoid epidemics of the nineteenth century, combined with an apparent inability or lack of interest on the part of the private sector to finance universal provision, led the state to take over the business of water supply infrastructure" (Bakker 2003a). It has been feared that this era came to an end in the wake of the widespread privatization of services and the growth, since the 1980s, of global water companies that have aggressively pursued a policy of marketing and privatizing

---

2 For a good overview of the Canadian debate about water, see Carty (2003).

water worldwide (Bakker 2003a, 2003b; Bakker and Hemson 2000; Barlow and Clarke 2002). After Hamilton became the first Canadian city to
privatize its water system in 1994, others (Goderich, Halifax, Moncton)
have experimented with various privatization and market schemes (Bakker 2003a; Buckley 2003), Toronto was considered a lucrative market and
obvious target for future privatization. While many municipal privatization schemes proved, in fact, less than successful for water companies,
they remain an option in a constantly expanding global water market. In
addition, the terms privatization—"the shift in control from the public
to the private sector"—marketization—"the full regulation of water by
market mechanisms"—and commodification—"often the restructuring of water management institutions and decision making processes"
(Bakker 2003b)—have to be seen as referring to an entangled process
of water provision, in which public and private actors, multinational
corporations, and individual citizens, municipal governments, and trade
unions may play various parts. In fact, in most cases, some mix of water
governance through public utility, the private sector, and community or
cooperative institutions seems not unusual (Bakker 2003a). In addition,
we know that the peculiarities of H_2O (in the hydrological cycle) and the
particularities of water (in the hydrosocial cycle) make it difficult at all
times to make water privatization a profitable enterprise (Bakker 2003a,
2003b). The issue that brought water to the fore of the public debate in
Toronto was one in which overall concerns of justice guided a specific
struggle around service provision.

Water and the City

In the common narrative on the relationship of water and cities, there
is an emphasis on the dependence of urbanization on the availability or
even abundance of water, the dependency on cyclical managed floods
for agriculture, and the location of cities along ship-carrying rivers. Water
was often transported into cities from far away, and cities were drained
at the cost of areas downstream. In some ways, this pattern also holds for
Toronto. Water has, for the past century, been taken from very far out in
Lake Ontario through a long pipe; it has been chemically and mechani-
cally cleaned, pumped many kilometres up land, and then returned to
downstream sewage plants whose runoff ends up in the lake again. This
grand *mechanical* cycle of water has been run on the principle of steadily

UNIQUELY ELEGANT, AS IT DOES NOT
DEPLETE SUB-SURFACE AQUIFERS.

FIGURE 8.2 Lakefront condominium construction site, South Etobicoke. Condominium towers, particularly along the waterfront, have been one of the most visible additions to the landscape and skyline of the city since the start of a residential building boom in the second half of the 1990s.

stepped-up supply and has largely been the technological spine in the huge gridiron of suburban expansion Toronto has known in the second half of the twentieth century.

Throughout that time, the regional system of watersheds has known another, less mechanized cycle of *natural* streams that originate in the alluvial Oak Ridges Moraine (ORM) that surrounds the urban region. The ORM is considered a huge rain barrel, whose layers of sand and gravel collect and clean rain water and discharge it through springs and sources into the streams and rivers that flow to the lake. While, in one sense, these mechanized and natural systems seem to be somewhat oppositional both in appearance and character, they really are more alike than one might think. The water that is taken from and discharged back into the lake remains, after all, just that: water, with all the unique and hard to manage properties of H_2O. The rivers and streams that flow from the ORM, on the other hand, have long become part of a huge and highly human-made system of flood control. In addition, their valleys also take on other non-natural urban functions, such as carriers of traffic, transportation, and information. They are, to use Erik Swyngedouw's term, true "urban cyborgs" (Swyngedouw 1996).

At a third level, these streams of water are also part of an intricate *symbolic* system of water use in the Toronto area. The ORM has become a terrain of struggle over development, the site of large-scale housing construction where people buy and sell homes in and close to nature and the purity of the ORM; the streams themselves have become sites of highly appreciated community clean-up and renaturalization efforts replete with reintroduced marshes, tree plantings, fish counts, and so on (Desfor and Keil 2000). The waterfront itself, where the land meets the lake, where all surface water in the region comes from and goes to, has become—once again—a giant selling point for residential properties, urban design dreams, and spectacular and speculative development. The symbolic properties of water—its alleged or real purity, its shiny backdrop to gigantic condominium developments along the shore, and its delivery through a publicly owned and managed system that has, so far, defied murky privatization schemes have become major battlegrounds of the public debate on urban development, management, and civic urbanity overall.

Toronto

The Canadian census of 2001 confirmed what had been evident to the residents of the Toronto region for many years: the outer ring of exurban municipalities in the four regional municipalities have had population growth at a rate four times that of the city (Statistics Canada 2002). This tendency was largely confirmed by the 2006 census. Assuming that much of this growth in human numbers translates into sprawling low density subdivisions, the tangible effects are even more pronounced than the statistics express. At the same time, Toronto's inner city and some of its old suburban edge cities, such as Etobicoke, Scarborough, and North York, have also undergone significant growth in condominium and townhouse development, which has brought many new residents to the old city core. Much of this growth is at or near the city's 40-kilometre waterfront.[3]

This urban and suburban growth has put tremendous strain on the service networks of the Toronto region. There are huge shortfalls in such areas as affordable housing provision, transit and transportation infrastructure, educational infrastructure, and landfill sites. Although the city

---

3 For an analysis of the political fallout of the suburban shift, see R. Alan Walks (2004a, 2004b).

lies on the shore of one of the largest bodies of surface fresh water in the world, the growth it experiences has also begun to put considerable pressure on these resources. At the same time, severe fiscal pressures have led the city to consider raiding a fund established for repair and replacement of water infrastructure for other municipal purposes (Moloney 2003).

Water, Development, and Growth in the GTA

Overall, a new water regime is in the making in Toronto, which—in more or less coherent fashion—creates a restructured relationship of the city with nature. In just over 200 years, Toronto has grown from a colonial outpost planted by the British in the wilderness to an urban region of more than 5 million people. Its water regime has likewise grown and adapted to changing circumstances. Progressive-era public health reforms in the early twentieth century established the universal provision of municipal drinking water and sewage treatment as a prerequisite for modernization. Throughout the nineteenth and twentieth centuries, the city expanded inland from the lake in concentric circles along water and sewage lines. Where the early twentieth century was a triumph of the discourse of *public health*, the mid and late twentieth century saw the triumph of the discourse of *technology*. With the problem of waterborne disease effectively under control, the focus shifted to the technologically based steady increase in the supply of water and volume of sewage treated. The scale of the human/nature articulation related to water increased in quantum leaps from the first water treatment plant built in the nineteenth century on Toronto Island to the R.C. Harris Filtration Plant of the first half of the twentieth century to the 1970s, when the York-Durham sewer opened a vast terrain to the north and east of the city to development. The urban explosion of the 1990s, fuelled by economic growth and relaxed political and planning controls, combined with the current anticipation of continued regional population growth of 100,000 per year, has led to a renewed discussion of expanding supply by extending the "big pipe" (McMahon 2000).

At the same time, there is at present increased attention to ecological matters, and the debate on growth has moved to centre stage. In suburban areas, the focus has been on the ORM, a band of hills that stretch 160 kilometres from west to east across the GTA, where dozens of rivers and creeks have their headwaters and which has become mythologized

[handwritten marginalia: HEAVILY; JOHN SEWELL INVOLVED IN THIS]

as the source of water in its purest form. Citizen groups from municipalities throughout the region mounted a several years long campaign
to protect the ORM from house builders. Starting in 2001 Ontario has
taken steps to declare much of the ORM off-limits to developers. On
the one hand, this can be seen as a victory for the environment—for
water in particular—and also a victory for movement politics that ignore
municipal boundaries and unite urban, suburban, and rural dwellers.
On the other hand, perhaps it perpetuates business as usual everywhere
else. The pure waters of the ORM are saved from house builders, while
the city of degraded nature and its filthy lake to the south are written
off as unsalvageable. In between the pure and the defiled (the ORM
and the city/lake), agricultural land continues to be consumed by sprawl.
While the recently established Greater Golden Horseshoe Greenbelt is
the most visible step towards forging a new urban and regional political
ecology in the Toronto region, it appears that its boundaries will be set so
as to allow several decades of continued sprawl development and its long
term effects will have to be seen. *[handwritten: WALKERTON – GOVERN. GAP – HYGIENE FAILURE]*

In the current post-Walkerton era, serious questions have been raised
throughout Canada about the infallibility of technical solutions, and
public health concerns about the safety of drinking water have been
voiced. There have been renewed calls in Toronto for action to clean
up the waterfront and river valleys. Environmental groups have emerged
throughout the Toronto region to fight against sprawl and protect natural
areas. This sudden and apparently fundamental change in the public
mind—in a province where a majority of voters have tolerated the
shifting technologies of power in a neoliberalized state architecture for
years—has also created a more critical stance towards the privatization of
water. There appears to be a widespread belief that "robust regulation"
is a prerequisite for effective water-supply management and a growing
awareness that private operators of water systems resist such regulation
(Bakker 2003b).

The View from the Centre: Toronto

In 2002, administrators and politicians in the City of Toronto, which
supplies water to its own city and to surrounding suburban municipalities, were accused by critics of intending to create the conditions for the
privatization of water services by changing the water governance regime.

A municipal proposal was on the table to establish a Toronto Water Board, fashioned along the lines of a so-called Municipal Service Board model. A previous in-house study that had floated various options of how to proceed had come under fire from the community, and amendments and changes were made as a consequence of public hearings to arrive at just this one model of the future regulation of water in Toronto.[4]

Critics of the proposed Water Board maintained that it would constitute the first step towards farming out water services and delivery to private firms. The establishment of a commission or corporation headed by a board of appointed—rather than elected—representatives is considered a major road toward privatization. Critics further cited lack of accountability, cronyism, and the right of the board to issue 20-year contracts (possibly to private companies) as major problems of the plan. They also raised the spectres of tax and water rate increases and less commitment to infrastructure investment as possible outcomes of the proposed re-regulation of water in Toronto (Water Watch 2007).[5] While this particular attempt at privatization was defeated, it should be noted that "the 'Big 3' of multi-national water companies—Suez, Vivendi, and RWE—have signaled their intent to secure control of 70 per cent of North America's public water services within the next ten years (Clarke 2003)."

The main thrust of the anti-privatization campaign had been brought forward by an organization called Water Watch, a loose coalition of the Toronto Civic Employees Union Local 416, Canadian Union of Public Employees Local 79, Canadian Environmental Law Association (CELA), Toronto-Central Ontario Construction Trades Council, the Council of Canadians, The Toronto and York Region Labour Council, the Metro Network for Social Justice, and the Toronto Environmental Alliance (TEA).[6] Thus, Water Watch turned out to be a remarkable scale-bending coalition of social justice and environmental groups. It included local labour organizations, the city's most important progressive environmental group (TEA), and regional labour councils and social justice groups as well as nationally active groups such as CELA and internationally active

---

4 Personal communication, Eduardo Sousa.
5 Information was taken from various smaller publications of the organization Water Watch (2007).
6 www.torontoenvironment.org.

organizations such as the Council of Canadians. In as far as this group represented social justice and environmental activists, as well as labour in the form of the public service unions that represented water workers, the main bureaucratic operatives who had much of the collective expert knowledge on water in the city were on side with the groups that organized against change. This made this struggle an environmental justice fight, as the main tenets of welfare statism and social solidarity were being defended and their defeat would have meant widespread social and environmental injustices (Debbané and Keil 2004).

The opposition to the threatened changes to Toronto's water regime did not consist only of organized groups of progressive activists, professionals, and their allies. There was widespread public support for the positions taken by Water Watch. A public opinion survey conducted for the coalition found that "[r]esidents of Toronto are unequivocal when it comes to the management of the Toronto water system. In overwhelming proportions and across all regions, they endorse public control over any forms of private management or contracting out." Clear endorsement of the status quo was expressed by respondents who were "overwhelmingly opposed to both the substance and the process of City Council's current deliberations over potential changes to the management of Toronto's water system" (Strategic Communications Inc. 2002).

In addition to the restructuring of water regulation in the city, huge lands adjacent to waterfronts and rivers are being brought under new forms of private control and more flexible and unaccountable forms of management, including simplified approval processes for development (Bunce and Young 2003). The ensuing (sub)urbanization-water complex is the subject of large-scale efforts to redefine the waterfront. A city document called *Making Waves: Principles for Building Toronto's Waterfront* (Dill and Bedford 2001) describes a new aquatic future "in purple prose thick with water metaphors" (Bunce and Young 2003): "[t]he benefits that will ripple out from a revitalized Central Waterfront will extend beyond its boundaries and will wash across the whole of the city" (Dill and Bedford 2001, quoted in Bunce and Young 2003). Let us now look a bit more closely at a specific case of water re-regulation in the northeastern suburb of Markham.

Markham's Suburban Water Regime

Immediately to the northeast of the City of Toronto is the suburban municipality of Markham. We have chosen to investigate it as a case study of water and suburbanization for a number of reasons. First, the Town of Markham owes its very existence as a booming edge city to water. Second, while in many respects Markham appears to be an ordinary Canadian suburban town, it is also a very particular product of global flows of capital and people. This self-proclaimed "High-Tech Capital of Canada" is home to the Canadian headquarters of multinational companies such as IBM and American Express, and it markets itself to prospective residents and businesses as a Silicon Valley of the North. Its residents also are multinational: many ethnic groups live there, including a large Chinese-speaking community that comprises 30 per cent of the town's population (Statistics Canada 2002). Finally, there is evidence in Markham of attempts at ecological modernization related to water that originate both in the local state and in civil society.

In the late 1950s, in the then tiny rural Village of Markham, local civic boosters dreamt of one day becoming a town with a population of 16,000 (Village of Markham 1959). By 2001, the population of Markham was 208,000—an increase of 20 per cent or 35,000 just since 1996 (Statistics Canada 2002)—and the town now anticipates reaching a population of 348,000 by 2026 (City of Markham 2008). Markham's modest dreams of the 1950s and its immodest real growth of the decades since the 1970s have both been shaped by water. The town is, at its closest, 10 kilometres from Lake Ontario to the south, and it lies from 120 to 220 metres above the level of the lake. Fifty years ago, none of its farmers or small-time house builders imagined that the hurdles of distance and elevation to bringing fresh water from the lake would ever be overcome. But overcome they were with the construction, by the Province of Ontario, of the mammoth York-Durham trunk sewer in the mid-1970s, a sewer that runs east-to-west through the entire length of Markham (and continues far to the west and north). Building the big pipe meant that treated drinking water could be pumped uphill to Markham (and beyond) from an intake and filtration plant on the shore of Lake Ontario in the City of Toronto, and sewage waste could flow downhill to a treatment plant on the lakeshore in the Town of Pickering, just east of Toronto. Without those water and sewage connections, Markham would never have (sub)urbanized beyond the

FIGURE 8.3 1990s residential development in Markham with sections of sewer pipe visible beyond house. Without the provision of Lake Ontario-based water and sewage infrastructure, the explosive growth of Toronto-area municipalities would not have been possible.

modest dreams of the 1950s. The solution to the "problem" of water was overcome by engineering, the application of technology, and the provision of infrastructure at a previously unimagined vast scale. Since the 1970s, property developers have covered Markham's prime agricultural land with tens of thousands of detached houses, prestige business parks, and shopping centres.

To town officials—planners and public works engineers who review developers' proposals for new neighbourhoods—water is under control in Markham. While at present there is a temporary capacity problem, this will be eliminated in the near future with the completion of an extension to the York-Durham sewer. Water is subject to a multi-scalar regulation by the state: the town's water is provided by the Regional Municipality of York;[7] York buys treated drinking water from the City of Toronto, which pumps it north from the so-called Palace of Purification (the R.C. Harris Filtration Plant) on the shore of Lake Ontario. Similarly, York Region is responsible for removal of sewage and waste water, which are treated at the Duffins Creek Sewage Treatment Plant in the Town of

7 The Region of York abuts the City of Toronto and is comprised of several towns and cities, one of which is Markham.

Pickering. Markham pays York for the sewage connection. Overall, standards for water and sewage infrastructure—both new construction and
the operation of existing structures—are set by the provincial Ministry of
the Environment. Provincial standards for drinking water are themselves
based on federal government guidelines.

In 2001, total water consumption in the town was 30.1 million cubic
metres, up 5.5 million cubic metres from just four years earlier. The total
amount of sewage generated (in 1997) was 24.8 million cubic metres.
The average Markham household pays $475 per year for water and
sewage services (City of Markham 2008). Planners and works staff in the
town pride themselves on going beyond the technical to embrace the
ecological in organizing water in subdivision layouts. In the mid-1990s,
Town Council adopted a growth strategy based on new urbanist planning
principles of building denser and on smaller lots. One reason behind
this remarkable policy shift was making more efficient use of costly
infrastructure, including water and sewage. It has also become standard
subdivision design in the town to provide storm water retention ponds in
new residential developments. Indeed, the provision of a water feature in
the form of a small pond has proven to be a successful sales feature.

However, this effort at ecological modernization is perhaps less successful in ecological terms than it appears. A Markham town councillor,
who is promoting a green agenda for the town, thinks the greening of
subdivision design is a very pale green, noting that many of the storm
water ponds were ill-placed relative to adjacent streams (Shapero interview 2002). Also, there are no management plans for them and many
have become pollution sinks, collecting runoff from driveways, roads,
and chemically treated lawns. Engineers and planners see no need to
explore alternative technologies in water and sewage infrastructure or
to question the fundamental ideology of rapid growth that, it could be
argued, is the essence of a place like Markham. The challenge facing
any green movement in such a boom town is to attempt to build new
and collective societal relationships with nature in a place that appears
to be the quintessential expression of unhindered growth, the privatization of space, social exclusion, and the maximization of consumption. In
particular, it seems that developing new relationships with water will be
especially challenging. The lake is so far from Markham that it is difficult
to make a connection in the everyday lives of citizens between the water

that comes out the tap or the flushing of a toilet and the lake that is both the source of the water that comes out of all of the taps and the recipient of all those flushing toilets. Water remains a "concrete abstraction" (Fitzsimmons 1989).

The Town of Markham has established two funds intended to support environmental projects. Its Environmental Sustainability Fund supports projects such as pesticide use reduction and green roofs. The town has put $300,000 into this fund and hopes to tap federal money by way of the Federation of Canadian Municipalities. It has also put $2.5 million into a Land Acquisition Fund, which will be used to acquire environmentally sensitive lands in partnership with the province and the local conservation authority. Also, the town is set to undertake a study that will look into how best to protect and preserve small watercourses, which tend to dry up when the land they drain is developed. Residents of Markham were also active in the fight to preserve the ORM, which straddles the town's northern border.

Conclusion

The regulatory regime of urban water in Ontario has suffered a few major blows in recent years, particularly the deadly water scandal of Walkerton, which threw provincial water policy into deepest crisis. An independent fact-finding task force reported in the spring of 2002 that the regulatory regime undermined by the provincial government had failed not just the people of Walkerton but had cast a shadow over the entire system of water supply in the province. A *Safe Drinking Water Act*, brought late in October 2002 by the Tory government, took up some of the recommendations of the provincial O'Connor Report (O'Connor 2002), particularly those that referred to the pumps and pipes part of the system, but it left unaddressed the larger ecological and social question of source protection. The regulation of the Toronto water regime has recently shown some pressure points both at the centre and at the edges. The previous Mayor and more market oriented councilors as well as some city staff championed a review of the city's water governance system. The outcome was a recommendation to create a Toronto Water Board, a governing body, which would consist of mostly appointed members.

The battle lines in this struggle are clearly drawn. Residents of the City of Toronto opposed the potential privatization of their water supply and delivery system and successfully fended off what were considered preliminary steps in that direction. It is understood that any change to the public status of water supply, demand management, and delivery would seriously endanger the safety and affordable availability of drinking water in Toronto. While the struggle over possible privatization was underway, the city's planners once again stepped up their efforts to build their city on the merit of the symbolic and aesthetic qualities of water, particularly in the form of its vacant land alongside the shore of Lake Ontario. In the meantime, exurbanization rages on with a development industry largely unchecked by government regulation and an active political endorsement of the continuation of large-scale, technologically conventional systems of water supply and reticulation as well as sewage systems that allow the continued overflow of the suburban ring into ever further copies of itself. At the same time, though, citizens in the outer suburbs of Toronto have begun to fight the degradation of their—exclusive—living arrangements at the city's edge.

The process of (sub)urbanization is both built on the availability of cheap water and is threatening to the hydrosocial cycle itself. This is all happening in the environment of neoliberal deregulation described above. Harvey noted that "[t]he neo-liberal state typically sought to enclose the commons, privatize, and build a framework of open commodity and capital markets. It had to maintain labour discipline and foster 'a good business climate'" (Harvey 2003, 184). Quoting Roy, Harvey concludes that privatization is the transfer of productive public assets to private companies: "Productive assets, suggests Roy, include natural resources, earth, forest, water, air. These are the assets that the state holds in trust for the people it represents.... To snatch these away and sell them as stock to private companies is a process of barbaric dispossession on a scale that has no parallel in history" (Roy, quoted in Harvey 2003, 161).

Ending with a note of caution about the neoliberalization of nature, we return to *Urinetown* one more time. After the daughter of the corporate tycoon who owned Urine Good Company topples her father and operates the regulation of water and sewage "as a public trust for the benefit of the public," it "wasn't long before the water turned silty, brackish, and then disappeared altogether." When the discipline of the market was gone, no other easy form of regulation was put in place in its stead, and ecological catastrophe threatened all life. The real lesson learned from Urinetown, then, is the fact that the way of living we have come to enjoy in urban regions such as Toronto has been made unsustainable by the consecutive dynamics of Fordist-Keynesian and post-Fordist-neoliberal capitalism. "This is Urinetown. Always it's been Urinetown! This place it's called Urinetown" (Hollmann and Kotis 2001, 34). Toronto, which is not *Urinetown*, must strive to reorganize its regional water ecology so that in future it will deserve the name *Morainetown*.

9
Transportation Dilemmas

The movement of people and goods in the Toronto region involves a vast network of users and providers with different and conflicting needs, desires, and motivations, and an equally tangled web of governing bodies regulating transport at different scales. The movement of commodities reflects the multiple and overlapping economic roles of Toronto as a place of both production and consumption, including its role as a centre for warehousing goods for distribution within and outside of the region. Overlaid on the movement of commodities are the millions of journeys made daily by individuals travelling from home to work, study, and shop.

Post-Fordist Toronto is an urban region of transportation contradictions. The region is strategically situated at the crossroads of rail and road networks that link it to northern Ontario and western Canada, to Quebec and Atlantic Canada, and to the United States and Mexico. The Toronto region dominates the rest of Canada from the perspective of transport, while at the same time there are serious inadequacies in its transport infrastructure. For example, it boasts a spectacular new $4 billion airport redevelopment built by a not-for-profit airport authority, while the buses of the public sector Toronto Transit Commission (TTC) operate long past their normal life expectancy on potholed public streets. Perhaps the biggest contradiction is that while there are serious transportation problems in the Toronto region, it is also a region that is, in some respects, very well served by transportation: the underfunded TTC manages to carry 1.3 million passengers every work day; when the region's 5 million residents go to the supermarket, they find it well stocked with food; it has the largest and busiest airport in the country, a network of superhighways, large intermodal rail yards, state of the art warehouse and distribution centres, a port, an extensive public transit network in its centre, and a well-organized transport sector.

At the turn of the twenty-first century, the existing transportation situation in Toronto has become a bottleneck for the continued globalization of the region, as global and local circuits of mobility are not well-coordinated and various scales of decision-making do not visibly interact for the regional good. The question to consider in this chapter is whether there is an emerging collective actor (or actors) to remedy the situation, or if the anarchic governance model of the recent past will continue.

Global City Transportation

Globalized city regions like Toronto are being reorganized rationally to improve the real or perceived needs of global capital accumulation through international trade and transnationalized production complexes into which each urban region wants to tap in order to increase its riches. We can call this the exchange value orientation of urban regions. However, such globalized superstructures must be interlinked with localized transportation and transit systems, which serve mostly the social reproduction and mobility requirements of resident populations and their use value oriented everyday needs. At the one extreme, we find airports and all associated fast and far-reaching forms of transportation that services the goods- and people-moving needs of corporations and states. At the other end, we find commuter roads, transit systems, street cars, buses, bike lanes, disabled transit systems, and "walking school buses."[1] These variously scaled systems are interlinked and interdependent. For most of us, at one point, both become necessary and welcome modes of getting around. For tourists and business travellers, academics, and diaspora populations, the two systems are almost indistinguishably intertwined at some moment or another. The enhancement of transportation infrastructures does not just conjure up glamorous images of airport lounges and fast-moving trains but also the transportation network designed

---

1 Walking school buses refers to groups of parents who deliver their children to school collectively on foot.

for material throughput—the movement and regulation of the urban region's metabolism (see Chapter 8).

A New Urban Geography

New rhythms and scales of production, exchange, and consumption, and the consequent impact on the movement of commodities, have generated a changing urban geography in the Toronto region. Commodities on the move in the GTA are supported by a concentration of new spaces and transport infrastructure that spread over a large terrain in the northwest part of the region. This sprawling transport complex can perhaps be considered as the counterpoint to the glamorous face of Global Toronto presented downtown and in the bourgeois urbanism of its gentrified inner city neighbourhoods. As air travel among global cities has increased and the number of flights between them continues to multiply (Smith and Timberlake 2002), it is not surprising that the new geography is centred at Pearson International Airport, by far the busiest airport in Canada in terms of passengers, aircraft movements, and cargo handled. Surrounding the airport, thousands of hectares of land are occupied by single-storey industrial buildings in the cities of Toronto, Mississauga, Brampton, and Vaughan. One of the largest facilities is the 280,000-square-metre Chrysler Bramalea Assembly Plant in Brampton. Overall, the GTA has the third largest concentration of industrial floor space in North America after Chicago and Los Angeles, and more than Vancouver, Calgary, Edmonton, Kitchener-Waterloo, London, Ottawa, and Montreal combined (Miller *et al.* 2001, 22).

Of particular significance to a study of regional transportation is the development of specialized logistics and supply chain management firms supported by new information technology. Current supply chain practices include equipping long distance trucks with Global Positioning Devices (GPS), facilitating the replacement of just-in-time (JIT) delivery with Quick Response (QR) delivery. QR is based on the daily delivery of goods to retailers and the premise of zero retail inventory (Raffan 2004, 67, 70).

This new urban geography includes the densest web of superhighways in the region. One of them, the 407 Express Toll Route (ETR), equipped with an all-electronic toll system, is owned and operated on a long-term lease by the private sector. A portion of another, Highway

New Transportation Technologies

An example of new methods in retailing that rely on sophisticated logistics technology is the Swedish-based multi-national fashion retailer Hennes & Mauritz (H&M). H&M, which operates more than 1,000 stores worldwide, entered the Canadian market in 2004 and by mid-2005 had eight stores, all in the GTA (two downtown and six in suburban malls; in 2009, the company had stores in 22 locations across the country). Goods are shipped from a central warehouse in Hamburg, Germany to a distribution centre in Montreal and then on to a warehouse/distribution centre in an industrial district in Brampton, Ontario, a municipality in the GTA. H&M guarantees new merchandise in every store every day (www.hm.com; Kok interview 2005).

An apparent trend in supply chain management is the development of logistics campuses "based upon a collection of multiple manufacturers focused on consumer products with similar distribution channels" (Miller et al, 41)." An example is the 56.6-hectare Brampton Distribution Centre, comprised of five buildings containing 260,000-square metres of floor space (www.Hopewell.com). The single largest tenant is Kraft Canada, which occupies a 93,000-square-metre building. Best Buy and Future Shop occupy 93,000-square-metres in two buildings, from which they supply all of their retail outlets in Ontario, Quebec, and Atlantic Canada. The Brampton Distribution Centre generates 145,000 truck movements annually. Individual retail chains have also built their own distribution centres in this part of the region. For example, Sears Canada has an 84,000-square-metre centre in Vaughan, which services most of its stores throughout Canada. Canadian Tire has a 111,000-square-metre warehouse and distribution centre in Brampton (one of five in the country) from which it provides its own in-house supply chain management.

Canadian Tire sources 60 per cent of its products in Canada. The rest comes in from around the world: mostly Asia. The GTA is the geographic and functional centre of national distribution of the company's retail network. The Brampton distribution centre with its hundreds of truck movements each day also provides jobs for close to 900 people who need to get to and from the facility daily. Like the airport, the centre, therefore, is a microcosm of the contradictory multi-scale transportation needs the region faces (McKenna interview 2005).

409, was sold to the Greater Toronto Airports Authority (GTAA) so that it could be included in the overall Pearson redevelopment project. The superhighway network links the Toronto region to American border crossings at Windsor, Sarnia, and Niagara, as well as to northern Ontario and Quebec. The transport complex in the northwest part of the GTA is also criss-crossed by major arterial roads that serve not only large-scale industrial and retail users but also the daily travel needs of the hundreds

FIGURE 9.1 Canadian Tire Distribution Centre in Brampton. This kind of industrial or commercial warehousing is typical for the just-in-time logistics common in urban regions today.

FIGURE 9.2 Highway 401, North York. While the TTC carries well in excess of 1 million passengers every day, the majority of journeys in the Toronto region are still made by automobile.

of thousands of residents of low-density suburban development, typical of that part of the Toronto region.

The past 50 years have seen a general shift in goods shipment in Canada from rail to truck; within the GTA, trucking has captured 80 per cent of the market share of transporting goods (Miller *et al.* 2001, 21). The railways have attempted to recapture market share by offering quick turn-around intermodal facilities and by promoting rail as an alternative to traffic-clogged highways. Canadian Pacific Railways (CPR) operates two intermodal rail facilities in the Toronto area. Their 280-hectare Vaughan Intermodal Facility on Highway 50 is the largest in Canada. Canadian National Railways (CNR) operates the MacMillan Yard, also in Vaughan, which is the most extensive general rail yard in Canada and includes a small intermodal facility.

Toronto Pearson International Airport

Toronto's major transportation feature is Pearson International Airport. This is not surprising as air transportation has become the magic word of global connectivity. It has also become the fastest growing mode of freight transportation (Switzer interview 2005). Air-based transportation has contributed to the development of what enthusiastic mainstream observers have called "the fast century" (Kasarda 1996). Airport expansion is among the most important *regional* tasks of world city infrastructural expansion: it is necessary and contested at the same time (Newman and Thornley 2005, 270).

Pearson is ranked as the twenty-ninth busiest airport in the world with 28.6 million passengers (preliminary 2004 figures from Airports Council International 2007), up 15.8 per cent over 2003, but still below the peak of 28.9 million reached in 2000. It handles roughly double the passenger volume of Vancouver Airport, the second busiest passenger airport in the country with 15.7 million passengers in 2004 (Vancouver Airport Authority 2008). In terms of total traffic movements, Pearson is the twenty-third busiest in the world (preliminary figures for 2004 from Airports Council International 2007). The latest figures for cargo indicate that 308,384.1 tonnes were handled in 2002 (Greater Toronto Airport Authority 2007), compared to Vancouver's 233,809 tonnes in 2004 (Vancouver Airport Authority 2008). To many leading thinkers and practitioners in the GTA, it is the airport itself that defines the urban region (Berridge interview 2005; Broadbent interview 2005). While most observers consider the non-descript and non-specialized nature of Toronto's economy (barring automotive assembly) as a strength and safeguard against sectoral downswings, they view the airport as its central hub. The region's geographic location makes the airport a more than regional asset, as it provides access to 60 cities in the United States and acts as a gateway to business and travellers both in and out of Canada and into North America east of the Mississippi, with 60 per cent of the American population within a one-hour flight away (Gillmor 2005, 63; Shaw interview 2005).[2]

As the GTAA acts as the crucial — almost extra-governmental — agency to build a regionally flavoured airport for global commodity exchange and passenger travel, the authority is unhappy about the way the region is run politically. Priding itself on its excellent tie-in with regional institutions, local economies, not-for-profit status, and community representation on its board, the GTAA is sharply critical of what, in the words of one of its leading operatives, is a lack of clarity in governance in the Toronto region. The agency has let the general public and regional decision-makers know in the past that it considers its model of organization and decision-making, its sense of having achieved regional inclusion, its aggressive private sector philosophy coupled with an ethics of civic altruism, and its accountability guaranteed by its board members to be an exemplary model of transportation — or perhaps general — governance (Shaw interview 2005). As the airport is often viewed as the prime key to the health of the regional economy, its governing agency is also held up as a model for how to get things done.

The GTAA sees itself as part of a contested space of political and economic, public and private, multi-scale decision-making bodies. This space is highly hierarchical and reflective of other power relationships in Canada's state and economic architecture. Municipal governments, for example, get short shrift in the administration of the airport's business, and their policies are often just appendices to decision-making processes that have already been made at higher levels of authority, both public and private. Despite the clearly expressed intention of GTAA leadership to integrate with the regional governance structure, local decisions on transit, for example, are often executions of necessary measures determined by needs produced unilaterally by the airport rather than coordinated multi-level planning or governance (Rieger interview 2005; Zbogar interview 2005).

---

2 "But Pearson itself is not a hub airport; 70 per cent of the passengers are destined for or departing from southern Ontario. The design of hub airports, like Atlanta's (where 80 per cent of the passengers don't leave the airport and are merely changing planes) is different from 'originating and destination' airports like Toronto" (Gillmor 2005, 68).

Airport Governance

Charismatic Texan Louis A. Turpen, previously CEO of the San Francisco airport, was invited by the Canadian government in 1995 to become president and CEO of the GTAA (Gillmor 2005, 63). Once hired, he operated on the assumption that things at the airport, and hence in the region, were not going very well. These deficiencies were to be blamed for the loss of business and major events such as the Olympics. From this analysis sprang the unique governance model of the GTAA, which is perhaps the least democratic but also perhaps the most effective (in terms of getting things done at all costs) regional governance institution in the area. It is with this governance model in place that Pearson underwent a $4.4 billion redevelopment of its Terminal 1 alone. Journalist Don Gillmor describes this succinctly:

> The key to redevelopment on a scale this large and complex was control, and the GTAA's structure ensured Turpen could do as he saw fit. In theory, the not-for-profit model freed airport development, which is necessarily long term, from the constraints of a short four-year political cycle, and insulated it from political whim. A purely private airport would subject the operations to the profit demands of shareholders. The private not-for-profit avoids both pitfalls but allows for little oversight and, in effect creates a fiefdom. Turpen's control is what made the project such an extraordinary model of efficiency, especially set against Pearson's dithering past. It is also what has attracted the biggest criticism: that Turpen was an arrogant dictator, a Napoleon overseeing an army of lesser Haussmanns. "You don't deal with Lou Turpen," a local politician says. "He just does his thing." (Gillmor 2005, 63).

As a "locational" strategy (Brenner 2004)—that is, as a strategy that wants to bind business in the area—the expansion of the airport under Turpen and the GTAA seemed to make intuitive sense to a broad coalition of decision-makers in the region, since this "gateway" produces jobs directly and indirectly (Harris 1994), and creates ancillary business around the airport specifically and in the entire region more generally. Yet such a strategy is also highly contradictory; it can never predict whether its effect is going to be to drain or to enrich the region with commodities, people, and ideas. No wonder that decision-making around the airport expansion was influenced by complex and sometimes contradictory interests. While local politicians want articulation with local business and communities, economic development officials see the importance of trade (Benham interview 2005); centrifugal and centripetal effects of a large and dynamic airport had to be reconciled. In this contradictory environment, the GTAA acts as a virtual monopoly and can therefore not be considered a model for other regional institutions. Rather, the experience with the GTAA points towards the necessity for regional institutions such as a transportation agency, which is representative and democratic throughout, rather than decisionistic and monopolistic in interest and behaviour (Crombie interview 2005).

Servicing the Capillaries: Getting Around in the Global City

Clearly, the most important segment of the regional transportation system is the extensive road network: the highways and arterial streets that criss-cross the region. An automobile region which, despite the impending crisis in Big Three car manufacturing, produces (and exports) cars far in excess of its own domestic market (Ontario has passed even Michigan as a location for automotive assembly) is also characterized by extensive car ownership and use. The suburbs, in particular, have been built almost entirely on the logic of automobile transportation for everyday work and play. Indeed, automobile transportation has been at the core of Canadian transportation policy overall, at least since World War II (Fowler and Layton 2002). Much of the interaction of global transportation with local circuits of activity is accomplished by cars, even as gridlock and environmental consequences, such as dramatically worsened air pollution, alert Torontonians daily to the problems caused by this mode of transportation. While the big automakers (GM, Ford, Chrysler, Toyota, Honda) and car part makers (Magna Corporation)[3] make their weight felt indirectly through creating or cutting employment in the region, there is little evidence that they directly steer regional transportation policy beyond lobbying for general infrastructural connections—mostly rail and road—to keep their JIT production processes flowing (McKenna interview 2005; Switzer interview 2005; Woo interview 2005).

3 Magna has become a regional dynasty with political and economic influence in the GTA and beyond. Austrian immigrant Frank Stronach, founder of Magna Corporation in Aurora, Canada, has long been one of Canada's highest paid corporate executives. His daughter, Belinda Stronach, attempted unsuccessfully to win the leadership of the national Conservative Party, changed parties subsequently, and was a federal minister in the government of Liberal Prime Minister Paul Martin before she resigned from politics and resumed the helm of her father's corporation.

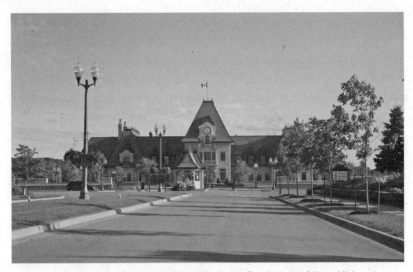

FIGURE 9.3 Magna Corporation headquarters in suburban Aurora. From here, one of the world's largest car parts manufacturers rules a global industrial empire of more than 80,000 employees in 24 countries.

As interest representation of the "movement industries" (Fowler and Layton 2002, 116) in regional planning issues goes, the Ontario Trucking Association (OTA) is the most active player. The OTA consistently acts on behalf of its membership in routine transportation policy processes and also in ad-hoc commissions and other governmental initiatives such as the "smart growth" planning process (Switzer interview 2005). The Canadian Auto Workers union (CAW), although a strong and progressive voice in ecological modernization discourses in larger Canadian public fora, has little interest in getting involved in regional transportation policy debates. Their organizational concerns tangentially touch transportation only insofar as the CAW's exemplary and progressive environmental politics involve thinking about ways to deal with car-related sustainability concerns (De Carlo interview 2005; Stanford 2005).

The TTC is always in the centre of public attention in Toronto. At least since its 1991 strike, after which ridership dropped dramatically and annual budget woes became a constant reminder of its precarious financial position, the public transit system in Toronto has been a source of anxiety for its workers, its clients, politicians, transit advocacy groups, and the general public. The transit agency often claims that it is unique in North America and perhaps in the world. While, on average, municipal

FIGURE 9.4 TTC headquarters, Davisville subway station. This building is the logistical centre of Toronto's extensive public transit system.

transit authorities recover 38 per cent of their cost at the fare box, the recovery rate of the TTC is 80 per cent (Rodo interview 2005).[4]

Two unrelated anniversaries bundled public debate regarding the TTC and crystallized these concerns in important ways. First, the 50-year anniversary of the opening of the TTC's first subway along Yonge Street in 2004 led to intense public discussion on the future direction the commission should take in developing a strong transit system in Toronto. Much of this debate concentrated on the expected nature of the extension of a system which is losing riders but which is expected to play a role in the city's demographic and economic expansion in the next generation. There was, however, much agreement among experts and the general public that the Ridership Growth Strategy (RGS), which had been implemented the year before, was the best way to consolidate the

---

4 While this claim is true in comparison to most cases, it must be pointed out that in some deregulated and privatized transit jurisdictions, such as Britain's, systems are operated largely without subsidies (Hensher and Brewer 2001). In North America, however, many rail-based public transit systems have been running at a loss, although some, such as those in Houston and San Diego, seem to be exceptions to that rule (Mackett and Edwards 1998; Kain and Liu 1999).

TTC's role at the current time, despite the warning by environmental-ists and transit advocates that the strategy may be underfunded (Perks interview 2003).

The more defensive strategy of the RGS, rather than potential large-scale expansion, was emphasized during the second anniversary, August 11, 2005, which marked a decade since the TTC's worst accident, when two trains collided and killed three passengers. The accident led to a fundamental restructuring of the TTC, since structural deficiencies in many areas were detected in its aftermath. The general philosophy of running the TTC switched to maintenance and a policy of keeping a status of good repair. Short- to medium-range planning moved almost entirely away from expensive subway line expansion after the Sheppard line was opened in 2002, despite constant pressure to expand the University/Spadina line to York University with its 50,000 students and 5,000 employees. Management, considered largely aloof and incompe-tent, was replaced by in-house practitioners and external transportation experts. Capital spending was redirected towards system maintenance and upkeep, and extensive changes were put in place to improve com-munication and training (Hall 2005).

The RGS, which was implemented in March 2003, is an outgrowth of the altered management goals and the changed political situation in the wake of the neoliberal reforms of the 1990s (Rodo interview 2005). Additionally, the RGS had its origin in the commission's expressed goal to bring its growth strategy in line with upper level and municipal state policy directives that started to congeal early in the new century. Citing the city's new Official Plan, the smart growth policies of the province, and the federal government's commitment to Kyoto, the TTC saw its role redefined in "providing travel to the people of Toronto" and to assist in the "'smart' reurbanisation of Toronto." Continuing funding instability was noted as a particular problem when long-term planning for stock and rails was needed, but a commitment to playing its part in making the region more sustainable was clearly expressed. The goal of the RGS is to increase system-wide ridership annually, in order to reach 500 million riders in 2011 (up from 415,000,000 in 2003). The RGS is touted as "a consistent, long-term staged program of providing priorities for, and investing in, existing transit services using proven technologies and operating strategies" and as a "realistic program of expansion at the TTC to put in place a transit

FIGURE 9.5 Davisville subway station, high density apartments in background. This image shows the intensified infrastructure of housing and transit in the centre of the urban region.

system that will attract new riders, and support the City's Official Plan vision for a transit-oriented re-urbanisation in Toronto" (Toronto Transit Commission 2003, E1–10). The TTC strategy, which is so clearly linked to the municipality's expansion plans, is a regional niche strategy, which builds on the specific advantages of public transit in the built-up core of the GTA. It is clearly the relationship of urban density and the need for cost recovery that drive TTC policies in this area (Rodo interview 2005). In this sense, it is the negative copy of transit policies beyond the "transit watershed" in the suburbs. Transit planners in Brampton, west of Toronto, for example, model their policies on specific linear needs between two distinct points rather than on comprehensive coverage based on urban density (Rieger interview 2005; Zbogar interview 2005).

Expressing the desire to participate in the reduction of automobile travel, a stated goal in most planning documents dealing with the GTA, the TTC sees an opportunity in minimizing the growth of auto use and its negative effects. This regional policy, by default, potentially supports plans at various scales of regional policy-making to achieve a new sustainability fix for the region and to solve major capacity problems in the regional transportation system. It is interesting, too, that the RGS does not refer explicitly to specific global growth strategies as the incentive for its own directions but cites regional sustainability goals and expansion of transit lifestyles as desired outcomes. Just as the TTC does not expressly pinpoint the overall growth goals of the global city as reasons for its policy, it also denies a role in social engineering (servicing and subsidizing transit-dependent non-car-owners), which it considers outside its mandate. Welfare effects of the ridership policy are considered largely beyond the potential of the transit authority (Toronto Transit Commission, 2003, 8). Let us now look at the larger picture of regional transportation governance in Toronto.

Government Transport Policy

Before focusing on transportation governance in the Toronto area as a regional policy field that attempts to identify notions of collective agency in the process, we will first briefly sketch the architecture of government transportation policies, which set the context for political and governance struggles in the region (for an overview of government transportation policy in Canada, see Fowler and Layton 2002).

Federal Transportation Policy

Since the 1980s the federal government, which has constitutional authority over transportation, has moved generally towards deregulation, while remaining strategically interventionist. Current federal transport policy is based on a "market-based transportation framework" in which "[c]ompetition and market forces will continue to guide the development of the national transportation system" (Transport Canada 2003, 19, 28). Examples of this policy trend include the privatization of Air Canada in 1988–89 and of CNR in 1995, and the transfer of ownership of the major airports in the country in the 1990s to non-profit private agencies (such as the GTAA in Toronto). Despite privatization and devolution, the federal government retains a strategic role in the planning and permitting of airports, as well as in security modernization, which became top priority after 9/11 (Warson 2003). In addition, the federal Ministry for Infrastructure and Communities has made its top priority the strengthening of both the globally oriented infrastructures of Canadian urban regions and the connectivity of communities (Godfrey interview 2004).

Provincial Transportation Policy

At a public information session held in Toronto in July 2004, David Caplan, then Minister of Public Infrastructure Renewal, stated that "good public infrastructure" is the basis of a good quality of life and a strong economy. Caplan estimated Ontario's infrastructure deficit to be $100 billion and stated that the province intended to implement a 10-year capital infrastructure plan in conjunction with private sector partners. According to Caplan, "better transportation systems are a crucial element" of the funding plan. Transit would be the first priority for moving people, while connecting the Greater Golden Horseshoe to "vital markets" (Caplan 2004) will be the priority regarding the movement of goods.

Schedule 6 of *Places to Grow*[5] (a map indicating transport infrastructure and titled "Movement of Goods") shows two new "economic corridors" widely interpreted to mean new superhighways that would cross the greenbelt. One, the Mid-Pen highway, would provide a new access route to the all-important Niagara border crossings to New York State. Interestingly, the transport maps included in *Places to Grow* indicate the border crossings at Niagara, Windsor, Sarnia, and in Eastern Ontario, suggesting that, from a transportation perspective, the region is defined as including all southern Ontario border crossings to the United States. The proposed Mid-Pen is a good example of the tangle of transport in the Toronto region. While it is promoted as necessary for continued export-based economic growth in southern Ontario (to allow trucks better access to the border), unless it is made a truck-only route, it will no doubt become as congested with mixed traffic as other super highways in the region. There is also the obvious conflict between the economic goals of the *Places to Grow* plan and the insertion of a major source of air pollution and, historically, a trigger of sprawl (a highway) into the most protected parts of the greenbelt (Woo interview 2005).

The detail of the province's spending plans became clearer in May 2005 when the Ministry of Public Infrastructure Renewal (now the Ministry of Energy and Infrastructure, since 2007) announced a $30 billion five-year public-private infrastructure renewal plan. Under the theme "Investing in the Economy," $6.9 billion was to be spent throughout the

---

5 Described in Chapter 6.

province by 2010 on highway improvements and border crossings (www. placestogrow.ca).

Local Transportation Policy

The often referenced telephone area code divide in the GTA between the inner city (416) and the outer regions (905) is evident also in the transportation policies of the local area municipalities. While the City of Toronto promotes the creation of lively pedestrian streetscapes and the upgrading of transit services in order to support its Official Plan goal of major intensification and population growth, the area municipalities promote their truck, rail, and airport cargo advantages as they compete among themselves for investment. A distinct culture of automobility in the 905 is counterposed against strong support for public transit in the more central districts of the Toronto region. Yet even there the politics of transportation can be very heated, as seen in the prolonged debate over the TTC's proposal to improve streetcar service on St. Clair Avenue West by creating an exclusive streetcar right-of-way. Transit advocates in the affected neighbourhoods were met by an equal number of automobile enthusiasts, one of whom declared at a public meeting that it was his "constitutional right to make u-turns in St. Clair." Still, we contend that while the transport policies of 416 and 905 appear generally to be increasingly divergent, when viewed at a regional scale they can be seen as working together in support of the stated elite goal of selling the Toronto city-region as a competitive city.

Regional Governance and Transportation:
The Search for Collective Agency

In Toronto, regional transportation in the period of globalization has been both surprisingly uncoordinated and predictably contested. There seems to be a dramatic disconnect between the (specialized) knowledge and experientially based (public) concern about problems that plague the region on the one hand, and, on the other hand, the political mechanisms through which they can be addressed. To many, this disconnect is a direct consequence of the depoliticized and technocratic nature of transportation policy, where powerful interests (the automobile industry, air and rail service providers, road builders, developers, transportation officials, unelected agencies such as the GTAA, etc.) fight over various models of capital accumulation and rational service provision. In this conversation, consumers and the environment appear merely as after-thoughts of a continuous modernization process that is based on shared elite goals of economic growth and expansion. Some policy-makers, however, see this disconnect as an expected outcome of democratic decision-making in a complex policy field with strongly divergent soci-etal and economic interests involved (Moscoe interview 2005). Either view may hide the bigger problem from the point of view of overall regional policy and unity: it is possible that the extant political system is structurally unable to create a set of policies that would consolidate the region and increase regional identity *through* transportation governance rather than *in spite of it*. While it is the almost unanimous belief of most regional decision-makers and opinion leaders in the region that good public transit is necessary, that its quality has an influence on Toronto's competitiveness, and that it has many ancillary benefits (such as making sprawl a less attractive alternative), decisions on transit funding are inco-herent as higher level governments have used piecemeal and "political" funding announcements for short-term political benefit rather than for the sake of improvements to civic infrastructures with potential benefits to the regional economy. Federal and provincial governments have been hesitant to commit full financial and organizational support to regional and local transportation in Toronto.

With the exception of the GTAA and provincially funded GO regional bus and train service,[6] regulation has been mostly hands-off and transfer payments to urban communities have lagged behind in international comparison. At the other end of the scale spectrum, municipal transit politicians have been largely caught in the "local trap" (Purcell 2005), which obstructs cross-jurisdictional solutions at the regional scale; this trap occurs where globally oriented movements of commodities and peo-ple meet the necessities of a strongly commuter-based regional economy

---

6 Under the provincial Tory government, GO Transit funding was downloaded temporarily between 1998 and 2001 to municipalities in the GTSB, which was GO Transit's governing body at that time. The province restored funding to GO in January 2002, when it became a provincial Crown Agency. Still, GO prides itself on consistently recovering "80–90 per cent of its operating costs from the farebox—the best financial performance for any transit system in Canada and one of the best in the world" (GO Transit 2003, 4).

that necessitates movement of supplies and labour in all directions. So far, all appeals to solve the transportation conundrum in the Toronto area are undoubtedly regional in nature while all attempts to consolidate action at the regional scale have so far suffered defeats.

When the conservative provincial government of Mike Harris amalgamated Toronto in the late-1990s, it failed to create a larger regional governance unit for planning and policy matters. Harris, whose government prioritized private automobile transportation, trucking, and road building—and virtually stopped all transfer payments to public transportation in the GTA—instead created a weak institutional hybrid, called the Greater Toronto Services Board (GTSB). Besides its role in allocating funding to regional GO Transit, this board had authority only to plan, not to implement. Its first head was former chair of the government of Metropolitan Toronto, Alan Tonks, who—after being elected to federal Parliament—made way for Gordon Chong, a conservative former Metro councillor. To the surprise of many, Chong's performance as the chair of the GTSB catapulted the agency into the limelight of public discourse on transit governance, just at the time when daily gridlock began to seriously hamper the system. When the GTSB was dismantled without a successor at the end of 2001, political wrangling started over whether the newly elected Liberal provincial government would create a Greater Toronto Transportation Authority (GTTA) in its stead. Alan Tonks has been credited with first floating this idea while he was the chair of the GTSB (*Novae Res Urbis*, Wednesday, March 20, 2005)

While for years no single authority replaced the GTSB, the discussion on individual and coordinated measures to control regional transportation movements has produced an endless string of more-or-less related proposals and innovations, such as a road toll on the inner city Gardiner Expressway, congestion pricing, comprehensive travel modelling, and the RGS discussed above (Eligh 2005). Some of these debates were located outside of government. Whereas various levels of government have failed to produce a coherent and coordinated regional transportation strategy, quasi-governmental and non-governmental organizations have entered the debate with proposals and lobbying agendas of their own. Most prominently, the Toronto Board of Trade has entered the fray in a series of publications (Toronto Board of Trade 2001a, 2002, 2003). In an initial report, *A Strategy for Rail-Based Transit in the GTA*, the board (2001a) produced two scenarios for public transportation, one that projects proceeding in a "business as usual" fashion, another that projects the development of a "wealthy city region." The latter scenario was built on the assumption of greatly increased public transit funding, which would draw, in its wake, ancillary outcomes, such as fewer cars on the road and a cleaner environment. Public-private partnerships would be used to accomplish the ambitious strategic goals of the strategy.

The Board of Trade's intervention adds up to a regional vision for transportation, where a giant modal shift is to occur along the lines of exchange value and being globally accumulation-oriented on the one hand, and the local use value orientation of transportation on the other hand. The most prized road networks of the region would be freed up for accumulation purposes and goods movement while public transit would be enhanced to take the overflow of commuters and other riders linked to local and regional—rather than global—circulation. The emphasis on rail over bus transport further suggests that critical connections between supra-local circuits of transportation and local capillaries is crucial to the board's proposal rather than local transit in its own right. These proposals finally arrive at a blueprint for a governance institution. (Toronto Board of Trade 2003; Roman 2004, 21)

The provincial government ultimately came through with founding a GTTA, later to be named Metrolinx. A draft regional transportation plan was released by Metrolinx in summer 2008 with a 25-year horizon and a $55 billion capital budget. The plan built on previous local, regional, and provincial transportation concept plans and funding announcements and proposed a mix of subway extensions, light rail and busway networks, and new highways. Less than 1 per cent of spending ($500 million) is earmarked for alternative forms of transportation like bicycling and walking. Noteworthy is the fact that, at the time of the release of the draft plan, capital funding beyond year 15 was purely speculative.

As could be expected, the plan sparked widespread public debate and a rehearsal of future philosophical and funding disagreements between different levels of government. While the chair of Metrolinx, Rob MacIsaac—former mayor of Burlington—points to the compatibility of his agency's plan with existing long-term planning, especially that of the TTC and the City of Toronto, inner city politicians and bureaucrats emphasize differences in direction and substance of both efforts. The main issue to be taken up in future discussions among the stakeholders seems to be the notion of rapid rail transit in Toronto. While the TTC and the city prefer street-based light-rail at the heart of their Transit City project, the Metrolinx plan suggests a stronger reliance on subway-type rail rapid transit and regional roads.

Conclusion

In a comprehensive comparative study of planning and governance in world cities, Newman and Thornley (2004, 256) have written:

> Planning, as defined by its professional associations across the world has objectives that seek to balance the aims of economic efficiency, social welfare, and environmental sustainability. On the ground, the balance between these aims expresses the pressure of different interests and lobby groups. The resultant planning priorities and strategic policy response depend on urban politics and the processes of governance.

This summarizes the forces at work in the planning of transportation infrastructure and governance systems in Toronto: it is possible that the political system—particularly the arcane regions of municipal politics—is structurally unable to create a set of policies that would consolidate the region and increase regional identity. Transit planning serves as an example here. While it is the shared opinion of many knowledgeable people in the region that better transit is needed; that its quality has an influence on Toronto's competitiveness; and that it has a lot of other social, health, and environmental benefits, decisions on transit expansion are piecemeal and political. That a regional community allows itself to be governed by such enlightened sluggishness (or perhaps "non-decision-making" under the name of democracy) is hard to grasp. While everything points to the necessity of regional solutions, municipal politics caught in the "local trap" (Purcell 2005) obstruct such solutions.

In the meantime, there is no lack of activity to keep plans of regional coordination of transportation needs on the front burner. While currently in a poor state, such coordination is absolutely necessary if the region wants to live up to its dreams of international competitiveness and meet its dire need of moving people and goods through the capillaries.

At the global end of the transportation universe, Toronto has been affected by the overall reassessment of transportation practices and border realities after 9/11 (for an elaboration, see Drache 2004); at the local end, it has been sucked into a vortex of hyper-growth-related problems of livability and efficiency of daily routines. In class, ethnic, and gender terms, the region's transportation infrastructure is getting increasingly sorted out as highly uneven and potentially unjust: high end, production-oriented supra-regional transportation networks—the airport, the partly privatized highway system—on one hand and a crumbling public transit system on the other. As the region has continued to play the role of Canada's premier global city, its underfinanced, increasingly decentralized transportation system, especially public transit, has mirrored the general problems of suburbanization and sprawl. This spatial configuration makes all non-individualized forms of transportation difficult to justify for efficiency reasons, which leads to the increase of unsustainable arrangements in the region overall (see Kennedy 2002; Kennedy *et al.* 2005). The disconnect between premium and everyday networks of transport in Toronto appears to be a bottleneck to the very economic competitiveness that largely drives public policy in the region. At present, however, no collective political actor appears capable or willing to bridge the disconnect and unstop the bottle.

10
Creative Competitiveness

"I never realized how much power we've got!"
(Co-chair of Pride Toronto interview 2006)

After the austerity period of the 1990s, strategies for "competitiveness" have shifted hands from dry business-attraction guys to cool high-tech, bohemian, artsy folks. Investing in creativity by promoting the arts, channelling money into urban design, encouraging a café culture and a lively street life, providing tax incentives to high-tech industries, or converting an old distillery into a cluster of art galleries will undoubtedly change the everyday mood of certain parts of the city and empower certain actors previously marginalized, be they artists or drag queens. Yet the not-so-hidden reason behind this creativity talk one can hear in the hallways of City Hall or at Board of Trade meetings is the hope to attract the "right type" of residents to Toronto: that is, the young, cool, educated, high-value-added worker of the knowledge economy.

The Creative City Program: Richard Florida Comes to Toronto When Harris's Neoliberal Conservatism Begins to Backfire

Economic development used to be under the exclusive purview of the federal government; it was only in the 1980s, and more heavily in the 1990s, that it became a provincial and municipal policy sector. Under the NDP provincial government of Bob Rae (1990–95), the chosen approach to economic development was to build on productivity coalitions

183

composed of state, business, labour, and community leaders, grouped according to economic sector. These groups were to get together and decide collectively on a strategy to develop their sector. However, following the harsh recession of 1990–93, the Rae government decided to focus on the shorter term objectives of unemployment and deficit control. These measures were very unpopular when Mike Harris took over the province in 1995. His approach to urban economic development, set in place by 2002, was inspired more by theories pertaining to economic and urban clusters (Bradford 2003):

- In 1998, he created the Ontario Jobs and Investment Board (OJIB) composed of business and government representatives. The board recommended continuing amalgamations and modernizing the *Municipal Act* in order to provide municipalities with tools for economic development by enhancing their capacity to mobilize the private sector for infrastructure financing, regional service delivery, and the formation of clusters.
- After his 1999 re-election, Harris established the Ontario SuperBuild Corporation, with a $20 billion budget over five years and a mandate to lead and coordinate public-private partnerships and to advise the cabinet on privatization opportunities.
- In 2001, a new bureaucratic unit of the Ontario Ministry of Economic Development and Trade was created for urban economic development, as well as a Prosperity Development Fund managed by OJIB. The Task Force on Competitiveness, Productivity, and Economic Progress was set up with the mandate to measure and monitor "Ontario's competitiveness, productivity, and economic progress compared to other provinces and US states and to report to the public on a regular basis. In the 2004 Budget, the Government asked the Task Force to incorporate innovation and commercialization issues in its mandate" (Institute for Competitiveness and Prosperity 2007).
- As of September 2002, selected municipalities were able to create tax incentive zones to entice companies while benefiting from the provincial Opportunity Bonds, through which the province subsidizes 50 per cent of interest costs for borrowing for infrastructure development. Both SuperBuild and the Ministry of Municipal Affairs and

Housing sponsored workshops for municipal and business elites on public-private partnerships.

In June 2002, Mayor Mel Lastman organized the Toronto City Summit in order to shape the urban agenda in the next decade. The SuperBuild program had tempered the effects of Harris's budget cuts and downloading, although the visibility of the crumbling of urban infrastructure nevertheless increased while homelessness and poverty became more and more obvious in the streets of the city. As Elyse Allan — former president and CEO of the Board of Trade — stated in a town hall meeting, the Board of Trade realized that there is a "need for more intimacy between business and the city" to "address the needs of citizens, not only of business," because "business competitiveness is intrinsically linked to the perceived competitiveness of the city," and, given that employees are very mobile, "they will move out to find a better quality of life" if nothing is done (Town Hall meeting 2004).

Such a statement captures the rationale behind the Toronto City Summit Alliance (TCSA), a coalition of "civic leaders in the Toronto region" (Toronto City Summit Alliance 2004) created in June 2002, in reaction to worries about the state of the city. The TCSA states that the reason for its existence is "to assess our urban region's strengths and challenges," and these challenges are defined as "expanding knowledge-based industry, poor economic integration of immigrants, decaying infrastructure, and affordable housing." It published a policy document in April 2003, entitled *Enough Talk: An Action Plan for the Toronto Region*, which was signed by 216 supporters and public figures. TCSA membership includes "private, labour, voluntary, and public sectors in the Toronto region," as well as a "network of hundreds of volunteers" (Toronto City Summit Alliance 2004). However, despite the participation of two labour groups and the United Way, it is clear that it is led by the globally oriented economic elite, including the Toronto Board of Trade and other consulting firms, such as the Boston Consulting Group. More specifically, the TCSA has a steering committee of 56 members, two staff members, 16 sponsors (including the five biggest banks of the country), and nine in-kind donors. Many of these TCSA actors have offices in the central core of the Toronto region, although there are also many representatives from businesses and public offices outside the central business district,

An Example of a "World-leading Research Alliance"

The Medical and Related Sciences (MaRS) centre occupies two square kilo-metres near the University of Toronto. It is a non-profit organization founded by John R. Evans, Torstar Corporation Chairman and Toronto City Summit active voice. Torstar owns *The Toronto Star*, one of the city's largest daily newspapers. The philosophy behind this research cluster is to ensure that Toronto becomes a world leader in innovation and commercial technologies. As a creative competi-tiveness strategy, MaRS aims at "systematically building a robust, sustainable entrepreneurial ecosystem that supports the development of young companies" by "directly intervening and assisting a number of emerging companies, with risk capital, management resources, strategic business tools and access to global markets; developing and maturing Canadian business talent" and "creat-ing powerful networks that will meaningfully connect the leadership of Canada's scientific, business, investment, and cultural communities to their international peers" (www.marsdd.com).

including the mayor of Oakville, a real-estate developer in the fast grow-ing suburb of Richmond Hill, and Magna International of Aurora in the automotive industrial core of Southern Ontario.

TCSA priorities are linked to demands for increased public funding for economic, infrastructural, cultural, and social development in Toronto, including:

- a new fiscal deal for the cities;
- improvement of the physical infrastructure, especially regional transportation and the waterfront;
- reviving tourism in Toronto;
- creating a world-leading research alliance;
- investing in post-secondary education;
- integrating immigrants into the economy;
- strengthening social and community infrastructure, especially afford-able housing and community services; and
- supporting arts and culture

A Toronto Board of Trade leader explained in an interview on Decem-ber 7, 2004 that business now has a more "sophisticated understanding of what is involved in competitiveness," that it is not only about lowering costs and taxes. For him, being competitive requires that government

"Helping great science become great business"

"Direct connection to public transit"

"An innovative space where best-in-class science and business come together"

GLOBAL SCALE

"Competitive on a global scale"

EllisDon

FIGURE 10.1 MaRS during its construction, 2004.

play a role by investing in infrastructure in order to generate opportunities for business to innovate (Director of Policy 2004). Competitiveness is seen as imperative, as the necessary response to globalization, one of Beck's (2007) three major risks. The current discourse does not question the need to be competitive. Another interviewee asked us, "Who can be against motherhood?", making an analogy between "natural" competitiveness and motherhood, since the former is not a zero-sum game: everyone can prosper without a cut-throat race for investment (Institute for Competitiveness and Prosperity 2004). The rationale justifying this race towards economic growth and prosperity—a modern version of boosterism—could generally be synthesized as follows: 1) private accumulation creates incentives for innovation; 2) growth increases the quality of life, which then attracts more potential for prosperity; and 3) growth creates a sense of community, because prosperity will eventually trickle down. While means have changed, objectives are no different from the "rollback neoliberal" period. This sense of urgency was captured in Margaret Thatcher's infamous phrase, "There is no alternative [to competition]." This sense of urgency is very clearly expressed in reports published by the Toronto Dominion Bank or the Board of Trade: *A Choice Between Investing in Canada's Cities or Disinvesting in Canada's Future*, an April 2002 report by the former; and *Strong City, Strong Nation: Securing Toronto's Contribution to Canada*, published two months later. The message sent by economic elites is clear: The economic vitality of Canada can only be secured through investment in cities.

The year 2002 was thus very important. In one instance, business interests in Toronto shifted away from austerity strategies *à la* Harris and sought to build bridges with labour and community groups in order to take charge of the problems that Toronto was facing following the 1990s neoliberal wreckage while remaining competitive. In another instance, American Richard Florida published a best-seller, *The Rise of the Creative Class*. A hip and talented self-marketing researcher, Florida travelled the world delivering and presenting speeches at conferences intended for an urban economic audience about the importance of attracting a highly educated population of creative workers (arts, design, fashion, high tech) to their cities. This creative class, he argues, prefers "cool" cities; therefore, wherever they choose to live is where money will flow. Such people look for recreational and lifestyle amenities, a clean environment, and cultural stimulation. This is where public money should go to foster economic development. The Creative Index combines the Talent Index, which measures the proportion of a city's population over 18 that holds a bachelor's degree; the Bohemian Index, which calculates the proportion of a city's employed labour force who work in artistic or creative sectors; the Mosaic Index, which tabulates the proportion of the city's foreign-born population; and the Tech-Pole Index, which notes the city's share of employment in high-tech industries relative to the national average. This became the benchmark against which Toronto has come to be assessed. Given the success Florida experienced in having his theories absorbed in Toronto, it was no surprise to see him move to the Prosperity Research Centre at the University of Toronto in the summer of 2007.

The cultural turn in urban economic development strategies was acknowledged as early as the 1980s (see for example Harvey 1989a). Cities, it was argued, tended to invest in hallmark festivals, in events showcasing ethno-cultural diversity, and in spaces of spectacular consumption. These strategies were indeed similar to Toronto's reformist tradition, which focused on green spaces, culturally vibrant neighbourhoods, and

FIGURE 10.2 Advertising on the site of the new Opera House. The federal government injected important sums of money on high visibility projects to encourage "art" in Toronto.

diversity as a defining character of the city. Henceforth, when ideas about the creative city surfaced in urban policy circles, Richard Florida had a receptive audience, particularly since the city's employees had gone through close to five years of budget cuts and austerity measures. Morale was low and talk of creativity was received like a breath of fresh air.

Within the municipal administrative and political structure, the creative city hype was translated into a Culture Plan, commissioned by City Council in May 2000. The Culture Division conducted a series of public meetings and focus groups in 2001–02. In addition in 2002, the federal and provincial governments announced that $233 million would go towards seven cultural regeneration projects (such as the new Opera House and refurbishment of the Royal Ontario Museum). These high-end cultural projects were at odds with Florida's emphasis on street-level culture, but they were nonetheless warmly welcomed by the city's cultural planners. The 10-year Culture Plan for the Creative City was adopted by Council in 2003. The plan focuses on resources, facilities, public-private partnerships, financing, heritage preservation, and creating a marketable world image of the city based on a "creative" identity. The plan—filled with

Liberty Village

Liberty Village, an area of 38.6 hectares located in the west end of Toronto, is a partnership between the Toronto Economic Development Corporation and Artscape that has transformed this industrial district. It has become a cluster of new media companies and artist studios, comprising about 500 businesses and 6,000 employees (www.lvbia.com). Organised as a Business Improvement Area (BIA) funded by a special tax levy applied to commercially assessed properties, it is one of Toronto's 60 BIAs. It is unclear, however, how the surrounding area of Parkdale benefits from this reconversion. While at the east end of the BIA there is a new development of 466 townhomes priced from $125,000 for a bachelorette to $399,000 for a three-bedroom unit, the high rise shown in Figure 10.3, looking west from the Artscape building, is home to much poorer residents.

references to the idea of the creative city—positions Toronto in competition with Montreal, Chicago, San Francisco, Milan, and Barcelona.

In partnership with civil society and semi-public organizations—Artscape, the Toronto Arts Council, and the Toronto Economic Development Corporation—the City of Toronto developed a series of programs aiming to foster creativity, including the Incubation Program, which subsidizes studio spaces for artists to prioritize the redevelopment of creative clusters such as Liberty Village and the Distillery District. Combined with the new Official Plan's adoption of beautification as a guiding principle, creative city ideas have made their way into many domains of city policies.

Creativity After Austerity: Impacts on Governance

"Who can be against competitiveness?" asked an employee of the Ontario Ministry of Industry (2004). We could use the same logic to ask "Who can be against creativity?" Both notions, competitiveness and creativity, are now so entrenched in the city's functioning that it would seem bizarre to question them. Resulting from the austerity of competitiveness strategies in the 1990s, Toronto has now shifted towards creative competitiveness. This has had important impacts on the manner in which decisions are made and how resources are channelled at City Hall. Indeed, under the reign of Mayor Lastman in the post-amalgamation years, streamlining was envisaged as giving more power to the mayor in order to fast-track

FIGURE 10.3 View of the surrounding neighbourhood from Liberty Village. There is a strong contrast between the art and high tech cluster of Liberty Village and the surrounding neighbourhood, which is ethnically diverse and poorer. Interactions between those who work and live in Liberty Village and those who live in the surrounding neighbourhood are very limited.

decision-making by increasing the use of private management boards, marketizing relationships between and among the City's departments, benchmarking city services against private-sector "competitors," and using market pricing techniques for city services.

This philosophy met with resistance from City employees, which culminated in a municipal workers' strike in 1999. Lastman responded with unsuccessful efforts to delegitimize their union. Within the context of the transition to the amalgamated city and the huge administrative overhaul this created at City Hall, municipal workers played a central role in maintaining a reformist tradition in amalgamated Toronto. Such consolidation led to the merging of important middle management positions across the city. In addition, a significant number of politicians and power brokers from the old suburban and Metropolitan Toronto governments were still in the transition process of adjusting to the mega-city, resulting in a marginalization of historically progressive municipal bureaucrats from the old core city. Moreover, Lastman's ideological conservatism and political nepotism—he brought many of his former North York staff with him into leading positions at City Hall—created a chilly climate for many reform-oriented bureaucrats. Some assume that the municipal governance culture at City Hall had irreversibly changed during these years towards a managerial culture led by ideas of efficiency and market orientation. We argue that there still is a sustained progressive impetus among the amalgamated city's employees, based on their history of social engagement ranging from the original trade union organizing in the nineteenth century to the more current social, multicultural, and environmental civic activism that motivates people to become public workers. For example, in Chapter 8 we described the important role played by municipal workers in preventing the privatization of Toronto's water and sewage systems. Ironically, it appears that the provincial Tories, despite their attempt to purge the city of radicals and progressives and thus purge their worst political enemies in the core of Toronto, gave them a larger playing field for their activities. The local state showed its resilience in the face of external attack, an incredible flexibility in handling its affairs, and an ability to rebound.

However, despite the remarkable capacity to maintain a progressive tradition at City Hall, city employees were beginning to lose hope as the Harris-Lastman suburban-style management view kept squeezing out all innovative initiatives. A series of workshops on creativity were organized in order to boost their morale. The creative city project, conceived as both a series of cultural planning measures and a management philosophy within the administration of the city, allows for a partial recuperation of the reformist institutional identities and roles that had been systematically degraded during the 1990s.

Nevertheless, emerging critiques cast doubt on the claim that creativity will deliver us from the wreckage of neoliberalism. Creative city programs are not so different from the 1990s-style entrepreneurialism and meritocracy promoted by Harris. Creation for the sake of creation has become a sort of conservative fashion orthodoxy. Yes, money is injected into arts and culture. Yes, brown fields are being redeveloped into hip Liberty Villages. Yes, the city seeks the advice of Pride Toronto and artists who were not considered legitimate actors in the recent past. Yes, the Royal Ontario Museum has a new starchitectural expansion. Yes, artists benefit from the marketing efforts deployed by the city and other branding actors.

FIGURE 10.4 The Michael-Lee Chin Crystal at the Royal Ontario Museum, Toronto. This striking extension to the museum was designed by architect Daniel Liebeskind and – while controversial – is considered a central part of the city's "cultural renaissance."

Yet, artists have to spend most of their time writing reports to justify how they spend their new grants and to assess the economic impact of their art through very complex performative calculations—or they have to do the work that recently fired social workers were doing in community centres and schools. Indeed, while school curricula have eliminated most electives and cultural courses, and while community centres have lost their grants, artists are now expected to do community art work with *their* operative grants. The city's grants policy states that this money is "a strategic tool used to achieve the City's social, economic and cultural goals" (City of Toronto 2007).

That is not to say that artists have no role in community arts programs that aim to improve equity and that they do not resist the "high culture" focus of the creative city programs. For instance, the Live With Culture campaign was launched in September 2005 and lasted until December 2006 to raise awareness about Toronto's cultural scene. Signature events were initiated by the City of Toronto in order to catch the wave that infused federal government investments into cultural regeneration projects, so as to underline Toronto as the Cultural Capital of Canada for 2005–06. The goal of the campaign was to integrate culture into the daily lives of Torontonians and visitors. At the end of the 16-month celebrations, a website—www.LiveWithCulture.ca—was created as a cultural agenda where people can announce cultural events across the city.

Responding to this high-profile event, a group of artists launched a Live Without Culture campaign. The aim of the project was to "rectify the damage done by the City of Toronto's misrepresentation of the artist's life … to offer a more realistic vision of what it means to experience culture. Sometimes, art makes you feel ugly and disillusioned, mean and slow, fat and tired. This reality needs to be presented to the public alongside the more peppy vision that is offered by the official campaign" (Vaughan 2006). Similarly, the Parkdale Tenants Association organized a "Lord of the Slums Bus Tour," coinciding with the opening of the *Lord of the Rings* musical, in order to show the world the other side of the glamorous cultural capital of Canada.

One problem with the creative city hype is that under the hopeful cover of creativity—rather than austerity—the same old neoliberal logic prevails: performance, marketization of public services, meritocracy, auditing, contracting out, and individualization. Clinging to the hopes of creative competitiveness to improve workplace productivity, focusing on the reproduction and attraction of a highly skilled labour force, developing innovative research incubators, and thriving on the marketable creativity of the city, many participants and sympathizers of the TCSA (with the support of City Hall) are banking on competitiveness for protecting the well-being of Torontonians. As Albo (1997) demonstrates, this competitive strategy requires: 1) converting the institutional structure from Keynesianism (and reformism) to a new development model based on competitiveness; 2) shifting existing resources from present usage to new promising sectors (biotech, high-tech, computer, life sciences, design); and 3) mobilizing new resources, such as the city's "marketable" diversity.

The problem with this model is that it concerns a limited number of sectors. Alongside the cluster strategy of "creative competitiveness" are large sectors dominated by a strategy of "competitive austerity," as well as a growth in the informal economy and related exploitation (Albo 1997). For instance, the low-income service sector is far from buying into the creativity mantra for its employees. Similarly, agricultural and bottom-of-the-line manufacturing workers do not benefit from the creative competitiveness hype, as such economic development strategy does not increase demand for their output nor does it affect the organization of work on the assembly line. The problem with the creative competitiveness consensus is that economic growth becomes the sole definition of prosperity and quality of life, just as "creative communities" exclude the majority of Torontonians who see culture valorized only to be commercialized.

Toronto, Inc.: Global Competitiveness for the City-region

In this chapter, we have highlighted the role of the TCSA in shifting the provincial economic strategy towards an explicitly urban economic development agenda based on public investments in quality-of-life issues. The TCSA builds on over two decades of city-regionalism. Momentum for city-regionalism first grew with the establishment of the Greater Toronto Area Task Force and the publication of its report in 1996 (GTA Taskforce 1996). The task force was chaired by Anne Golden, then president of United Way of Toronto and founding member of the TCSA. Its report and the transcript of its public consultations clearly linked regionalism and global competitiveness. As an example of the terms of the debate at the time, consider the following excerpt from a *Toronto Star* editorial:

> For years, we have prided ourselves as living in "the city that works." By "city," we usually mean that broad swatch of metropolis from Burlington to Oshawa north almost to Lake Simcoe: Ontario's supercity, the Greater Toronto Area (GTA), or just Toronto. In the past, we've been the locomotive of growth for both the province and country. Our collective initiative, drive and creativity have made us the capital of English Canadian commerce and culture. Our sense of civility and our community of thriving neighborhoods have made us the envy of the world. Today, however, the city is in the doldrums. We lack a vision, a concerted plan to take us into the next century.... Politically, we have outgrown our structure of municipal government—a lasagna of councils and boards with overlapping responsibilities and boundaries that no longer make sense. The structure encourages waste and discourages accountability. (Honderich 1995)

The recommendations of the GTA Task Force report, particularly the creation of a regional government, were not followed by the provincial government. Instead, six local municipalities were amalgamated into the Municipality of Metropolitan Toronto (which had been incorporated in

1953), creating in 1998 the new City of Toronto at a scale much smaller than the GTA.

If amalgamation was not what the GTA Task Force was envisaging, its work nevertheless set the tone for the economic development strategies developed in the following decade. Two important shifts took place. First, despite the absence of a regional government structure, competitiveness came to be closely associated to the scale of the city-region, the boundaries of which are elastic and unclear—sometimes it is referred to as the GTA, others times as the Greater Golden Horseshoe, but rarely is it only the amalgamated city. A civic association, the TCSA, took the lead in crafting an urban economic development strategy at the regional scale. Second, the means through which economic growth is to be fostered have changed. From an austerity strategy characterizing the Tory period (1995–2003), Toronto has adopted a creative city logic privileging innovation, design, and culture as both objects of investments and the philosophy of its public management. In other words, the drive towards the creative city represents a set of initiatives synthesized in the Culture Plan as well as a way to manage city employees through a series of performance indicators and innovation-rewarding techniques very similar to the New Public Management philosophy popularized in the 1980s and 1990s.

Despite a strong consensus around creative competitiveness in Toronto and in Ontario, barring some stinging criticisms on the Left, there remain disagreements among the elites, the TCSA, and City Hall. While most people talk the creativity talk, when it comes down to reorganizing a business or levying new taxes, it becomes less attractive to some. Similarly, the spotlight on the high-tech nerd, the gay consumer, or the opera lover does not necessarily please the old-time businessman used to selling a hockey game to his clients rather than a seat for the latest opera. Indeed, when the city gained $18 million in 2004 from a voluntary 3 per cent levy in the tourism sector as a destination marketing fee, the hotel sector was not keen on spending this money to promote cultural events. They preferred instead old-fashioned destination marketing strategies, such as major league sports tickets. This controversy illustrates the lack of consensus on creative strategies when it comes down to finding ways to put them into practice. The fact that the 3 per cent levy remained voluntary means that it was not implemented as a measure fully included in the Culture Plan. This resulted in giving more leeway to those who resist this shift towards culture in economic development strategy.

Perhaps one of the most visible tensions between strategies promoted under the logic of creative competitiveness is synthesized in the branding exercise initiated by Tourism Toronto in the summer of 2005. In response to the SARS crisis, an effort was mounted to devise a brand identity for the city. The bulk of the $4 million branding exercise was provided by Tourism Toronto, which contracted an American marketing firm. Surprisingly for people at City Hall (which had adopted "Diversity, our strength" as its motto), the theme of diversity and multiculturalism was not appreciated by American test audiences. The result of this effort was the Toronto Unlimited campaign (Toronto Tourism 2006), which was subject to immediate criticism from Mayor Miller.

Conclusion

In the end, despite resistance and internal tensions, creative competitiveness is now the dominant logic guiding actions at City Hall and in many civic organizations. In many ways, it is seen as the best of both worlds: the world of efficient management and economic growth, as well as the world of entertainment, fun, and quality of life. Glenn Murray, former Winnipeg mayor and vocal advocate for the New Deal for Cities said in an interview in 2006:

> Most gay people come here because it's dense, urban, comfortable with diversity; there's a lot of weird people here and you can just fit in real comfortably. There's a lot of that sense that you can live a life here that's hard in South Porcupine. So there's a sense of urbanity, of density. I think there is also a sense that globally this is a place to come and make money to have a big house—the McMansion Syndrome. And I think that's true too. I think they can co-exist. (Murray interview 2006)

Because Toronto's city-region offers such diversity in urban form and lifestyles, argues Glenn Murray, it has enormous attractive potential, which the creative competitiveness logic seeks to nourish. The problem, as we argued in Chapter 7, is that glamorous zones tend to remain in the city centre, at the expense of the in-between city, despite efforts made by community arts programs to bring culture closer to the people. The problem with those programs is that they put a heavier burden on artists themselves. Stuck between auditing requirements for their grants and performing community work with almost no support from social workers, artists are transformed into resources for, for instance, taking youth out of the streets. Many of them are happy with this social involvement, but they also struggle to find time to create artwork. Transferring the burden of social work onto artists is an example of the individualization of responsibility characteristic of neoliberal management. Rather than having a state-sponsored support system, the creative competitiveness logic "downloads" social work onto artists.

11
Millermania

When David Miller was elected mayor in November 2003, a wind of hope swept the city. The broom that served as the icon of his campaign promising a "Clean City"—clean streets, clean air, clean management practices—was also meant to clear the way for a new political era. The Tories, under Ernie Eves, had just faced a disgracing defeat at the provincial level, and Liberal Paul Martin had just taken over as prime minister of Canada. In Toronto, the arrival of David Miller meant the end of the post-amalgamation Mel Lastman years. It also meant the return of reformism or, as we argue, of neoreformism. The Toronto of the new millennium is not governed as it was in the 1970s in the "glorious" years of the "Stop the Spadina Expressway" battle. Toronto went through the austerity period of the long 1990s and re-emerged as a progressive city with a neoliberal twist.

This chapter explores how neoliberalism evolved from an exogenous and ideological force to an endogenous and normalized element of governance under neoreformism. David Miller incarnates this synthesis of reformist ideals implemented with neoliberal tools in a city where myriad aspects of neoliberalism have become the norm in many corners of everyday life.

Taking out the Broom

Some symbols do not die. In November 2003, Councillor David Miller campaigned for mayor on a platform of cleaning Toronto. The night of

FIGURE 11.1 David Miller with a broom and David Miller by the lake, 2003. On the night of the municipal election, David Miller used the broom as an icon of his victory. Standing by Lake Ontario, Miller announced his desire to beautify the city and give it a design image.

his victory, he was photographed raising a broom in the air. The city was in the midst of a corruption scandal, and Miller promised integrity by cleaning up City Hall. Community activists in central city neighbourhoods and urban environmentalists were adamantly fighting the construction of a fixed link to the Toronto Island, because they feared it would open the door to the expansion of the central Island Airport. Miller pledged to cancel the construction of the bridge, should he be elected. The TCSA and other business-led groups like the Toronto Board of Trade were making more and more noise about the dilapidated state of the city and its negative impact on the quality of life. Miller committed himself to cleaning the streets of the city and making it more beautiful.

The broom thus seemed a logical symbol for this campaign. Miller as Mayor ushered in a new era, the end of the Harris-Lastman antireformist years. Yet, the broom also recalled other popular mayors who campaigned on the theme of cleanliness, Rudolph Giuliani being the most famous. Elected mayor of New York City in 1994 on the promise of cleaning it of corruption, immorality, and crime, Giuliani's most famous project was the Disneyfication of Times Square. He pushed out prostitution, porn shops, homeless people, and drug dealing, replacing them with Disney megastores and other sites of suburbanized consumption. Giuliani became famous for his zero tolerance philosophy towards crime and his law-and-order platform. Miller did not advocate the same measures and did not subscribe to the same discourse, yet he also vowed to clean the city. This discourse pleased both business elites and middle-class reformists. Indeed, when John Sewell was elected mayor in 1978, he also campaigned against the old ways of doing things at City Hall and with regard to policing and corruption in particular.

In 2003, municipal elections took place in the midst of wide discontent towards the provincial Tory government and a change of leadership at the federal level. In Toronto, five major candidates ran for mayor. Tom Jakobek, the city's budget chief for 10 years, was a conservative candidate who was rapidly defeated as his involvement in a corruption scandal became public. John Nunziata ran a campaign on the theme of morality and health, mixing his opinion that prostitution is "filthy" with ideas about decriminalizing marijuana, improving public transit, and forcing homeless people off the street and making them seek professional care. Barbara Hall, the erstwhile frontrunner and logical candidate of the old reform forces who had lost against Mel Lastman, ran a weak campaign and appeared politically spent.

David Miller slowly but surely developed into the candidate to beat. His steadfast insistence on a few issues that captured the public's attention—such as the Island Airport debate—carried him past the other contenders through the summer of 2003. Miller's fiercest opponent was the former CEO of Rogers Communications, John Tory. Often depicted as bland, dispassionate, and a typical backroom dealer, Tory had served as a senior advisor to the federal PC party under Brian Mulroney and Kim Campbell. He also served as principal secretary to Ontario PC Premier Bill Davis and as a fundraiser for Mike Harris and had worked on the election campaigns of conservatives David Crombie and Mel Lastman. His campaign priorities were much the same as Miller's: restoring faith in City Hall, fighting non-violent crime such as graffiti and loitering, and cleaning up Toronto's streets. But his means were different: he vowed to run the city like an efficient business with a strong leader. This meant, for instance, hiring students to pick up litter and clean graffiti, installing a zero tolerance philosophy towards small crime and disorder, and banning postering across the city.

Miller carried the day with 43 per cent of the vote, ahead of Tory with 38 per cent, and Hall who was far behind with 9 per cent. He was seen to be the most promising candidate on the Left but also proved acceptable to many people in the centre of the electorate. Jane Jacobs supported him, as did other prominent public figures including Margaret Atwood, Michael Ondaatje, and Robert F. Kennedy Jr. With his campaign organized by professionals such as conservative John Laschinger and liberal Peter Donolo, as well as with the advice of public intellectuals such as architect Jack Diamond, Miller's public support surged prior to the election. Indeed, within the business community, John Tory only had uncertain support, given his error record during federal PC campaigns. Miller was seen to be a strong leader, sensitive to improving global competitiveness by enhancing the quality of life in Toronto. Despite his leftist record, many in the business sector liked him. His sincerity and charisma inspired trust and hope, especially following the more flamboyant and erratic style of Mel Lastman. In many ways, he embodied a different type of populism, focusing on quality of life, beauty, cleanliness, and creativity.

FIGURE 11.2 David Miller cartoon, cover of *Eye Weekly*, November 8, 2003. Miller was seen as a superhero of the Left, reconquering City Hall.

From Small Town Common Sense to Neoreformism in the Global City

Under Mike Harris as premier of Ontario, a small town and suburban-based political culture gained more voice, and, as a result, the exurban ring around Toronto became the dominant political space in the province. Part of this political shift was also a turn to a mindset that ostensibly associated more with the likes of small and medium businesses than with the needs of a downtown global city economy. Harris was first elected on the basis of strong support in small town, small enterprise Ontario, with a populist rhetoric enhanced by subtle references against the economic, cultural, and political power of cosmopolitan and transnational Toronto. Interestingly, whereas amalgamation of the central core of the region was arguably meant to reduce the power of reformists and their slow-growth agenda while avoiding the creation of a regional governmental institution that business did not want, the outcome did not so much result in a gain of power for small and medium businesses but for transnational capital. In creating a business-friendly climate for the city-region, Harris's Tory government became closely linked with the transnational capitalist class in Toronto (Sklair 1997). Through its embrace of neoliberal economic policies, it eventually evolved to work hand in hand with the interests of Toronto's globalized sectors (banking, finance, auto, entertainment, real estate, airport and logistics, etc.). This was perhaps nowhere as obvious as in its decision to launch its 2003 budget at the headquarters of Magna Corporation, the global auto parts maker.

During the anti-statist period of the long 1990s, neoliberalism was largely legitimated ideologically through a discourse on the exigencies of globalization and the need to work on Ontario's global competitiveness. For instance, amalgamation was justified by the Harris government on such ideological terms. Its goals were to:

- strengthen the fiscal and economic position of Toronto and the GTA;
- strengthen Toronto's position for global economic competition;
- remove a tier of government for accessibility and accountability;
- complete the unification of services to stop municipalities from competing with each other; EQUITY.
- make use of community councils and volunteer committees, which cost less than real government; and
- eliminate duplication and waste. (Quoted in Milroy, Campsie *et al.* 1999, 164–65)

However, the longer the Harris regime lasted, the greater became the number of big business representatives, such as large segments of the Toronto Board of Trade, who expressed their concerns about the possible negative impact of rapid restructuring and local government underfunding on social peace in the city. The Board of Trade did not approve of Harris's downloading package, shifting—among other things—welfare costs to

TABLE 11.1 **Three Political Periods in Toronto, 1972–2008**

The reformist period (1972–1995): From the first election of reformists at City Hall in the former City of Toronto, to the election of Mike Harris's Tories in the province of Ontario in 1995. During this period, the central city was dominant in city-regional politics. The main line of conflict was between developers and local residents (who were represented at City Hall by reformists).

The anti-statist neoliberal period (1995–2003): From the election of Mike Harris to the defeat of the Tories in 2003. During the long 1990s, Toronto experienced the suburbanization of city-regional politics with the dominance of pro-growth, neoliberal, and suburban interests. The main line of conflict was between economic growth (not only land development, but economic growth understood more broadly) and the quality of life.

The neoreformist period (2003–present): Starts with the election of Mayor David Miller and Paul Martin's New Deal for Cities. This period is characterized less by a suburbanization of city-regional politics and more by the creation of a city-regional consensus (between globally and locally oriented capital, labour, and politicians) on the necessity to focus on the quality of life in Toronto as a competitive asset for city-regional economic development.

the relatively inelastic property tax base of the city, a move that could prove disastrous if the local economy were to fall on bad times. From the Board of Trade's perspective, the expected adverse effects of these fiscal reforms, or Local Services Realignment, were mitigated both by the government's SuperBuild program, through which it directly invested billions of dollars in infrastructure, and by a cap on commercial property tax increases. However, these measures did not prevent the quality of life of Torontonians from facing serious deterioration. In contrast to Rae's hapless NDP government, which coincided with a local and global recession that severely limited its actions, the Harris government was aided by both a favourable economic context and Toronto's tradition of conservative philanthropy, which acted as a buffer against the worst excesses of its regime.

During the Harris years, business actors and transnational capital began to actively shape regional politics, particularly via the TCSA. Players representing big capital had been fairly absent from the regional and local political scenes up until recently, as they traditionally focused their lobbying activities towards the federal level. Why, then, did transnational capital begin to be active at the city-regional level?

First, transnational economic actors believe that the competitiveness of the city goes hand in hand with the competitiveness of their businesses.

They were indeed becoming worried about the adverse effects of neoliberal cutbacks on the quality of life in Toronto. Further, in forging alliances with other actors in the city (labour, communities, small and medium businesses), and through acting in the name of Toronto, they may have greater agency with which to influence the federal government, drawing on the latter's desire to invest in the urban policy field. Moreover, the city-regional scale has the advantage of being only weakly institutionalized. Businesses can thus more easily control that political space. The TCSA is very successful in using reformist language—sustainability, diversity, quality of life, local democracy—in order to press an agenda of urban competitiveness.

The struggle against amalgamation had mainly been organized by middle-class reformists in the former City of Toronto and was based on a dichotomous discourse that associated "local democracy, sustainability, and quality of life" with the central city and "absence of democracy and domination of land developers" with the suburbs. Miller and—what we would call—neoreformists in the amalgamated city discursively associate local democracy, sustainability, regionalism, and competitiveness. Miller himself embodies this synthesis. Clearly on the Left of the political spectrum, his past and current actions reveal his reformist (slow-growth) vision, particularly his opposition to the central city airport expansion. However, he benefited from the support of globally oriented elites during his electoral campaign. One might have expected that his closest rival, former CEO of Rogers Communications John Tory, would have gathered more support among other big businessmen. Yet Tory, as well as leftist candidate Hall, were both playing on the same polarized strategies as they had done previously, that is, reformism against neoliberalism. In contrast, Miller seemed more successful in fostering a new consensus between the two poles.

Neoreformism promotes a vision of urbanity that incorporates many aspects of the neoliberal project. Toronto is thus shifting from a period of downloading and austerity to the opening of new revenue sources for municipalities under the *City of Toronto Act* and the New Deal for Cities and Communities. A city with a viable, festive, multicultural urban centre is greatly appreciated by economic developers as much as by reformists. This vision, however, excludes many sectors of civil society, who remain voiceless, powerless, or simply too radical. The goals of reinvesting in

---

Two Iconic Urban Struggles: (1) The Spadina Expressway Saga

In the mid-1960s, the Metropolitan Toronto Transportation Plan proposed a north-south expressway through the western central parts of Toronto. It was approved by the OMB. Yet as construction began, Jane Jacobs led and nurtured grassroots opposition in those neighbourhoods it was meant to traverse. When Premier Bill Davis withdrew his support for the road in 1971, construction was halted. What is now known as Allen Road is the only remnant of what would have been the Spadina Expressway.

This grassroots struggle lent momentum to the reform movement that transformed the political landscape in Toronto. Reformists treasured mixed urban spaces, citizen participation, and use value more than exchange value. They were aided by a heavy provincial hand in municipal affairs, particularly in controlling land development. This meant that locally oriented segments of the business sector did not have an important say in local politics, especially when compared to their American counterparts (Garber and Imbroscio 1996).

---

infrastructure and increasing the quality of life are largely defined along the norms of the urban consumer-oriented middle class and are widely anchored in the governmentality of suburbanized neoliberalism. This trend was programmatic under the conservative regimes of Mayor Lastman and Premier Harris. However, it remains active under Miller. For example, at the end of May 2004, Miller decided to evict squatters from under the Bathurst Street bridge. The Ontario Coalition Against Poverty (OCAP) responded with severe criticism since he had not proposed any concrete solutions with which to address the housing crisis. They wrote:

> Three important conclusions must be drawn from these sickening developments. Firstly, all the excuses and explanations offered by Miller's functionaries to justify these acts of social cleansing are nonsense and the real reason for them is crystal clear. The development industry has plans for the centre of the City that the homeless and poor are standing in the way of ... The second lesson we must draw is that David Miller, the pseudo reformer, is as ready to serve the needs of the developers and persecute the homeless as was Mel Lastman, the overt conservative ... Lastly, these attacks can only be stopped if we mobilize to fight back ... For 6 months the City has been sending cops and employees under the bridge to threaten eviction but have backed down when we've showed it won't happen quietly. The larger sweeps that are being prepared can be turned back if homeless people and those who stand with them are ready to make the political price higher than Miller is ready to pay. (Ontario Coalition Against Poverty, 2004)

Two Iconic Urban Struggles: (2) The Island Airport Controversy

Built in 1939, the Island Airport was originally meant to be the city's main airport, until Pearson International Airport took over. The Island Airport is owned by the Toronto Port Authority, based on a federal, provincial, and municipal tripartite agreement. In 2002, under Mel Lastman, the agreement was modified to permit construction of a bridge to link the island with the rest of the city. The fixed link was fiercely opposed by local community groups who feared it would give the airport market opportunities to expand its operations. This would have meant more air traffic over downtown Toronto, given that the Island Airport is more conveniently located than Pearson. What prevents it from expanding is said to be the absence of a fixed link since its only access is still by ferry.

Despite opposition, contracts were signed with contractors and airlines. However, the day after the November 2003 municipal election, the new mayor, David Miller, asked council to pass a motion retracting its support for the bridge. With this withdrawal, the federal government cancelled the construction and compensated the Port Authority with $35 million. Most of this money was used to settle with companies that were under contract for the construction.

THE ISLAND AIRPORT EXPANSION.
IT'LL BE LIKE THE AIR SHOW.
ONLY 365 DAYS A YEAR.

THE ISLAND AIRPORT AFFECTS OUR FUTURE. A FUTURE only one candidate is thinking about. David Miller knows there is a lot at stake in the race for our next mayor. And it's not just the waterfront.

It's about courage. It's about showing leadership in the face of some really tough decisions.

This election is also about the future of this city. Ultimately, the city we leave our children.

When Ms. Hall and Mr. Tory say they fully support the expansion of the Island Airport, they are not just supporting the

WHO'S FOR DESTROYING OUR WATERFRONT?

BARBARA HALL

JOHN TORY

destruction of our waterfront. They are simply not thinking about the future of our city. David Miller is.

That's because, of all the candidates, David is the only one who opposes any expansion of the Island Airport. And for a lot more reasons than we could fit on this page. ☞

FIGURE 11.3 David Miller's campaign leaflet, 2003.

OCAP's fighting words are at odds with the general perception of middle-class citizens that urban "problems" or those who personify them—the homeless or street people—need to be managed so that they allow other residents of the city to go about their daily business without being harassed or confronted. This is a typical and usually unresolved problem of urban life to which a new register has now been added. In the current period of neoliberal normalization, ideological references are less present. In neoreformist Toronto, we witness a reappropriation of social critiques of neoliberalism. On the one hand, the language of local democracy, sustainability, and quality of life is more readily used by elites. On the other hand, civil society actors are reappropriating the neoliberal project by being drawn into new forms of socialization, such as the consensus-building project of the TCSA. This apparent consensus has the effect of delegitimizing more radical forms of critiques and politics, like those put forth by OCAP or anti-globalization activists.

The Millermania Continues?

In the 2006 elections, despite some criticism from the Left and little opposition from the Right, David Miller was re-elected with 57 per cent of the vote. Although under constant barrage from conservative councillors under the leadership of Lastman acolytes Case Ootes and Denzil Minnon Wong and pundits such as *The Toronto Star*'s Royson James, who regularly blame Miller for incompetence and inaction, his track record is significant. In his first three years in power at City Hall, he developed a "From Streets to Homes" outreach strategy and signed an affordable housing agreement with Ottawa and Queen's Park. This resulted in 900 new units of affordable housing being slated to be built. In terms of public transit, he secured $500 million for the purchase of environmentally friendly buses and also bought new subway cars. At the same time, to stimulate economic development, he adopted a plan to reduce the business tax ratio every year for the next 15 years and lobbied the provincial government for a reduction of the education tax. He focused on the film industry with the construction of a new film studio and the appointment of a Toronto Film Commissioner responsible for promoting the city as a world film capital.

What happened to the broom? Miller did clean the streets: there are more litter pickers, street sweepers, and street vacuums and more trees, murals, and newer building facades. The Island Airport expansion was cancelled the first day he arrived in office in 2003, and he still puts public transit high on his priority list as a way to improve Toronto's air quality. As of 2005, after incidents of gun violence, more police officers have been

TABLE 11.2 Main Political and Economic Transformations by Decade, 1980s-1990s-2000s

1980s Reformism		1990s Anti-statism		2000s Neoreformism
Boom → Bust →		Recession → "CSR" →		Reclaiming the active state
Eggleton		Rowlands, Hall, Lastman		Miller
FTA/NAFTA → Deindustrialization →		Toronto: Capital of rustbelt → "Megacity" →		Recapturing the global city
"Good business climate" →		Local neoliberalism →		The creative city
		Olympic Dreams		SARS

sent into the streets. The city has identified 13 priority neighbourhoods where social investments are to be made to fight "place effects" such as social decay and gang violence. As for a clean City Hall, Miller has remained fairly silent on how to fight corruption, aside from the appointment of the first Integrity Commissioner in 2004, whose role is maintaining "the public's confidence in City Hall and in ensuring that the codes of behaviour and ethics governing elected officials are objectively communicated and applied" (City of Toronto 2008). With the new *City of Toronto Act* providing the city with extended powers—passing by-laws, planning, representation of the city, taxing, delegating powers—a code of conduct and a lobbyist registry have been set up, although the ombudsman and the auditor general still hold important roles.

Despite criticism, Miller remains a popular mayor. This is particularly important given the weak level of power that he enjoys. Indeed, the mayor of Toronto is no more than the chair of City Council. He was recently able to set up an executive committee, as did his Montreal counterpart, which gives him more steering power within Council. However, given that Toronto municipal elections are non-partisan, he cannot count on the automatic vote of his party at Council in order to push his ideas. In this context, the mayor has to be very skilled at convincing councillors to agree to his policies. He does enjoy symbolic power in the public eye; charisma is thus a very powerful resource.

Miller has been able to build and maintain consensus on cleaning the city of pollution, with a green plan and transit measures that continue to rely on both Left and Right support. During 2007, however, he faced major challenges from the populist Right on Council when he wanted to put into use the new taxing powers that the *City of Toronto Act* had given him. In July that year, he attempted to introduce two new taxes on land transfers and vehicle registration. Losing the support even of some of his allies, he was defeated in a 23–22 decision, with crowds of irate real estate agents and car dealers populating the public sections of the Council chamber. The taxes, so Miller argued, were necessary since the city faced a \$575-million budget crisis for 2008. In order to maintain the level of service commitment, the mayor scrambled to find new revenue sources and end the city's dependence on property taxes.

Among other things, Miller and his supporters on Council—in particular, TTC Chair Adam Giambrone—played a game of brinksmanship after the defeat of the new taxes and threatened, at one point, to mothball the underutilized Sheppard subway in the northeast of the city. More serious was Miller's decision to close community centres and make their services unavailable on Mondays in order to save money. This last move cost him much sympathy, even among supporters.

Still, after much public debate and political wrangling, the Municipal Land Transfer Tax and the Personal Vehicle Ownership Tax were passed on October 22, 2007, going into effect on February 1, 2008. While they created an important income stream for Toronto, in the end the resolution of the budget crisis relied on the mobilization of provincial transfer funding, in the area of transportation in particular.

The erstwhile defeat enabled Miller to ask the police to cut \$10 million from their budget. The conservative Right resisted lowering the number of street officers, and Miller had no political choice but to support Police Chief Bill Blair's promise not to lay off officers. In the context of an ongoing debate on gun violence, exacerbated since the unintended shooting of 15-year-old Jane Creba, a bystander during a gang shootout on Yonge Street on Boxing Day 2005, the killing of student Jordan Manners at a Toronto high school, and the shooting deaths of two innocent passers-by in late 2007 and early 2008, Miller has been vocal on the need to stop gun smuggling from the United States while cracking down on gang violence. The mayor's community safety plan focuses on providing opportunities to youth and working with neighbourhood groups on place-based social cohesion building mechanisms.

Even though human security is a broad concept that includes such aspects of well-being as economic stability, health care, and public safety, it is mostly the latter that is responsible for inciting fear in people. Indeed, murders and shootouts are highly visible. They stimulate fear due to their random nature, which often then translates into higher demand for increased police presence on the streets. Beck (2007) has highlighted human security as a major risk of our times. Unfortunately, human security is too often narrowly understood simply as public safety and counter-terrorism and can serve to legitimate reactionary politics. The challenge of progressives in this context is to address these fears more appropriately than can the conservative Right. Will Miller succeed?

12
Changing Toronto

Ya, you see everyday
All the people standing at the train station
Left, right, left, right, left, right
We don't talk to each other now
What an alien nation
Up, tight, up, tight, up, tight
I hope one day some things can get better
I hope some way our hearts can change the weather
As we walk this yellow road
And try to shake the load
In this 4-1-6 area code

K-os, *Flypaper*

Mayor Miller weathered the storms of 2007 and charged ahead with a renewed sense of purpose and direction, but the shadows of that less-than-perfect year were with him as he tried to rescue the big picture of his second term in office. When *Toronto Life* magazine published its list of 25 "most influential Torontonians" in November 2007, Miller was not among them. In this select group are mostly white old men who continue to be the skeleton of the city's permanent government. Visible minorities and women, such as Toronto's chief financial officer Shirley Hoy, *National Post* gossip journalist Shinan Govani, author Margaret Atwood, and capitalist Heather Reisman, are noted exceptions. One particular power broker stands out: "optimist" David Pecaut, who heads the hyperactive Toronto City Summit Alliance, which has all but established itself as an alternative government in such strategic areas as immigrant settlement, economic development, and urban sustainability.

With urban power moving from straight government to governance, the rise of the City Summit Alliance is not a surprise, as welfare and planning functions of municipal affairs are taken up more and more by private and third sector actors. What is more surprising, perhaps, is the recurrence of a kind of pre-reform politics that have long been considered unimportant, at least in the core of the city. While the downtown elites have been successful in deflecting attention on development away from the giant wall of condominiums at the waterfront towards the sprawl of the outer suburbs, the millstones of public opinion have finally ground the airy goals of the Official Plan into the grist of conventional cycles of hyper-fuelled growth and lately decline.

In City Council, the right-leaning councillors, a group orbiting around former deputy mayor Case Ootes, although conservative upstart Karen Stintz has recently been a visible spearhead for the group as has Denzil Minnon Wong, have coalesced into a mostly ineffective but noisy opposition, which often uses obstinate and obstructionist politics, giving them the reputation of being somewhat bratty (see in particular columns by *The Globe and Mail's* columnist John Barber, who takes them to task on a regular basis). Yet, in their populist backlight, they emboldened a homeowner revolt against what appears to be the public interest of the city. Leading the charge against Miller's attempts to use the newly granted taxing powers of the *City of Toronto Act* in the summer of 2007, this group of conservative local politicians has become a thorn in the side of the mayor's political executive. The anti-tax forces are a strange amalgam of conservative politicians (e.g., Ootes and Minnon Wong), who play a broken record of fiscal conservatism and appeal to the homeowners' many suspicions about what "their" taxes pay for (welfare, treatment of drug addicts, immigrants, transit, clean air, etc.), and some of the least productive sectors of the urban economy, the car dealers and real estate brokers who suck endless windfalls out of the boundless—but highly uneven—urban growth process. Their strong presence at council meetings at City Hall during the deliberations on the new taxes was a clear expression of a new form of rather regressive politics that threatens to set back the progressive metropolitan change just coming to terms with the bare necessities of global city formation in Toronto. It showed that the political right in Toronto could effectively mobilize resistance to what seemed a decent plan—to make those who have the money to make major purchases pay more taxes rather than spreading the burden around to all tax payers, rich and poor. The homeowner democracy of the property owners, which revealed itself here, goes by the principle "one-house-one-vote," not "one-person-one-vote." It is driven by the socially most regressive sector of the capitalist class, which mobilizes basic knee-jerk instincts in the property-owning general public, who fear taxes almost as much as they fear transit riders and tenants, inner city kids, and urban culture. It may be a throwback to the nineteenth century in how it links political rights directly to property rights rather than other forms of human and citizenship rights. Homeowner democracy makes property the measure by which—popular—power is accounted for both materially and discursively. This kind of power gains organizational form in the Real Estate Board and the Taxpayers Association (Sandberg 2007). It is predictable that this tendency will grow as the economic crisis forces a general conservatism on the hegemonic polity of Toronto.

The real estate economy is the most exposed sector in the global city and certainly the core of its downtown and particularly its exurban growth machines, as well as the backbone of its infrastructure expansion, although that is mostly paid for by the taxpayer (MacDermid 2009). It raises its head defensively against the modest reforms proposed by Miller and the NDP hegemony on City Council, but it really has little to offer by way of a comprehensive metropolitan strategy to deal with the triple challenge to economic prosperity, human security, and ecological sustainability that the city faces. By contrast, any business-led coalition would certainly have to include some other players such as the auto industry, the creative industries, the high tech sector, etc. And it will have to include organized labour as well as territorial (neighbourhoods, community), topical (environmental, cultural), and ethno-cultural civic groups. Whether Pecaut and his philanthropic army of City Summiteers will be able to provide a cohesive strategy to forge such an alliance remains to be seen. As the Miller regime progresses, the Toronto Board of Trade keeps offering advice from the sidelines that may become white noise to the mayor and his team or may strike a chord with larger groups of Torontonians. The board did this before when it sniped at the Harris Tories and Mel Lastman, who were selling out the city by the kilo. Later, the board threw its weight around in debates over the need for public transit. One such typical insertion into public discourse was the advice, at budget time in early 2008, to bring in a five-year infrastructure surcharge on residential property taxes to create long-term budget sustainability. After pinpointing unionized labour as the biggest cost factor (and hence culprit) in budget overruns and property tax hikes, the board assumes a position of higher public interest: "All of us continue to feel the impact of Toronto's infrastructure gap, as residents and business people, through gridlock, rundown community facilities or sinkholes in major highways. It is undermining both our competitiveness and our quality of life" (Wilding 2008, AA8).

Given the stark choices the city seems to face as neighbourhoods and communities drift apart socio-economically and culturally during a period of economic uncertainty, the next few years will be decisive. Will there be a set of new social movements around transit, the environment, and labour backing the NDP councillors' and the mayor's progressive course, but pushing for more extensive politics of redistribution of wealth in this city? Or will the Right use their moment in the media sun to muster up more populist support to build up a viable candidate to unseat Miller in 2010 and regroup around a new urban regime? There has already been some excitement about this option among the police, who flatly denied the mayor's request for budget cuts with their usual recourse that more cops are needed on the streets to keep social order in a deteriorating Toronto. If the Toronto Board of Trade counts on restraint and flexibility when it comes to the renewal of public service collective agreements in the future, it may not be wise to count on the police, as they have already drawn a battle line in the sand.[1]

For now, the mayor—and governance in Toronto more generally—faces another, deeper challenge. Growth, the mantra that has driven the Official Plan review of the last few years, has been elusive even during the fat years of economic expansion until the emerging financial and economic crisis. While the thousands of new condominiums that spring up everywhere suggest a steep increase in Toronto's population, they seem to have led only to gentrification without any remarkable population gain overall (Lehrer and Wieditz 2007). Fewer newcomers than expected— only 21,787 people—swelled the ranks of Torontonians between 2001 and 2006. One obvious reason is the ongoing process of gentrification in the city's traditional ethnic working-class neighbourhoods, such as Riverdale, Parkdale, and Little Italy (Walks 2006a, 2006b, 2005, 2007). Some areas, like the Dufferin corridor in the city's west end, are experiencing a

---

1 In February 2008, in anticipation of the new provincial Family Day holiday, the police placed an ad in *The Toronto Star* in which the mayor was personally attacked for not giving them that day off.

dramatic demographic exodus, as larger multi-generational families make way for smaller, more affluent family units (Gerson 2007).

Yet the apparent decline in the city's population growth rate is also linked to a more troubling set of developments. A group of researchers at the University of Toronto have documented that Toronto increasingly falls apart into "three cities" of diverging futures. Not only does "who lives where" depend "on the socio-economic status of the residents of each neighbourhood," these different neighbourhoods have also been growing more rapidly apart in the last generation. In 20 per cent of all census tracts in Toronto, individual incomes rose by 20 per cent or more in the years 1970–2000. In 43 per cent, increases or decreases were less than 20 per cent. But, shockingly, in 36 per cent of all neighbourhoods, individual incomes dropped by 20 per cent or more during that time (Hulchanski 2007, 1). More disturbingly, the same study notes that the number of middle-income earners has declined during the study period, as there has been "a 34 per cent drop in the proportion of neighbourhoods with middle incomes between 1970 and 2000" (Hulchanski 2007, 5). Most of this collapse of the middle was absorbed in the growing ranks of relatively poorer Torontonians. Where there was once a fairly even distribution of income, there is now a sharp—and rapidly growing—divide of fortunes in Toronto neighbourhoods. As this is a socio-economic and socio-spatial phenomenon, all thinking about future growth in Toronto must confront a double challenge of social class division and geographical segregation. That this is overlaid with a hardening pattern of ethno-cultural segregation adds to the complexity and explosiveness of the situation. In their study of racial segregation in Canadian cities, Walks and Bourne (2006, 286) have found that "Toronto stands out as the CMA with both the largest visible minority population and the greatest proportion of its population in highly concentrated tracts (mixed minority and polarized)." While the study provides no evidence for ghettoization in Canadian cities like that experienced in the United States or even Britain, it points to the correlation of a severe housing shortage with immigration and concentration of poverty. Thus, the built form of the city, according to Walks and Bourne, as well as forms of tenure, may be read as predictors of poverty as there is "a strong and consistent relationship ... between concentrations of apartment housing and higher levels of low income." They conclude that "the implications for policy thus point to the need for countering growing

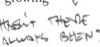

hasn't there always been?

TCSA
Toronto Shwit Alliance

income inequality and addressing the lack of affordable rental housing"
(2006, 286, 295).

Toronto's fluid global city grid of socio-economic relations is now
congealing into a distinct set of three trajectories where polarization
between the first and third city of winners and losers overshadows the
potential stability of the middle income earners between. The city, as
well as its burgeoning social welfare sector—which includes the United
Way, dozens of foundations, religious organizations, and corporate-
sponsored actors, such as the TCSA—have set their sights on a number
of priority neighbourhoods, where they are testing place-based strategies
of community development. The assumption that these are bad places
in need of repair from within concentrates money and attention on
large parts of the "third city," which fully encompasses the priority
neighbourhoods. Having entirely embarked on neoliberal strategies of
urban growth and prosperity, the city and its key actors are helping daily
to widen the gulf between rich and poor, only to lament its existence
later. In contrast to other periods in Canadian history, no large scale
models of systemic change to address these inequalities are forthcoming.
As of now, the neoliberal party continues at the expense of those who are
left behind by the tremendous polarization of the city. How this will be
further impacted by the current crisis remains to be seen.

It is remarkable, though, that some citywide initiatives and planning
schemes have taken up the segmentation of Toronto and have tried to reconnect the scattered and splintered enclaves and ghettos of race and class
in new and innovative ways. Among those plans, we should mention the
city's and the TTC's ambitious Transit City concept, which sees priority
neighbourhoods connected by a sweeping network of light transit routes.
One of the intersections of this new network may be Jane and Finch, an
area we studied in Chapter 7. Another such citywide initiative which speaks
both to the deficiencies of place and the possibilities of space is the Mayor's
Tower Renewal Project, ostensibly designed to help overhaul the building
stock in the in-between city. Both these transit and housing strategies address the insularity and lack of services in the priority neighbourhoods at a
scale more in line with the production of the inequalities themselves.

In this book, we have looked at the recent historical processes that
have shaped Toronto at the end of the first decade of the twenty-first
century. This urban region, which Frances Frisken (2007) recently

described aptly as a "public metropolis," formed by waves of deliberate and often progressive public policy, has experienced a century of sometimes explosive spatial and demographic growth and change. We have looked at these developments since the 1990s through the lenses of human security, economic prosperity, and environmental sustainability. In Chapter 1, we argued that Toronto's current state was symptomatic of, but also setting, trends that are now common not just in Canada but worldwide. Cities are where most people live, and in metropolitan regions, most of the changes of neoliberal, globalized capitalism are being decided, acted upon, and executed. It is possible, even, to view the expansive oil sands developments in Alberta as part of the urban ecological and economic complex that cities constitute today. As Canada faces an urban future, Toronto is one very influential model to understand how certain developments will shape up elsewhere. — PRIME MOVER

Chapters 2 to 4 retell the story of neoliberalization in Toronto. The crisis of the "city that works" in the late 1980s triggered a series of developments that made and broke two provincial governments, both neoliberal, one on the Left and the other on the Right of the political spectrum. The social-democratic restructuring of planning and urban governance failed as the reform of the *Planning Act* and the regional governance recommendations fell by the wayside when the NDP was driven from power in 1995. The Common Sense revolutionaries under Mike Harris developed an alternative idea on how to restructure the urban region, as they amalgamated the municipalities of Metropolitan Toronto into the megacity in 1998. By itself, amalgamation violated traditions of local democracy, and it destroyed the vanguard status of the old core city of Toronto as a progressive community equipped to deal with diversity better than the suburbs that surrounded it. But amalgamation alone was not the main problem. In contrast, it created a potentially equalizing dynamics, which could have helped redistribute wealth and poverty. The problem for Toronto was the rigid program of neoliberalization brought about in revolutionary style by Harris and politically legitimized by a series of measures that anchored the inflicted cold social pain in a warm ocean of populism. The ten years between 1995 and 2005 cemented divisions of class and power into the three Torontos we described above in following Hulchanski and his research group. During that time, economic opportunity, ecological sustainability, and human security took a direct setback.

The transformations were not just political. Since the mid-1980s there has been a dramatic shift in the ethnocultural composition of Toronto. The fastest growing immigrant communities in Toronto, those from South and East Asia, are also now among the most segregated and most vulnerable in the city. "Old" immigrant neighbourhoods are rapidly encompassed into the gentrifying first city, as the new immigrant enclaves—and perhaps ghettos—are concentrated and increasingly segregated in some older suburbs, such as Malvern or Rexdale. As the case of the African-centred schools showed, Toronto has now embarked on a post-universal, perhaps also post-colonial, social policy direction as it has acknowledged, and perhaps accepted, the wildly diverse opportunities that children from different ethnocultural backgrounds are facing in the immigrant metropolis.

In Chapters 4, 5, and 6, we examined the transformations that have characterized the rapidly globalizing city through the making of a new metropolitan structure, diversity, and official planning. In each case, the evolving issues of neoliberalization translated into challenges to human security, sustainability, and economic security. In Chapters 7, 8, and 9, we expanded our view on these challenges to the regional scale, as we scrutinized changing urban form, ecological problems, and transportation dilemmas. In each of those chapters, the tremendous regional governance challenges for the region have become obvious. In recent years, the spatial fix that was reached more-or-less reluctantly under the Harris regime has given way to a looser understanding of what the Toronto region entails. As the traditional 416/905, central city/suburban split in the region gave way to the new realities of economic integration under globalization, political agents followed suit. From the inside out, powerful economic actors such as the Summit Alliance and the Board of Trade alongside planners, urban theorists, and environmental activists pushed regional agendas (Boudreau *et al.* 2007). From the top down, the Liberal provincial government redefined the Toronto region as extending beyond the GTA or census area boundaries and established planning legislation at the scale of the Greater Golden Horseshoe, which wraps around the western tip of Lake Ontario and includes large swaths of now protected green areas on the Niagara Escarpment, the Oak Ridges Moraine, and the tender fruitlands of the Niagara Peninsula. This new scale of regionalism recognizes the networked quality of regional growth centres in and beyond the core of Toronto and thinks in terms unknown to previous provincial legislators. For the City of Toronto, the crucial question is how it will want to fit into this new super-region. One important sector where this fit will be put to the test is transportation and transit, where a new regional agency, the GTTA or Metrolinx, has been created to coordinate and mediate conflicting interests of moving people in the region.

In Chapters 10, 11, and 12 we explored political realities after the Lastman years. Paying particular attention to the emerging regime under Mayor David Miller, we examined the new political fortunes of a unified but still divided city. In a series of political analyses, we argued that Miller's mayoralty was the necessary reaction to anti-urban provincial policies and a resurgence of a new urbanity in the city centre. As Toronto remade itself with cultural policy and references to creativity and spectacle, its neighbourhoods drifted apart socio-economically and socio-culturally. Crises produced by SARS,[2] gun violence, and transportation gridlock shocked the complacent growth machines and forced policy-makers and the public to address the entire territory of the city rather than the select few neighbourhoods in the city centre. Miller's priority neighbourhoods were one highly publicized attempt to broaden the view of our urban policy regimes to include areas that normally get short shrift in the allocation of resources and all the attention of the police.

Thomas Courchene (2007) asked recently how Canadian global cities might fare in the age of a knowledge-based economy. As is usual in such considerations, globalization and the accompanying economic shifts are portrayed as a set of opportunities to which cities need to rise as they struggle with traditional constraints. We have taken up this question in a different and broader, not just economic, sense and have recalibrated it to the everyday life experience and politics of people in the Toronto region. What we have found, at least for Toronto, is a continuing challenge for the rapidly diversifying urban population to succeed economically, while integrating socially and culturally, in a region that faces huge sustainability challenges in the years ahead. The recent changes to life in Toronto have thrown up new constraints that have led to socio-spatial polarization, ecological pressures, and threats to human security. To paraphrase Karl Marx freely, we can say that while Torontonians make their own

---

2 For discussion of the effects of SARS on the global city in Toronto, see Ali and Keil, 2008.

FIGURE 12.1 Lasts Longer Than You Do billboard, Toronto. This image captures the landscape of the new Toronto, where the downtown looms over a large sea of low- to mid-rise developments.

city, they don't make it entirely at their own will. The constraints of rapid economic restructuring and now recession, globalization, and ecological crisis weigh heavily on the good citizens of Canada's largest urban region. *Changing Toronto* sounds a serious warning that, while the open neoliberal attack on the city has ended, much remains to do to stem the tides of social polarization, racialization, and environmental injustice that characterized this period. Beyond the deluge, though, there is also the possibility of a new city, which re-embarks on a radically different politics of social solidarity, cultural heterogeneity, and sustainability. This is our City of Hope.

References

Books and Articles

Abers, Rebecca. 1998. Learning Democratic Practice: Distributing Government Resources Through Popular Participation in Porto Alegre, Brazil. In *Cities for Citizens: Planning and the Rise of Civil Society in a Global Age*, ed. Mike Douglass and John Friedmann, 39–65. Chichester: John Wiley and Sons.

Airports Council International. 2007. www.aci.aero.

Albo, Greg. 1997. A World Market of Opportunities? Capitalist Obstacles and Left Economic Policy. *Ruthless Criticism of All that Exists: Socialist Register 1997*. Merlin: London/Humanities: New Jersey.

Alcoba, Natalie. 2008. Trustees Vote 11–9 in Favour of Afrocentric School. *The National Post* (January 29).

Ali, S. Harris. 2004. A Socio-Ecological Autopsy of the E. coli O157:H7 Outbreak in Walkerton, Ontario, Canada. *Social Science and Medicine* 58: 2601–12.

Ali, S. Harris, and Roger Keil. Eds. 2008. *Networked Disease: Emerging Infections in the Global City*. London: Wiley-Blackwell.

Amselle, Jean-Loup. 1996. *Vers un multiculturalisme français. L'empire de la coutume*. Paris: Aubier.

Arnstein, Sherry. 1969. A Ladder of Citizen Participation. *Journal of the American Institute of Planners* 35(4): 216–24.

Association of Municipalities of Ontario. 1994. *Ontario Charter: A Proposed Bill of Rights for Local Government*. Toronto: AMO.

Avana Capital Corporation. 2000. The Toronto Charter. Toronto: Avana Corporation, www.torontocharter.conv.

Ballantyne, Derek. 2004. Public lecture, Toronto, November 26.

Bakker, Karen. 2003a. Liquid Assets. *Alternatives* 29(2):17–21.

——. 2003b. A Political Ecology of Water Privatization. *Studies in Political Economy* 70: 35–58.

——. 1996. Privatising Water, Producing Scarcity: The Yorkshire Drought of 1995. *Economic Geography*, 76(1): 2000.

Bakker Karen, and D. Hemson. 2000. Privatizing Water: Hydropolitics in the new South Africa. *South African Journal of Geography* 82(1): 3–12.

Barber, John. 1997. Lastman's Win Pushes Old Toronto Out the Door. *Globe and Mail* (November 11): A13

Barlow, Maude, and Tony Clarke. 2002. *Blue Gold: The Battle Against Corporate Theft of the World's Water*. Toronto: Stoddart.

Beck, Ulrich. 2007. *Weltrisikogesellschaft*. Frankfurt: Suhrkamp.

Biro, Andrew, and Roger Keil. 2000. Sites/Cities of Resistance: Approaching Ecological Socialism in Canada. *Capitalism, Nature, Socialism* 11(4): 96.

Bish, Robert L. 1971. *The Political Economy of Metropolitan Areas*. Chicago: Rand
McNally.

Bish, Robert L., and Robert Warren. 1972. Scale and Monopoly Problems in Urban
Government Services. *Urban Affairs Quarterly* 8: 97–122.

Boltanski, Luc, and Eve Chiapello. 2006. *The New Spirit of Capitalism*. New York:
Verso.

Bond, Patrick. 2004. Water Commodifica'·on and Decommodification Narratives:
Pricing and Policy Debates from Joha· ·ie ·burg to Kyoto to Cancun and Back.
Capitalism, Nature, Socialism 15(1): 7 26

——. 2003. The Limits of Water Commod   ation in Africa. *Journal für Entwicklungspolitik* 19(4): 34–55.

Boudreau, Julie-Anne. 2000. *The Megac*   *aga: Democracy and Citizenship in this
Golden Age*. Montreal: Black Rose Bo

Boudreau, Julie-Anne, Pierre Hamel, Be   d Jouve, and Roger Keil. 2007. New
State Spaces in Canada: Metropolitai   tion in Montreal and Toronto Compared. *Urban Geography* 28(1): 30–53.

——. 2006. Comparing Metropolitan Governance: The Cases of Montreal and
Toronto. *Progress in Planning* 66: 7–59.

Bourdieu, Pierre. 1998. *Acts of Resistance: Against the Tyranny of the Market*. New
York: The New Press.

Bourne, Larry. 2004. Beyond the New Deal for Cities. *Research Bulletin #21*. Toronto: Centre for Urban and Community Studies, University of Toronto.

Bradford, Neil. 2003. Public-Private Partnership? Shifting Paradigms of Economic
Governance in Ontario. *Canadian Journal of Political Science* 36(5): 1005–33.

Bramley, Glen, and Christine Lambert. 1998. Planning for Housing: Regulation
Entrenched? In *Urban Planning and the British New Right*, ed. Philip
Allmendinger and Huw Thomas, 87–113. London and New York: Routledge.

Brender, Natalie, and Mario Lefebvre. 2006. *Canada's Hub Cities: A Driving
Force of the National Economy* (July), www.conferenceboard.ca/documents.
asp?rnext+1730.

Brenner, Neil. 2004. *New State Spaces: Urban Governance and the Rescaling of
Statehood*. Oxford: Oxford University Press.

Brenner, Neil, and Roger Keil (Eds.). 2006. *The Global Cities Reader*. London and
New York: Routledge

Brenner, Neil, and Nik Theodore. 2002. Cities and the Geographies of "Actually
Existing Neoliberalism." *Antipode* 34(3): 349–79.

Broadbent, Alan. 2008. *Urban Nation: Why We Need to Give Power Back to the
Cities to Make Canada Strong*. Toronto: Harper/Collins.

Brooks, Stephen, and Lydia Miljan. 2003. *Public Policy in Canada: An Introduction*.
4th ed. Toronto: Oxford University Press.

Brown, Louise, and Brett Popplewell. 2008. Board okays black-focused school.
Toronto Star (January 30), www.thestar.com/News/GTA/article/298714.

Buckley, Michelle. 2003. *Water Privatization and Re-Regulation in Hamilton,
Ontario*. Major Paper, MES Program, Faculty of Environmental Studies, York
University.

Bunce, Susannah. 2004. The Emergence of "Smart Growth" Intensification in Toronto: Environment and Economy in the New Official Plan. *Local Environment: An International Journal of Justice and Sustainability* 9(2): 177–91.

Bunce, Susannah, and Douglas Young. 2004. Image-Making by the Water: Global City Dreams and the Ecology of Exclusion. In *International Network of Urban Research and Action*, ed. Raffaele Paloscia, *The Contested Metropolis: Six Cities at the Beginning of the 21st Century*. Basel: Birkhäuser.

Canada External Advisory Committee on Cities and Communities. 2006. *From Restless Communities to Resilient Places: Building A Stronger Future for All Canadians*. Final report of the External Advisory Committee On Cities and Communities. Ottawa: Infrastructure Canada.

Canada-Ontario Immigration Agreement. 2005. www.cic.gc.ca/EnGLIsh/ department/laws-policy/agreements/ontario/can-ont-index/asp.

Canadian Press. 2005. Stop Black Youths at Random, Toronto Councillor Suggests. *Globe and Mail* (August 16): A6.

Canadian Urban Institute. 1994. *Background Paper with Respect to the Question on the Ballot: City of Toronto Municipal Elections, November 1994*. Toronto: The Canadian Urban Institute.

Caplan, David. 2004. Public address. July 28, Toronto.

Carty, Bob. 2003. Hard Water: The Uphill Campaign to Privatize Canada's Waterworks. *The Water Barons*, by the International Consortium of Investigative Journalists, a Project of the Center for Public Integrity, Washington, D.C. http://projects.publicintegrity.org/water/report.aspx?aid=58.

Cash, Andrew. 2006. Can Faith Make Them Vote? Anger and Alienation Grip City's Poor and Immigrant Northwest. *NOW* (January 19–25): 20.

Caulfied, Jon. 1994. *City Form and Everyday Life: Toronto's Gentrification and Critical Social Practice*. Toronto: University of Toronto Press.

City of Markham. 2008. Official website of the Town of Markham. www.city.markham.on.ca/Markham.

City of Toronto. 2002a. *Plan of Action for the Elimination of Racism and Discrimination*. www.toronto.ca/diversity/plan.htm.

——. 2002b. *Staff Report—Refusal Report: Official Plan and Zoning By-law Amendment Application No. 100034 (ATS 2000 0001) and Site Plan Approval Application No. 30'056 for 2195 Yonge Street*. Staff Report: February 11.

——. 2001a. *Development of a City of Toronto Declaration and Plan of Action Regarding the Elimination of Racism in Relation to the United Nation World Conference Against Racism, Racial Discrimination, Xenophobia and Related Intolerance (UN-WCAR)*. www.toronto.ca/legdocs/2001/agendas/council/cc010424/pof4rpt/cl009.pdf.

——. 2001b. *Preliminary Report, Application to Amend the Official Plan and Zoning By-law, Minto YE Inc., 2195 Yonge Street, Terms of Reference for Focused Review of Yonge-Eglinton Part II Plan*. Staff Report, March 15.

——. 2000a. *Towards a New Relationship with Ontario and Canada*. Toronto: Chief Administrator's Office.

——. 2000b. *Toronto at the Crossroads: Shaping our Future*. Directions Report.

——. 2000c. *Toronto at the Crossroads: Shaping our Future*. Summary.

Clarke, Tony. 2003. Water Privateers. *Alternatives* 29(2): 10–15.

Colour of Poverty. 2008. www.povnet.org/node/2095.

Commission on Planning and Development Reform in Ontario (John Sewell, Chair). 1993. *New Planning in Ontario, Final Report*. Toronto: The Commission.

Committee for Economic Development. 1966. *Modernizing Local Government*. New York: Committee for Economic Development.

Community Social Planning Council of Toronto. 2000. *An Act for the New Millenium?* Toronto: Community Social Planning Council of Toronto.

Conway, Janet. 2004. *Identity, Place, Knowledge: Social Movements Contesting Globalization*. Toronto: Fernwood Publishing

——. 2000. Knowledge, Power, Organization: Social Justice Coalitions at a Cross-roads. *Studies in Political Economy* 62: 43–70.

Courchene, Thomas. 2007. Global Futures for Canada's Global Cities. *IRPP Policy Matters* 8(2).

Corbett, Lois. 2000. *Towards a Greater Toronto Charter and the Environment*. Toronto: Avana Corporation.

Croucher, Sheila L. 1997. Constructing the Image of Ethnic Harmony in Toronto, Canada: The Politics of Problem Definition and Nondefinition. *Urban Affairs Review* 32(3): 319–47.

Dale, Stephen. 1999. *Lost in the Suburbs: A Political Travelogue*. Toronto: Stoddart.

Davis, Mike. 2006. *Planet of Slums*. London: Verso Press.

Debbané, Anne-Marie, and Roger Keil. 2004. Multiple Disconnections: Environmental justice and urban water in Canada and South Africa. *Space and Polity* 8(2): 209–25

Desfor Gene, and Roger Keil. 2004. *Nature and the City: Making Environmental Policy in Toronto and Los Angeles*. Tucson: University of Arizona Press.

——. 2000. Every River Tells a Story: The Don River (Toronto) and the Los Angeles River (Los Angeles) as Articulating Landscapes. *Journal of Environmental Policy and Planning* 2: 5–23.

Desfor, Gene, Stefan Kipfer, Roger Keil, and Gerda Wekerle. 2006. From Surf to Turf: No Limits to Growth. *Studies in Political Economy* 77(Spring): 131–56.

Dikeç, Mustafa. 2007. *Badlands of the Republic: Space, Politics and Urban Policy*. Madlen, MA: Blackwell.

Dill, Paula M., and Paul J. Bedford. 2001. *Making Waves: Principles for Building Toronto's Waterfront*. Toronto: City of Toronto.

Doucet, Michael J. 2001. The Anatomy of an Urban Legend: Toronto's Multicultural Reputation. http://ceris.metropolis.net/virtual%20library/other/doucet3.html.

Drache, Daniel. 2004. *Borders Matter: Homeland Security and the Search for North America*. Halifax: Fernwood Publishing.

Drainie, Bronwyn. 1998. Them Against Us. *Toronto Life* (May): 76–82.

Duménil, Gérard, and Dominique Lévy. 2001. Periodizing Capitalism: Technology, Institutions, and Relations of Production. In *Phases of Capitalist Development: Booms, Crises, and Globalizations*, ed. Robert Albritton, Makoto Itoh, Richard Westra, and Alan Zuege, 141–62. New York: Palgrave.

Edwards, Peter. 2003. *One Dead Indian: The Premier, the Police, and the Ipperwash Crisis*. Toronto: McClelland and Stewart.

Edwards, Peter, and David Grossman. 2005. Did Jealousy Lead to Shooting? *Toronto Star* (August 5): A1.

Edwards, Peter, and Tabassuma Siddiqui. 2005. Three Charged in Boy's Shooting. *Toronto Star* (August 6): A16.

Eligh, Blake. 2005. Software Model Simulates Future Travel Patterns. *Novae Res Urbis* 9(10): 1–6.

Erie, Stephen P. 2004. *Globalizing L.A.: Trade, Infrastructure, and Regional Development.* Stanford: Stanford University Press.

Eye Weekly. 2003. Cover image. November 8.

Filion, Pierre. 2000. Balancing Concentration and Dispersion? Public Policy and Urban Structure in Toronto. *Environment and Planning C: Government and Policy* 18(2): 163–89.

Fishman, Robert. 1987. *Bourgeois Utopias: The Rise and Fall of Suburbia.* New York: Basic Books.

Fitzsimmons, Margaret. 1989. The Matter of Nature. *Antipode* 21(2): 106–20.

Florida, Richard. 2002. *The Rise of the Creative Class: And How It's Transforming Work, Leisure, Community, and Everyday Life.* New York: Basic Books.

Fowler, Edmund P., and Jack Layton. 2002. Transportation Policy in Canadian Cities. In *Urban Policy Issues: Canadian Perspectives*, ed. E.P. Fowler and D. Siegel, 155–71. Oxford: Oxford University Press.

Frisken, Frances. 2007. *The Public Metropolis: The Political Dynamics of Urban Expansion in the Toronto Region, 1924–2003.* Toronto: Canadian Scholars' Press.

Frisken, Frances, Larry Bourne, Gunter Gad, and Robert A. Murdie. Governance and Social Well-Being in the Toronto Area: Past Achievements and Future Challenges. Research Paper 193, Centre for Urban and Community Studies, University of Toronto.

Galabuzi, Grace-Edward. 2006. *Canada's Economic Apartheid: The Social Exclusion of Racialized Groups in the New Century.* Toronto: Canadian Scholars' Press.

——. 2004. Social Exclusion. In *Social Determinants of Health: Canadian Perspectives*, ed. Dennis Raphael, 235–252. Toronto: Canadian Scholars' Press.

Gandy, Matthew. 2002. *Concrete and Clay: Reworking Nature in New York City.* London: The MIT Press.

Garber, Judith A., and David L. Imbroscio. 1996. "The Myth of the North American City" Reconsidered. Local Constitutional Regimes in Canada and the United States. *Urban Affairs Review* 31(5): 595–624.

Garreau, Joel. 1991. *Edge City: Life on the New Frontier.* New York: Doubleday.

Garrett, Mike. 2001. *Building the New City of Toronto: Three Year Status Report on Amalgamation, January 1998–December 2000.* Toronto: Chief Administrative Office, City of Toronto.

Gerson, Jen. 2007. The Dufferin Exodus. *Toronto Star* (March 16): A1.

Gandhi, Unnati. 2005. "Anybody Can Have a Gun" in Northwest Toronto. *Globe and Mail* (August 10): A1, A8.

Girardet, Herbert. 1992. *GAIA Atlas of Cities: New Directions for Sustainable Urban Living.* London: GAIA Books.

Gillespie, Kerry. 2006. $30M for "At-risk" Youth. *Toronto Star* (February 13): A1.

Gillmor, Don. 2005. Terminal Velocity. *Toronto Life* 39(2): 54–79.

Globe and Mail. 2003. Miller Pledges to Make Clean Sweep (image). November 11: A11.

——. 2003. I See Paris, London (image). November 15: M4

GO Transit. 2003. *Go Transit: The Year in Review, 2002–03.* Toronto: Greater Toronto Transit Authority.

Goonewardena, Kanishka, and Stefan Kipfer. 2005. Spaces of Difference: Reflections from Toronto on Multiculturalism, Bourgeois Urbanism, and the Possibility of Radical Urban Politics. *International Journal of Urban and Regional Research* 29(3): 670–78.

Gottman, Jean. 1961. *Megalopolis*. New York: Twentieth Century Fund.

Greater Toronto Airport Authority. 2007. www.gtaa.ca.

Greater Toronto Services Board. 2000. *GTA Countryside Strategy*. Toronto: Queen's Printer.

GTA Task Force. 1996. *Greater Toronto Report of the GTA Task Force*. Toronto: Queen's Printer.

Guimera, Roger, Stefano Mossa, Adrian Turtschi, and Luis A. Nunes Amaral. 2005. The Worldwide Air Transportation Network: Anomalous Centrality, Community Structure, and Cities' Global Roles. *PNAS* 102(22): 7794–99.

Hajer, Maarten, and Arnold Reijndorp. 1995. *In Search of New Public Domain: Analysis and Strategy*. Rotterdam: NAi Publishers.

Hall, Joseph. 2005. Ten Years After. *Toronto Star* (August 6): B1, B4–5.

Hannam, Kevin, Mimi Sheller, and John Urry. 2006. Editorial: Mobilities, Immobilities and Moorings. *Mobilities* 1(1): 1–22.

Hardt, Michael, and Antonio Negri. *Empire*. Cambridge, MA: Harvard University Press.

Harris, Nigel. 1994. The Emerging Global City: Transport. *Cities* 11(5): 332–36.

Harvey, David. 2005. *A Brief History of Neoliberalism*. Oxford: Oxford University Press.

——. 2003. *The New Imperialism*. Oxford: Oxford University Press.

——. 2000. *Megacities Lecture 4: Possible Urban Worlds*. Amersfoort, Netherlands: Twynstra Gudde Management Consultants.

——. 1989a. *The Condition of Postmodernity: An Enquiry into the Origins of Cultural Change*. Oxford: Blackwell

——. 1989b. From Managerialism to Entrepreneurialism: The Transformation in Urban Governance in Late Capitalism. *Geografiska Annaler* 71(B): 3–17.

——. 1989c. *Urban Experience*. Oxford: Blackwell.

Helly, Denise. 2004. Are Muslims Discriminated Against in Canada Since September 2001? *Journal of Canadian Ethnic Studies* 36(1): 24–47.

——. 2003. Canadian Multiculturalism: Lessons for the Management of Cultural Diversity. Paper presented at Canadian and French Perspectives of Diversity. Conference Proceedings, October 16, 2003. www.pch.gc.ca/pc-ch/pubs/diversity2003/index_e.cfm.

Hensher, David A., and Ann M. Brewer. 2001. *Transport: An Economics and Management Perspective*. Oxford: Oxford University Press.

Heynen, Nik., James McCarthy, W. Scott Prudham, and Paul Robbins (Eds.), 2007. *Neoliberal Environments: False Promises and Unnatural Consequences*. London; New York: Routledge.

Hollman, Mark, and Greg Kotis. 2001. *Urinetown: The Musical*. Lyrics from liner notes. RCA Victor CD.

Honderich, John. 1995. A New Vision for our Supercity. *Toronto Star* (January 7): A1.

Huffman, Tracy. 2005. Police Boost Presence to Combat Violence. *Toronto Star* (August 8): B1.

Hulchanski, J. David. 2007. Ghettos of the Rich and the Poor: Is this Where Toronto is Headed? *Mapping Neighbourhood Change in Toronto*. University of Toronto. www.gtuo.ca.

——. 2004. How Did We Get Here? The Evolution of Canada's "Exclusionary" Housing System. In *Finding Room: Options for a Canadian Rental Strategy*, ed. J. David Hulchanski and Michael Shapcott, 179–94. Toronto: CUCS Press.

Hume, Christopher. 2003. Minto towers design needs no apology. *Toronto Star* (February 10): B3.

——. 2001. Getting High. *Toronto Star* (January 27): M5

Hurst, Lynda. 2001. Who is High Risk? *Toronto Star* (October 20): A30.

Isin, Engin H. 1998. Governing Toronto Without Government: Liberalism and Neoliberalism. *Studies in Political Economy* 56: 169–91.

Isin, Engin, and Jo-Anne Wolfson. 1999. *The Making of the Megacity: An Introduction*. Working Paper No. 21. Toronto: Urban Studies Program, York University.

Jacobs, Jane, and Mary W. Rowe. Toronto: Considering Self-Government. *The Quarterly* 1(3); www.ideasthatmatter.com/quarterly/itm-1-3/tcsg.html.

Jeanneret-Gris, Charles Édouard. *The Athens Chapter*. New York: Grossman Publishers.

Jenson, Jane. 1989. "Different" But Not "Exceptional": Canada's Permeable Fordism. *Canadian Review of Sociology and Anthropology* 26: 69–94.

Jessop, Bob. 2001a. What Follows Fordism? On the Periodization of Capitalism and Its Regulation. In *Phases of Capitalist Development: Booms, Crises, and Globalizations*, ed. Robert Albritton, Makoto Itoh, Richard Westra, and Alan Zuege, 283–300. New York: Palgrave.

——. 2001b. Kritischer Realismus, Marxismus und Regulation: Zu den Grundlagen der Reulationstheorie. In *Ein neuer Kapitalismus?*, ed. Mario Candeias and Frank Deppe, 16–40. Hamburg: VSA Verlag.

Jones, Victor. 1942. *Metropolitan Government*. Chicago: University of Chicago Press.

Joyette Consulting Services. 2005. *Black Creek West Community Capacity Building Project: Phase III Towards Resource & Capacity Development. Action Plan*. Toronto: Joyette Consulting Services.

Kain, John F., and Zvi Liu. 1999. Secrets of Success: Assessing the Large Increases in Transit Ridership Achieved by Houston and San Diego Transit Providers. *Transportation Research A* 31(4): 601–24.

Kasarda, John D. 1996. Transportation Infrastructure for Competitive Success. *Transportation Quarterly* 50(1): 35–50.

Keating, Michael. 1995. Size, Efficiency, and Democracy: Consolidation, Fragmentation, and Public Choice. In *Theories of Urban Politics*, ed. D. Judge, G. Stoker, and H. Wolman, 117–34. Thousand Oaks, CA: Sage.

——. 2007. Empire and the Global City: Perspectives on Urbanism after 9/11. *Studies in Political Economy* 79: 167–92.

——. 2005. Progress Report: Urban Political Ecology. *Urban Geography* 26(7): 640–51.

——. 2003. Progress Report: Urban Political Ecology. *Urban Geography* 24(8): 723–38.

——. 2002. "Common Sense" Neoliberalism: Progressive Conservative Urbanism in Toronto, Canada. *Antipode* 34(3): 578–601.

——. 2000. Governance Restructuring in Los Angeles and Toronto: Amalgamation of Secession? *International Journal of Urban and Regional Research* 24(4): 758–81.

——. 1998a. Toronto in the 1990s: Dissociated Governance? *Studies in Political Economy* 56 (Summer): 151–67.

——. 1998b. Globalization Makes States: Perspectives of Local Governance in the Age of the World City. *Review of International Political Economy* 5(4): 616–46.

——. 1998c. *Los Angeles: Globalization, Urbanization, and Social Struggles*. Chichester: John Wiley and Sons.

Keil, Roger, and S. Harris Ali. 2006. Multiculturalism, Racism, and Infectious Disease in the Global City: The Experience of the 2003 SARS Outbreak in Toronto. *Topia* 16: 23–50.

Keil, Roger, and Julie-Anne Boudreau. (2006). Metropolitics and Metabolics: Rolling out Environmentalism in Toronto. In *In the Nature of City: Urban Political Ecology and the Politics of Urban Metabolism*, ed. Nik Heynen, Maria Kaika, and Erik Swyngedouw, 41–62. London and New York: Routledge.

Keil, Roger, and John Graham. 1998. Reasserting Nature: Constructing Urban Environments after Fordism. In *Remaking Reality: Nature at the Millennium*, ed. Bruce Braun and Noel Castree, 100–25. London and New York: Routledge.

Keil, Roger, and Rianne Mahon (Eds). (2009). *Leviathan Undone? Towards a Political Economy of Scale*. Vancouver: UBC Press.

Kennedy, Christopher A. 2002. A Comparison of the Sustainability of Public and Private Transportation Systems: Study of the Greater Toronto Area. *Transportation* 29(4): 459–93.

Kennedy, Christopher A., Eric Miller, Amer Shalaby, Heather Maclean, and Jesse Coleman. 2005. The Four Pillars of Sustainable Urban Transportation. *Transport Reviews* 25(4): 393–414.

Khosla, Punam. 2003. *If Low Income Women of Colour Counted in Toronto*. Toronto: The Community Social Planning Council of Toronto.

Kingwell, Mark. Excuse Us, But Is Civility Dying? *Toronto Star* (December 11): E1.

Kipfer, Stefan. 1998. Urban Politics in the 1990s: Notes on Toronto. In *Possible Urban Worlds: Urban Strategies at the End of the 20th Century*, ed. Richard Wolff, Andreas Schneider, Christian Schmid, Philip Klaus, Andreas Hofer, and Hansruedi Hitz, 172–79. Basel: Birkhaeuser.

Kipfer, Stefan, and Roger Keil. 2002. Toronto Inc? Planning the Competitive City in the New Toronto. *Antipode* 34(2): 227–64.

Klein, Naomi. 2007. *The Shock Doctrine: The Rise of Disaster Capitalism*. Toronto: Alfred E. Knopf.

——. 2000. *No Logo: Taking Aim at the Brand Bullies*. Toronto: Knopf Canada.

Kymlicka, William. 1995. *Multicultural Citizenship: A Liberal Theory of Minority Rights*. Oxford: Oxford University Press.

Larner, Wendy. 2000. Neo-liberalism: Policy, Ideology, Governmentality. *Studies in Political Economy* 63: 5–25.

Leach, Allan. 1996. *Statement to the legislature*. www.ontla.on.ca/web/house-proceedings/hansard_search.jsp?locale=en&go+AdvancedSearch.

Lefebvre, Henri. 2003. *The Urban Revolution*. Minneapolis: University of Minnesota.

——. 1991. *The Production of Space*. Cambridge, MA: Blackwell.

——. 1972. *Das Alltagsleben in der modernen Welt*. Frankfurt am Main: Suhrkamp Verlag

Le Galès, Patrick. 2002. *European Cities: Social Conflicts and Governance*. Oxford: Oxford University Press.

Lehrer, Ute. 1994. The Image of the Periphery: The Architecture of FlexSpace. *Environment and Planning D: Society and Space*, 12(2): 187–205.

Lehrer, Ute, and Thorben Wieditz. 2007. The New Gentrification: Condo-boom in Toronto. Paper presented at the International Seminar, New-build Gentrification: Forms, Places, Processes, University of Neuchatel, Switzerland, November 15–16.

Leitner, Helga, Jamie Peck, and Eric S. Sheppard (Eds.). 2007. *Contesting Neoliberalism: Urban Frontiers*. New York: Guilford Publications.

Lieser, Peter, and Roger Keil. 1988a. Zitadelle und Getto: Modell Weltstadt. In *Das Neue Frankfurt: Städtebau und Architektur*, 183–208. Frankfurt: Vervuert.

——. 1988b. Frankfurt: Die Stadt GmbH & Co.KG. *Stadtbauwelt*, Special Issue 100: 2122–27.

Little, Bruce. 1994a. Ontario's Secret Boom Belt. *Globe and Mail* (December 6): B1.

——. 1994b. Toronto Struggles to Recover. *Globe and Mail* (November 14): B1.

Lipietz, Alain. 2001. The Fortunes and Misfortunes of Post-Fordism. In *Phases of Capitalist Development: Booms, Crises, and Globalizations*, ed. Robert Albritton, Makoto Itoh, Richard Westra, and Alan Zuege, 17–36. New York: Palgrave.

Logan, John, and Harvey Molotch. 1987. *Urban Futures: The Political Economy of Place*. Toronto: University of Toronto Press.

Lorinc, John. 2006. *The New City*. Toronto: Penguin Group Canada.

MacDermid, Robert. 2009. *Funding City Politics: Municipal Campaign Funding and Property Development in the Greater Toronto Area*. Toronto: The CSJ Foundation for Research and Education and Vote Toronto.

Mackett, Roger, and Marion Edwards. 1998. The Impact of New Urban Public Transport Systems: Will the Expectations Be Met? *Transportation Research A* 32(4): 231–45.

Magnusson, Warren, and Andrew Sancton. 1983. *City Politics in Canada*. Toronto: University of Toronto Press.

Makin, Kirk. 2003. Police Engage in Profiling, Chief Counsel Tells Court. *Globe and Mail* (January 18): A1.

Mallan, Caroline. 2001. Six Years Later. *Toronto Star* (June 9): K1–3.

Martiniello, Marco. 1997. *Sortir des ghettos culturels*. Paris: Presses de sciences politiques.

McArthur, Keith. 2003. Airports Look to the Ground for Fun and Profit. *Globe and Mail* (August 30): B-1.

McBride, Stephen. 2005. *Paradigm Shift: Globalization and the Canadian State*. Halifax: Fernwood.

McKenzie, Judith I. 2002. *Environmental Politics in Canada*. Toronto: Oxford University Press.

McLeod, Judi. 1999. Portrait of a Poverty Pimp. *Toronto Free Press* (August 17–30): 5.

McMahon, Michael. 2000. *Oak Ridges Moraine: Environmental Challenge and Opportunity*. GTA Forum co-sponsored by Centre for Urban and Community Studies, University of Toronto; Ryerson University; Urban Studies Program, York University.

Miller, Glenn, Daniela Kiguel, and Sue Zielinski. 2001. *Moving the Goods in the New Economy: A Primer for Urban Decision Makers*. Ottawa: Canadian Urban Institute, Human Resources Development, Transport Canada.

Milroy, Beth Moore. 2002. Toronto's Legal Challenge to Amalgamation. In *Urban Affairs: Back on the Policy Agenda*, ed. Caroline Andrew, Katherine A. Graham, and Susan D. Phillips, 157–78. Montreal and Kingston: McGill-Queen's University Press.

Ministry of Municipal Affairs and Housing. 2008. Protecting the Greenbelt. www.greenbelt.ontario.ca

———. 1996. *A Guide to Municipal Restructuring*. Toronto: Publications Ontario.

Moloney, Paul. 2003. Council Seeks to Tap Water Fund. *Toronto Star* (February 26): B3.

Municipality of Metropolitan Toronto. 1994. *The Liveable Metropolis: The Official Plan of the Municipality of Metropolitan Toronto*. Toronto: Municipality of Metropolitan Toronto.

Needham, Richard. 1974. A Writer's Notebook. *Globe and Mail* (July 15): 6.

Newman, Peter, and Andy Thornley. 2004. *Planning World Cities: Globalization, Urban Governance, and Policy Dilemmas*. Basingstoke: Palgrave Macmillan.

Novae Res Urbis. 2005. March 30.

O'Connor, Dennis R. 2002. *Report of the Walkerton Inquiry*. Toronto: Ontario Ministry of the Attorney General.

Ontario Coalition Against Poverty. 2004. *Stop the City's Social Cleansing: Call the Mayor Now*. www.ocap.ca/ocapnews/bathurst.html.

Ontario Municipal Board. 2002. *Decision/Order No. 1263*. September 18.

Ontario Office for the Greater Toronto Area. 1992. *Shaping Growth in the GTA*. Toronto: Queen's Printer.

Ornstein, Michael. 2000. *Ethno-Racial Inequality in the City of Toronto: An Analysis of the 1996 Census*. Toronto: Access and Equity Unit, Strategic and Corporate Policy Division, Chief Administrator's Office.

Ostrom, Vincent, Charles M. Tiebout, and Robert Warren. 1961. The Organization of Government in Metropolitan Areas: A Theoretical Inquiry. *The American Political Science Review* 4: 831–42.

Peck, Jamie. 2006. Liberating the City: Between New York and New Orleans. *Urban Geography* 27(8): 681–713.

———. 2001. *Workfare States*. New York: Guilford Press.

Peck, Jamie and Adam Tickell, 2002. Neoliberalizing Space. *Antipode* 34: 381–404.

Peterson, Paul. 1981. *City Limits*. Chicago: University of Chicago Press.

Prudham, Scott. 2004. Poisoning the Well: Neoliberalism and the Contamination of Municipal Water in Walkerton, Ontario. *Geoforum* 35: 343–59.

Purcell, Mark. 2008. *Recapturing Democracy: Neoliberalization and the Struggle for Alternative Urban Futures*. London and New York: Routledge.

———. 2005. Scale, Urban Democracy, and the Right to the City. Paper presented at the Conference on the Political Economy of Scale, York University, Toronto, February 4.

Raffan, James. 2004. Four O One Liner. *Canadian Geographic* 124(5): 62–72.

Regional Municipality of Peel. 2005. GTAA Nomination and Ad Hoc Committee Minutes GTAA-2005-1. www.region.peel.on.ca/council/subcomm/gtaa/2000s/2005/gtaamin-2005-03-10.htm.

Richmond, Jonathan. 2004. *Transport of Delight: The Mythical Conception of Rail Transit in Los Angeles*. Akron, OH: University of Akron Press.

Robinson, Jennifer. 2006. *Ordinary Cities*. London and New York: Routledge.

Roman, Joseph. 2004. Riding the Rails to Prosperity: The Toronto Board of Trade and the Attempt to Remake Public Transit in the Greater Toronto Area. Unpublished paper, Department of Political Science, Carleton University, Ottawa.

Rose, Nikolas. 1999. *Powers of Freedom: Reframing Political Thought*. New York: Cambridge University Press.

Rowe, Mary W. (Ed.). 2000. *Toronto: Considering Self-government*. Owen Sound, ON: Ginger Press Inc.

Royal Commission on the Future of the Toronto Waterfront (Honourable David Crombie, Commissioner). 1992. *Regeneration: Toronto's Waterfront and the Sustainable City. Final Report*. Ottawa: Minister of Supply and Services.

Rubin, Thomas A., James E. Moore, and Shin Lee. 1999. Ten Myths about US Urban Rail Systems. *Transport Policy* 6: 57–73.

Sahely, Hall R., Shauna Dudding, and Christopher A. Kennedy. 2003. Estimating the Urban Metabolism of Canadian Cities: GTA Case Study. *Canadian Journal of Civil Engineering* 30: 468–83.

Salutin, Rick. 2001. In Harm's Way: Death and Politics in Ontario. *Globe and Mail* (July 20): A13.

Sancton, Andrew. 2000. *Merger Mania: The Assault on Local Government*. Montreal and Kingston: McGill-Queen's University Press.

Sandberg, Tor. 2007. Toronto's Trouble: Taxes or Democracy? *Rabble*. http://can.mailarchive.ca/politics/2007-08/4514.html.

Sandercock, Leonie. 1998. *Making the Invisible Visible: Insurgent Planning Histories*. Berkeley and Los Angeles: University of California Press.

Saunders, Doug. 2005. Extreme makeover: slum edition. *Globe and Mail*, December 3, p. F7.

Sewell, John. 2006. Local Government. *Local Government Bulletin* 62. www.localgovernment.ca/show)bulletin.cfm?id=168.

——. 1997. The Mourning After. *NOW Magazine* (November 13–19): 16.

Sheller, Mimi, and John Urry. 2006. The New Mobilities Paradigm. *Environment and Planning A* 38: 207–26.

Shields, John, and Bryan M. Evans. 1998. *Shrinking the State: Globalization and Public Administration "Reform."* Halifax: Fernwood Publishing.

Sieverts, Thomas. 2003. *Cities Without Cities: An Interpretation of the Zwischenstadt*. London and New York: Routledge.

Simmons, Jim, and Larry Bourne. 2003. The Canadian Urban System, 1971–2001: Responses to a Changing World. *Research Bulletin #18*. Toronto: Centre for Urban and Community Studies, University of Toronto.

Sklair, Leslie. 1997. Social Movements for Global Capitalism: The Transnational Capitalist Class in Action. *Review of International Political Economy* 4(3): 514–38.

Smith, David, and Michael Timberlake. 2002. Hierarchies of Dominance among World Cities: A Network Approach. In *Global Networks, Linked Cities*, ed. S. Sassen, 93–116. London and New York: Routledge.

Smith, Neil. 1996. *The New Urban Frontier: Gentrification and the Revanchist City*. London and New York: Routledge.

Soja, Edward. 1996. *Thirdspace: Journeys to Los Angeles and Other Real-and-Imagined Places*. Cambridge, MA: Blackwell.

Stanford, Jim. 2005. Take the Bus. *Facts from the Fringe* 105. www.caw.ca/news/factsfromthefringe/issue105.asp.

Statistics Canada. 2007. *Portrait of the Canadian Population in 2006: Subprovincial Population Dynamics*. www12.statcan.ca/english/census06/analysis/popdwell/Subprov4.cfm

——. 2002. *2001 Census of Canada*. www12.statcan.ca/english/census01/home/index.cfm

Stewart, Keith. 1999. *Greening Social Democracy? Ecological Modernization and the Ontario NDP*. PhD Diss., York University.

Strategic Communications Inc. 2002. *Managing Toronto's Water: A Public Opinion Poll Commissioned by Toronto Water Watch*. Toronto: Water Watch.

Studenski, Paul. 1930. *The Government of Metropolitan Areas in the United States*. New York: National Municipal League.

Swyngedouw, Erik. 2003. Privatising H$_2$O: Turning Local Water Into Global Money. *Journal für Entwicklungspolitik* 19(4): 14.

——. 1996. The City as a Hybrid: On Nature, Society, and Cyborg Urbanization. *Capitalism, Nature, Socialism* 7(2): 65–80.

Sywngedouw, Erik, and Nik Heynen. 2003. Urban Political Ecology, Justice, and the Politics of Scale. *Antipode* 35(5): 898–918.

Swyngedouw, Erik, Maria Kaika, and Esteban Castro. 2002. Urban Water: A Political-Ecology Perspective. *Built Environment* 28(2): 124–37.

Teeple, Gary. 1995. *Globalization and the Decline of Social Reform*. Toronto: Garamond Press.

Thompson, William I. 1984 [1971]. At the Edge of History. In *Toronto Remembered: A Celebration of the City*, ed. William Kilbourn, 330. Don Mills, ON: Stoddart.

Tiebout, Charles M. 1956. A Pure Theory of Local Expenditures. *The Journal of Political Economy* 64(5): 416–24.

Todd, Graham. 1995. "Going Global" in the Semi-periphery: World Cities as Political Projects. The Case of Toronto. In *World Cities in a World-System*, ed. Paul Knox and Peter Taylor, 192–213. Cambridge: Cambridge University Press.

Toronto Board of Trade. 2003. *The Case for a Greater Toronto Transportation Authority*. Toronto: Toronto Board of Trade.

——. 2002. *Strong City, Strong Nation: Securing Toronto's Contribution to Canada*. Toronto: Toronto Board of Trade.

——. 2001a. *A Strategy for Rail-Based Transit in the GTA*. Toronto: Toronto Board of Trade.

——. 2001b. Remarks by Kerrie MacPherson and Elyse Allan. 2001 Provincial Pre-Budget Hearings. Toronto, February 21.

Toronto City Council Policy Council of Toronto. 2001. *Diversity Advocate*. Toronto: City of Toronto.

Toronto Community Housing Company. 2006. *Community Management Plan 2006/2007/2008*. Toronto: Toronto Community Housing Company.

——. 2004. *An Introduction to Toronto Community Housing*. Toronto: Toronto Community Housing Company.

——. 2002. *Community Management Plan 2003–2005*. Toronto: Toronto Community Housing Company.

Toronto District School Board. Trustees Approve Four Recommendations for Improving Success for Black Students. www.tdsb.on.ca/about_us/media_room/room.asp?show=allNews&view=detailed&self=9563.

Toronto Dominion Bank. 2002. *A Choice Between Investing in Canada's Cities or Disinvesting in Canada's Future: Special Report.* Toronto: TD Bank. http://unitedwaytoronto.com/whoWeHelp/reports/pdf/TD_report.pdf.

Toronto Region Immigrant Employment Council. www.triec.ca/index.asp?pageid=5.

Toronto Star. 2000. Toronto Needs Its Own Charter. *Toronto Star* (June 30): A22

Toronto Transit Commission. 2003. *Ridership Growth Strategy.* Toronto: TTC.

Transport Canada. 2003. *Straight Ahead: A Vision for Transportation in Canada.* Ottawa: Government of Canada.

Tully, James. 1995. *Strange Multiplicity: Constitutionalism in an Age of Diversity.* Cambridge: Cambridge University Press.

United Way. 2005. *Strong Neighbourhoods: A Call to Action.* Toronto: United Way of Greater Toronto.

——. 2004. *Poverty by Postal Code: The Geography of Neighbourhood Poverty in the City of Toronto, 1981–2001.* Toronto: United Way of Greater Toronto.

Urquhart, Ian. 2001. "He Established That Things Can Change": Mike Harris' Political Style is for Confrontation rather than Consultation. *Toronto Star* (June 9): K1–3.

Van der Pijl, Kees. 2001. International Relations and Capitalist Discipline. In *Phases of Capitalist Development: Booms, Crises, and Globalizations,* ed. Robert Albritton, Makoto Itoh, Richard Westra, and Alan Zuege, 1–16. New York: Palgrave.

Vaughan, RM. 2006. Live Without Culture: An Apology, on the Occasion of a Recent Art Project. In *The State of the Arts: Living with Culture in Toronto,* ed. Jonny Dovercourt, Christina Palassio, and Alana Wilcox. Toronto: Coach House Books.

Vancouver Airport Authority. 2008. www.yvr.ca.

Vicino, Thomas J., Bernadette Hanlon, and John Rennie Short. 2007. Megalopolis 50 Years On: The Transformation of a City Region. *International Journal of Urban and Regional Research* 31(2): 344–67.

Village of Markham. 1959. *Proposed Official Plan of the Village of Markham.* Markham, ON: Village of Markham.

Wackernagel, Mathis, and William Rees. 1996. *Our Ecological Footprint: Reducing Human Impact on the Earth.* Gabriola Island, BC and Philadelphia, PA: New Society Publishers.

Walks, R. Alan. 2007. The Boundaries of Suburban Discontent? Urban Definitions and Neighbourhood Political Effects. *Canadian Geographer* 51(2): 160–85.

——. 2006a. Aestheticization and the Cultural Contradictions of Neoliberal (sub)Urbanism. *Cultural Geographies* 13(3): 466–75.

——. 2006b. The Causes of City-Suburban Political Polarization? A Canadian Case Study. *Annals of the Association of American Geographers* 96(2): 390–414.

——. 2005. The City-Suburban Cleavage in Canadian Federal Politics. *Canadian Journal of Political Science* 38(2): 383–413.

——. 2004a. Suburbanization, the Vote and Changes in Federal and Provincial Representation and Influence between Inner Cities and Suburbs in Large Canadian Urban Regions, 1945–1999. *Urban Affairs Reviesw* 39(4): 411–40.

——. 2004b. Place of Residence, Party Preferences, and Political Attitudes in Canadian Cities and Suburbs. *Journal of Urban Affairs* 26(3): 269–95.

Walks, R. Alan, and Larry S. Bourne. 2006. Ghetto's in Canada's Cities? Racial Segregation, Ethnic Enclaves, and Poverty Concentration in Canadian Urban Areas. *Canadian Geographer* 50(3): 273–97.

Walkom, Thomas. 2004. Saving Any Greenbelt Takes Guts. *Toronto Star* (August 24): A17.

Warson, Albert. 2003. Canada's Airports Take Off. *Building* 53(4): 24–29.

——. 2001. A Development Battleground. *Building* 51(4): 18–22.

Water Watch. 2007. Water Watch Organization. www.torwaterwatch.org.

Wilding, Carol. 2008. Infrastructure Surcharge: Making Tough Choices to Build a Better City. *Toronto Star* (February 11): AA8.

Winfield M.S., and G. Jenish. 1998. Ontario's Environment and the "Common Sense Revolution." *Studies in Political Economy* 57: 129–47.

Wood, Patricia K., and Liette Gilbert. 2005. Multiculturalism in Canada: Accidental Discourse, Alternative Vision, Urban Practice. *International Journal of Urban and Regional Research* 29(3): 679–91.

York, Richard, and Eugene A. Rosa. 2003. Key Challenges to Ecological Modernization Theory. *Organization and Environment* 16(3): 273–88.

Young, Douglas (2006) Rebuilding the Modern City After Modernism in Toronto and Berlin. Unpublished dissertation, York University, Toronto.

Websites

The following websites were consulted during the research:

www.aci.aero
www.canadiancities.ca
www.competeprosper.ca
www.gtaa.ca
www.hm.com
www.hopewell.com
www.LiveWithCulture.ca
www.localgovernment.ca
www.lvbia.com
www.mapquest.com
www.marsdd.com

www.ocap.ca/ocapnews/bathurst.html
www.placestogrow.ca/
www.toronto.ca/culture/grants.htm
www.toronto.ca/integrity/index.htm
www.toronto.ca/water/water_watch/
    index.htm
www.torontoalliance.ca
www.torontoenvironment.org/water
www.torontotourism.com
www.yvr.ca

Meetings

BCWAPCC Meeting, January 31, 2006.
TCHC Meeting. November 26, 2004.
TCHC Meeting. November 27, 2004.
Town Hall Meeting, organized by Toronto Board of Trade, February 25, 2004.

Interviews

Benham, Kyle. Toronto Economic Development Department, Business Retention
    Unit. Toronto, May 13, 2005.
Berridge, Joe. Partner, Urban Strategies Inc. Toronto, March 16, 2005.
Broadbent, Alan. Chairman, Maytree Foundation. Toronto, March 23, 2005.
Crombie, David. President and CEO, Canadian Urban Institute. Toronto,
    March 3, 2005.
De Carlo, Nick. Canadian Auto Workers. Toronto, March 16, 2005.
Director of Policy, Toronto Board of Trade, December 7, 2004
Godfrey, John. Minister of State (Infrastructure and Communities), Government of
    Canada. Toronto, November 26, 2004.
Institute for Competitiveness and Prosperity, February 10, 2004. Interview granted
    on agreement of confidentiality.
Kok, Jeroen. Hennes and Mauritz, Inc. Brampton, August 30, 2005.
McKenna, Neil. Director, Transportation, Operations and Transportation, Can-
    adian Tire. Brampton, September 12, 2005.
Moscoe, Howard. Chair, Toronto Transit Commission. Toronto, March 9, 2005.
Murray, Glenn. President, Canadian Urban Institute. December 22, 2006.
Perks, Gordon. Toronto Environmental Alliance. Toronto, December 3, 2005.
Pride Toronto. Toronto, November 1, 2006. Interview granted on agreement of
    confidentiality.
Rieder, Barry. Anglican Church of Canada. Toronto, July 15, 2005.
Rieger, Doug. Project Leader, Transit, City of Brampton. Brampton, August 30,
    2005.
Rodo, Vincent. General Manager, Toronto Transportation Commission. Toronto,
    September, 2005.
Shapero, Erin. Councillor, Town of Markham. Markham, February 13, 2002.
Shaw, Steve. Greater Toronto Airport Authority. By telephone, March 10, 2005.
Sousa, Edward. Personal communication.
Switzer, Doug. Manager Government Relations, Ontario Trucking Association.
    Toronto, August 30, 2005.
Thomas, Barry. Toronto Community Housing Program, August 17, 2005.
Urban Economic Development, Ministry of Industry, Ontario, February 12, 2004
Woo, Leslie. Ontario Growth Secretariat. Toronto, February 23, 2005.
Zbogar, Henrik. Project Leader, Acceleride, City of Brampton. Brampton, August
    30, 2005.

Index

strain on service networks, 150–51
gun violence, 210, 211
Hajer, Maarten, 106, 108
Hall, Barbara, 48, 54, 55, 58, 76, 201
Harcourt, Mike, 18–19
Harper, Stephen, 71
Harris, Mike, 24, 33, 53, 54
    support from suburbs and small
        towns, 202–203
    see also Common Sense Revolution
Harvey, David, 24–25, 39, 40, 159
Hayek, Friedrich, 24
Helly, Denise, 94
heterogeneity and civility, 48–49
homeless persons, 25, 26, 55, 92, 185
Hulchanski, David, 124
human security, a broad concept, 211
Hume, Christopher, 112, 115
hydrosocial cycles (water in cities), 142,
    143

*If Low Income Women of Colour
    Counted in Toronto* (Khosla), 128
immigrants
    access to higher skilled jobs, 95–96
    *Canada-Ontario Immigration
        Agreement* (2005), 96
    discrimination against, 85–86, 91–92
    immigration policy changes, 85, 126
    integration of, 86
    location in the city, 86, 88
    poverty, 86, 91, 217
    segregation, 220
    Toronto's multicultural self-image
        and policies, 86–87
    unemployment rates, 91
"in-between cities," 22, 35, 119–120, 140
    Jane and Finch, *see* Jane and Finch
        area
    studies of Thomas Sieverts, 120–22
income inequality, growing, 217–18
infrastructure funding program
    (Ontario), 145
inner city
    donut effect in U.S. cities, 57
    Toronto in 1970s, 40–41
    Toronto in 1990s, 33
    Toronto today, 119, 150, 163

Integrity Commissioner, 209
intensification as antidote to sprawl, 108
intergovernmental relations and big
    cities, 21
Isin, Engin, 28–29
Island Airport, 200, 201, 207

Jacobs, Jane, 40, 80, 126, 202, 206
Jakobek, Tom, 201
James, Royson, 208
Jane and Finch area
    as an in-between city, 124
    branded as undesirable, 126–27
    demographic profile, 127–28 (tables
        on 130, 131, 132, 133)
    deracialization of immigration
        policy, 126
    Edgely Village, 125–26
    experimentation in planning and
        design, 125–26
    founded on modern ideas of 1950s to
        1970s, 122, 124–26
    issues faced by residents, 128
    maps, 123, 129
    perception of crime, 128, 130
    place and idea, 122, 126–27
    poverty levels, increasing, 128
    public housing, 124–25, 126, 127,
        130–33
    see also Black Creek neighbourhood;
        Glenfield-Jane Heights
        neighbourhood

Keynesian-Fordist regime, 24
Khosla, Punam, 91–92, 128
Kingwell, Mark, 48–49
Kipfer, Stefan, 31

Lambert, Christine, 109
Lastman, Mel, 185, 215
    election as Toronto mayor in 1997,
        55–58, 76
    fast crises, 77, 78
    fight with city employees, 190–92
    flamboyant style, 54, 202
Layton, Jack, 19, 80
Leach, Al, 72–73
Lefebvre, Henri, 30

neomarxist political economy view, 22, 25–28
perspectives on neoliberalism in Ontario, 62, 63
resistance to urban neoliberalism, 31–32
"roll-back" vs "roll-out," 26–27, 39, 66
state role, 24, 26, 28–29, 31
neoliberalization
all levels of government, 22–23, 32
of cities, 20, 22–31, 32, 33, 39–40, 60–65
Harris government in Ontario, see "Common Sense Revolution"
nature and, 144–45
neoliberalism and, 24–25
water supply and, 143, 159–60
neoreformism, 204, 205–208
characteristics, 204, 205–208, 209
middle-class orientation, 205–206
New Deal for Cities, 71, 80–81
New Deal for Toronto, 96
New York, centre of neoliberalism, 40
Newman, Peter, 180
Nguyen, Paul, 139–40
North York, 54, 58
North York Centre, 104
Nunziata, John, 201

Oak Ridges Moraine (ORM), 147, 149, 150, 151–52
campaigns to protect, 152, 158
official plan
characteristics and functions, 101
plan for amalgamated Toronto, see TorontoPlan
Olympia & York (O&Y), 43
Ontario
downloading to municipalities, 56, 59, 60–61, 71, 203–204
governments 1961–present, 49
Harris government, 24, 33, 50, 51, see also "Common Sense Revolution"
Rae government, 183–84, 204
transportation policy, 175–76
Ontario Coalition Against Poverty (OCAP), 23, 25, 53–54, 91, 206, 207

Ontario Housing Corporation (OHC), 124–25
Ontario Municipal Board (OMB), 113–14
Ontario Trucking Association (OTA), 170
Ootes, Case, 208, 214

Pacific Mall, Markham, 89
Parkdale Tenants Association, 194
Pecaut, David, 50, 213
Penney, Mac, 53
Personal Vehicle Ownership Tax, 210
Pinochet, Augusto, 24, 39
Places to Grow Act (Ontario, 2005), 34–35, 99, 117–18, 175
planning
changes 1995–2005, 34–35, 100, 118
political nature, 100, 180
public participation, 108–110
urban and regional levels, 99–100
see also official plan; regional planning; TorontoPlan
Planning Act (Ontario), 101
point tower, favoured by planners, 107–108
police, 128, 130, 139, 208–209, 216
powers increased by anti-terrorism law, 94
racial profiling, 93–95
political periods in Toronto (1972–2008), 204
political right in Toronto today, 214–215
Port Authority in Toronto, 50
Porto Alegre event organized by TCHC, 132–33
poverty
correlated with housing shortage, 217
immigrants, 86, 91–92, 95, 217
racialization of, 91–92, 95, 128
Poverty by Postal Code (United Way), 128, 136
priority neighbourhoods, 136, 137, 138, 140, 209, 218, 221
privatization of water supply
danger stopped in Toronto, 141, 150, 152–54, 158, 159
efforts towards, 147–48

About the Authors

Julie-Anne Boudreau is Associate Professor at the Center for Urbanisation, Culture, and Society of the National Institute for Scientific Research in Montreal. She holds the Canada Research Chair on the City and Issues of Insecurity. Her recent work focuses on fear in the city and fear of the city.

Roger Keil is the Director of the City Institute at York University and Professor at the Faculty of Environmental Studies at York University, Toronto. Keil is the co-editor of the *International Journal of Urban and Regional Research* and a co-founder of the International Network for Urban Research and Action.

Douglas Young is Assistant Professor of Social Science and teaches Urban Studies at York University, Toronto. He has worked as an architect, planner, and developer of non-profit housing co-operatives.